1938: Modern Britain

1938: Modern Britain

Social change and visions of the future

MICHAEL JOHN LAW

Bloomsbury Academic
An imprint of Bloomsbury Publishing Plc

B L O O M S B U R Y
LONDON · OXFORD · NEW YORK · NEW DELHI · SYDNEY

Bloomsbury Academic

An imprint of Bloomsbury Publishing Plc

50 Bedford Square	1385 Broadway
London	New York
WC1B 3DP	NY 10018
UK	USA

www.bloomsbury.com

BLOOMSBURY and the Diana logo are trademarks of Bloomsbury Publishing Plc

First published 2018

British Library Cataloguing-in-Publication Data
A catalogue record for this book is available from the British Library.

ISBN: HB: 978-1-4742-8500-1
PB: 978-1-4742-8501-8
ePDF: 978-1-4742-8499-8
ePub: 978-1-4742-8502-5

Library of Congress Cataloging-in-Publication Data
A catalog record for this book is available from the Library of Congress.

Cover design by Liron Gilenberg
Cover image: Tower of Empire, Empire Exhibition, Bellahouston Park, Glasgow © RIBA

Typeset by Deanta Global Publishing Services, Chennai, India
Printed and bound in Great Britain

To find out more about our authors and books visit www.bloomsbury.com. Here you will find extracts, author interviews, details of forthcoming events and the option to sign up for our newsletters.

CONTENTS

LIST OF ILLUSTRATIONS

Figures

Tables

Maps

ACKNOWLEDGEMENTS

Writing a book seems, when you are doing it, to be a very solitary task. In truth, many people have helped me with *1938: Modern Britain*.

I would like to thank the editorial staff from Bloomsbury Academic, who provided encouragement at the beginning of this project and consistent, professional support thereafter. I am grateful for the good advice provided by Mark Clapson and Peter Catterall and would like to thank Martin Doherty and the University of Westminster for providing funding for the illustrations for the book. Geoff Levett and Phil Hatfield have had to bear the brunt of putting up with me talking about this book for the best part of two years.

My family have always been supportive of my work, whether it is as an academic or in my previous business life, and without them it would be hard to imagine I could have had any success as a writer. Particular thanks to Pippa, who read the drafts of this book and steered me away from some overwritten sentences and clumsy grammar.

MJL

CHAPTER ONE

Partial history

The history of 1938 is well known. It was an interesting year, too interesting in some ways as the competing claims of appeasement and the preparations for war filled the newspapers. In the headlines were Chamberlain's meetings with Hitler, *Kristallnacht*, the Spanish Civil War, and at home, Air Raid Precautions and planning for the evacuation of children from London in the event of a war. Each of these news items brought home the foreboding possibility of another world war. However, among all these profound world events, something else far less obvious at the time was happening, a modern world in rapid development, a process that was to be halted by the Second World War and the years of austerity that followed it.

The starting point for this book was an idea that there was something hidden and odd about 1938 that most studies of the period have ignored and that warranted further investigation. My initial prompt was coming across *Modern Wonder*, a set of lively weekly magazines from 1937 and 1938, in a Brighton junk shop. As promised in the title, the magazine's brightly coloured covers and exciting features delivered a vision of the future of science and technology. Their enthusiastic articles described a world yet unaffected by wartime fears.

This find provoked two pieces of informal research. First was to use Google's 'Ngram' viewer, which searches digitized books and magazines to calculate the relative frequency of a word's use over time. British sources showed a peak in use of the word 'modern' in the late 1930s and early 1940s, reflecting a long upward trend over many decades. Second was a search on eBay, the internet marketplace, for material featuring both of the terms 'modern' and '1938'. This returned many interesting items for sale, including books, magazines, cigarette cards and postcards from an Empire exhibition in Glasgow. Contrary to what I had expected, instead of material on the latest navy destroyer or fighter planes, the search mostly produced representations of civilian technologies. There were pictures of giant American telescopes and magazine features on the secrets of electric trains. Perhaps some national cognitive dissonance was in play, Britain not wanting to believe war was coming.

A more systematic investigation of British newsreels, newspapers and magazines revealed many different major projects in progress in 1938. Not connected to the war, they showed a modern society in development. Construction projects for schools, hospitals, airports and office blocks were in full swing. Publishers launched new magazines, exhibitions were held to boost imperial pride or to sell televisions to expectant, wealthy customers and increased working-class mobility prompted new types of leisure.

This modernity was apparent to some at the time. Cicely Hamilton, novelist, travel writer, commentator and former suffragette, wrote about the changes she had seen in the previous fifteen years.[1] She contrasted everyday life in 1938 with Stanley Baldwin's famous explanation of what his country meant to him, contained in a 1924 speech.[2] Baldwin based his national view on a nostalgic, bucolic, rural scene, a much-in-vogue 'deep' England.[3] Hamilton, in contrast, proposed that, in 1938, the people's 'inheritance is tram, tube and motorbus, not the plough team breasting the hill'.[4] Setting aside nostalgia, she contended that 'the real modern England is essentially urban, living by the office, the factory, the shop'.[5] More famously, George Orwell, writing in 1940, saw Britain's future in the suburban way of life established in the late 1930s: 'It is a rather restless, cultureless life, centering round tinned food, *Picture Post*, the radio and the internal combustion engine.'[6] Hamilton and Orwell's examples are reflected in the choice of case studies for this book.

As the title of this chapter proposes, this book is a partial history of modern Britain in 1938. I use the term 'partial' in two of its senses: first to suggest the writing of one part of the history of this year and second to indicate that the account contained here is far from impartial. I have made no attempt to produce a balanced history of that time and place. My thesis is that the impact of extraordinary political events has distorted our understanding of the history of the late 1930s. It has overshadowed the modernity experienced, in most cases, by Britain's wealthier middle-class citizens. As Kate Caffrey, an author of popular history, puts it, 'There is a natural tendency to change tempo as soon as the writers sniff the approach of the war, to make a dash for the finish. ... As soon as one steps outside politics it seems to me the closing years had received rather rough treatment.'[7] Caffrey made this observation in 1978. Since then, there have been many new studies of the 1930s that have taken a more thematic and less temporal view of the decade. However, there is still some truth in her idea; the historiography of the end of this decade continues to be dominated by the profound world events of 1938 and 1939.

In recent years, there have been three leading books that consider the social and cultural history of Britain between the wars, each with their own distinctive approach. Richard Overy's *The Morbid Age – Britain*

Between the Wars is a learned study of British intellectuals' response to war, fascism, slump and modernity.[8] This excellent account does not share much ground with this book, but brings into play the pessimism that some contemporary commentators associated with modernity. This is worth further consideration. It would be fair to say that the partial account of late 1930s Britain written here disregards the negative aspects of modernity. For example, in welcoming increased working-class mobilities in cars and charabancs (see Chapter 7) this book does not dwell on the thousands of deaths experienced by motorists, cyclists and pedestrians in the 1930s. In considering Britain's increasing interest in flight (see Chapter 8) it ignores its military connotations and the implications of bombing on civilian populations.[9] Martin Pugh's *We Danced All Night – A Social History of Britain Between the Wars* reviews the two decades thematically, evoking the feel and tone of the period from contemporary sources and memoirs.[10] Of the twenty-one chapters, each of which is devoted to a separate topic, only one, 'Work, Unemployment and Class Conflict', is devoted to the deep problems of the period. His book has made a number of compromises to embrace so much ground and so much change in one volume. Pugh does not concern himself with the preparations for likely war in 1938, allowing him to concentrate on the positive aspects of the 1930s. His viewpoint is closer in tone to this book, but in its attempt to be an all-embracing social history over twenty years that experienced dramatic changes, *We Danced All Night* obscures as much as it reveals. Finally, Juliet Gardiner's *The Thirties: An Intimate History* solves half of Martin Pugh's problems by concentrating on a single decade. As the subtitle suggests, she uses personal accounts as the means of providing great levels of detail in her account.[11] The book is organized temporally and within that by theme. It concludes, conventionally, with an account of life in 1938 and 1939 that concentrates on the anticipation of and preparation for the coming war.

Each of these books faced a choice in its periodization, which is the tendency of historians to attribute particular characteristics to a block of time or a cycle of events.[12] This practice, as Marc Bloch puts it, applies 'wrong labels which eventually deceive us about [their] contents'.[13] Periodization is not necessarily illogical. For example, a common periodization is made by selecting the years between the two world wars. It would be foolish to think that the periods before and after the First World War were not different from each other. It would be just as foolish to think Britain was not changed by the Second World War, so defining a period that was bookended by such great events makes complete sense if you wish to take a temporal view. It is also common to separate the interwar period into its constituent decades. This is tempting, as the contrast between the years before and after the Wall Street Crash and its repercussions painted each decade in its own particular hue. Dividing history into decades and giving them an overarching characteristic is also commonplace in popular discourse. In the twentieth century, the 'roaring' twenties, the 'hungry thirties' and the 'swinging sixties' come easily to mind.

Periodizing by decades is appealing but has its consequences.[14] First and most obviously, it ignores continuities from previous and to subsequent decades. A good example of this is the idea that Britain, and in particular London, only began to swing in the 1960s. In reality, a little more thought shows that many of the 'swinging' features such as teenage fashion and premarital sex were present in previous decades.[15] Second, this approach encourages the practice of fitting facts to the spirit of the decade, ignoring inconvenient truths. Simplistic historical accounts of the two decades between the wars seem to be divided by skirt lengths and hairstyles as much as anything else. In reality, the 1920s and the 1930s are difficult to periodize successfully. In the 1920s, the spirit of the flapper and bright young thing must be set against poverty, industrial decline and the General Strike.[16] In the 1930s, the dreadful impact of a widespread slump and its social implications must be contrasted with the rise of suburban consumerism and Americanization. This difficulty was first managed by Marxist scholars writing what came to be known as 'pessimistic' accounts that focused on slums and the slump followed by preparations for an inevitable war. Revisionist, 'optimistic' histories largely ignore this aspect of the 1930s to focus on the raised living standards and changed consumption practices achieved by the majority of Britons.[17] The decade-by-decade approach has a distinct advantage over interwar histories where there is a tendency for a kind of historical compression; there is just too much going on in these action-packed twenty years to allow the exploration of subtle changes. The result is a flattened, squeezed landscape. Life in 1920 was, in so many ways, different from life in 1938, mostly caused by interrelated changes to income, demographics, technology and popular culture. At the time of writing, it would require us to imagine life in 2017 to be similar to 1997 despite the rapid changes brought about by internet technologies in the period.

This book focuses on Britain in 1938. A cursory review of library catalogues for twentieth-century British history suggests that selecting a specific year is quite a common approach. Choosing one year avoids some of the problems of looking at a whole decade but creates others by provoking another form of potential error. This is the idea of a year having a unique characteristic. For example, two nostalgic histories of Britain in 1938 take the approach that it was special because it marked the end of the interwar period, a way of life that had passed forever.[18] This conclusion was reached by using selective evidence, choosing the facts to support this specific thesis. This book takes a different approach that emphasizes the modern aspects of the year and eschews nostalgia. This book circumvents the problem of selective evidence through the construction of a deliberately partial history. It is not intended to be a balanced and complete review of the year; in fact, it is quite the opposite. Specific periodizations offer authors an attractive possibility. Charles S. Maier calls out his fellow historians on this temptation: 'That is one reason why debates over periodization usually follow a predictable and sometimes dreary course. [It] entails a series of claims that a development hitherto taken to mark one era ... [such as] the cultural markers of modernity can be observed in an earlier one and has just been overlooked. Significant developments thus seem to creep backward through time.'[19] Maier's critique could be applied to this book, as it identifies some aspects of modernity in 1938 that prefigure later developments. The reader can judge whether these claims propose too much, or the argument is as 'dreary' as Maier thinks it might be.

This book's inquiry into Britain in 1938 uses six case studies of projects from that year that exemplify modernity. The first question to consider on this approach is why use case studies as the viewing frame at all? There were other options. Richard Overy, as might be expected in a study of intellectual opinion, relies on contemporary writing and published diaries and memoirs. Martin Pugh, who had the broadest canvas to cover, synthesizes many accounts of the period to achieve his aim. Juliet Gardiner emphasizes the personal by employing diaries, memoirs and scholarly accounts. The advantage of studying projects (using the term in a wide sense) is that they capture an attempt to achieve change. These disruptions each constitute in their own way a component of what can broadly be summed as modernity. Marshall Berman's examination of a new highway project in the Bronx taken from his childhood memories is an evocative example of a project that had a transformative effect.[20] Projects do not necessarily have to be about construction, they can also be about less concrete ideas using less concrete. A second question is to ask how typical are the case studies of the overall state of modernity in 1938? The chosen case studies emphasize dramatic peaks in the landscape of 1930s life. Some reveal aspects of life that were encountered by wide sections of British society; others show experiences for the lucky few. However, the intention here is to destabilize previous well-held views rather than to produce a comprehensive record.

I selected the case studies in this book by reviewing topics making the news in 1938. This news, as seen by the *Times, Manchester Guardian, Illustrated London News* and other publications, was not from the headlines, but from the inside pages. Searching these sources for the word 'modern', an option not available to previous generations of historians, provided clues. From a long list of about thirty possible projects, I chose five for this book because I thought them interesting and because they had good supporting archival material. A possible case study on the opening of a new factory foundered because of the paucity of material available in the company's official archive. One case study is based on my earlier research. Each case study uses an assembly of archival sources and published material from the period. Present-day academic work is used to provide further commentary and colour.

Britain's obsession with technology and modern life was apparent from at least the middle of the nineteenth century and was accelerated by the impact of the First World War.[21] Even taking this trend into account, 1938 was an unusual year in which Britain was exceptionally bothered by being modern, featuring in newsreels and in reading material of all sorts ranging from cigarette cards, popular science magazines, schoolboy weeklies and annuals, and technical journals. In a book titled 'Modern Britain' it is worth explaining exactly what 'modern' means, although it should be made clear that this book does not attempt to theorize modernity. As historical geographer Miles Ogborn has pointed out, this is a difficult task: '[Modernity's] periodization, geographies, characteristics and promise all remain elusive.'[22] This book recognizes certain characteristics of modernity that are sometimes contradictory. These include the introduction of order and chaos through change, the destruction and remaking of space and place, and time/space compression.[23] The case studies examine the condition of modernity in Britain in 1938 and its interaction with key elements of a changing culture. The elements I have chosen are Class and Wealth, Americanization, Consumption, Network Development and Urban Formation.

As far as class and wealth is concerned, it would be foolish to suggest that the key beneficiaries of the products of modern life in 1938 were any group other than the wealthier middle classes. This group's increased leisure time and disposable income provided them with the means and opportunity to, for example, drive their cars into the countryside, buy cine-cameras and own push-button radios and new televisions. Working-class modernity in the 1930s was most directly experienced through work, such as in the mechanization of agriculture and the production methods employed in new factories.[24] It was also seen in widespread access to radios, charabanc visits to modern pubs that welcomed working-class customers and in the mass attendances at an exhibition of the modern world, to take three examples from this book. The partial nature of this book, which emphasizes the modern aspects of 1938 life for a relative few and ignores the poverty, poor work conditions, unemployment and slum housing of many, places it in the optimistic history category. In the book's defence, working-class history of this period has been well explored.[25] In contrast, the history of middle-class Britain in the 1930s has often only been exposed through discussions on suburbanization.[26]

Americanization was a key aspect of the experience of modernity in the 1930s. It had been so for the previous eighty years as cheap American goods arrived in Britain and the rise of American economic and political power became a problem for the mighty British Empire.[27] In the interwar period Americanization took many forms. There was a direct influence of wealthy American citizens on British 'society' and from large American businesses such as Hoover and Firestone. These companies wished to jump Britain's tariff barriers and established themselves on the new arterial roads leading out from London.[28] Less direct, but more pervasive, was the impact of American culture. American music had been a popular import since the arrival of ragtime in the late nineteenth century. The gramophone and later the Hollywood musical ensured that by the 1930s, American jazz and swing music dominated the British scene, although some adaptation for British audiences took place generating a strong sense of hybridity.[29] Hollywood movies were very popular in Britain in the 1930s and influenced language, fashion and behaviour. The widespread consumption of American novels and story papers reinforced their impact.[30]

Increased real incomes and levels of consumption across the British middle and lower middle classes were one of the key economic features of the 1930s. New light-engineering industries promoted and responded to a growing demand for consumer durables, fuelling the transformation of the regional economies of England's south and midlands. The greater availability and social acceptance of instalment credit also made consumption more accessible. The result was a notable increase in the purchase of cars, washing machines, vacuum cleaners and the like.[31] Increased consumption met with greater leisure time, and more money was spent on travel and holidays than in previous decades.[32] Religious leaders and commentators saw consumerism as a problem and often linked it to the domestication and secularization brought about by the rapid suburbanization of Britain's major cities in the 1920s and 1930s. George Orwell thought that suburbanites knew more about car engines than about the Bible.[33]

The formation of networks is a consequence of modernity and a promoter of time/space compression. In the pre-modern world, local networks were formed around the family and the village, with perhaps occasional visits to a market town, where new commercial connections could form. Developments in transport transformed this simple state of affairs. Railways allowed for the rapid urbanization and suburbanization of Britain, together with many unforeseen changes to society. This theme was repeated with the introduction of motorized trams and buses, and in the 1930s a much wider use of motor cars and, for the wealthy, aeroplanes.[34] One of the key characteristics of these developments was that they were brought about by untrammelled capitalism, the inefficient results of which are still evident in, for example, London's over-complex train network. New technologies formed invisible networks in the first part of the twentieth century with the introduction and then widespread acceptance of the telegraph system and radio.[35] The partial and temporary collapse of capitalism in the early 1930s, which was coupled with an admiration for the (imaginary) success of the communist system, ensured that planning came to the fore in the 1930s. In Britain, the state began to have greater influence on regulating networks such as radio, telegraph, airlines and road haulage.[36]

The impact of destruction and construction on the built environment and physical networks was most clearly seen in Britain's cities. The tearing down and rebuilding of urban space dislocated traditional communities, obliterated memory and tradition, and replaced it with a cleaner and more regulated world.[37] Some of this order generated further chaos as urban life became more hectic. For example, in a tube station in the rush hour, an ordered system directed passengers in specific ways to trains running to timetables, but all around there was an overwhelming sense of uncontrolled movement. In the 1930s, urban redevelopment focused its attention on two key features. First, councils and private enterprise built large-scale, shared housing projects for both the poorest and wealthiest sorts in flats and apartments, the previous occupants moving to the suburbs.[38] Second, developers built large, Americanized office blocks.[39] Such projects changed Britain's cities by replacing some of the slums and reordering the city.

* * *

1938: Modern Britain has an explanatory opening which describes how Britain explored its own sense of modernity in the last full year before the Second World War. It is followed by six case-study chapters that interrogate the relationship between modernity and the social and cultural elements described above. A concluding chapter collates these ideas to build a picture of the modern world of 1938.

CHAPTER TWO

Representations of modern life in 1938

You are the future builders of great scientific and mechanical marvels.[1]

This chapter considers how, in 1938, ideas of modernity, expressed through public interest in science and new technologies, were mediated by popular and technical books and magazines and, less consciously, in the presentation of cigarette cards. Typically, this literature followed a 'modern wonder' discourse in which readers were in awe of the power and speed of sublime technology. Most of this material was aimed at men and older boys, positioning them as the inheritors of a masculine tradition that uniquely could master the technological world of the near future. *Kodak* magazine, written for tyro photographers, bucked this general theme, employing women writers to explain new technologies to readers of both genders. The chapter examines a variety of modern wonder, technology and scientific publications and concludes that public interest in them was unusually raised in 1938 and that they show a tension between imperial pride and an admiration for increasingly dominant American technologies.

FIGURE 2.1 *Churchman's Cigarettes, 'Modern Wonders #22' – High-Power Grid-Glow Tube, 1938, Image Credit: Author's Collection.*

Being modern defies most attempts at strict periodization. Not always though. For example, historian David Kynaston suggests that 'Modernity Britain' arrived in 1957.[2] Putting aside the use of modernity as an adjective, this specificity also ignores the experiences of the previous generation who in their lives, habits and hobbies were also modern, just as their parents had been in the Edwardian period and their parents before them. Each generation from the industrial revolution to the present day has thought themselves modern, although signal events and advances in technology accelerated the pace at specific times. Railways, safety bicycles, cars and planes generated radical time/space compressions and societal changes. Rapid growth in urban and suburban settlements in the nineteenth and twentieth centuries transformed Britain's class and gender structures and working and domestic life. All these processes and events pushed the experience of modernity forward.

All periods are modern in their own way, but the late 1930s were distinguished by a heightened sense of modernity in public discourse. One way of looking at this effect is to use Google's 'Ngram' tool, which analyses digitized books and calculates the frequency of words occurring in texts published over the years.[3] The results are quite crude, as Google has not digitized all books and the meaning of words change over time, but it provides a sense of the direction of travel for a specific word.[4] Using this tool to examine the word 'modern' in British English over the last 150 years shows that it reached a peak, not as one might expect in 1967, but two decades earlier in 1944. The use of the word accelerated throughout the 1930s. It seems likely that some of this rise was triggered by the impact of the Second World War, but the trend was also strong early in the decade before the realities of large-scale aerial bombardment on civilian populations had become fully apparent.[5] Use of 'modern' is on the rise again in recent years, perhaps reflecting disruptions resulting from the rise of the internet. This analysis does not necessarily suggest that 1938 was more modern than 1932; however, the idea of being modern occurred more frequently in public discourse towards the end of the decade. This was seen in many books, magazines and ephemera from 1938, and it is noticeable when one's attention focuses on this particular year.

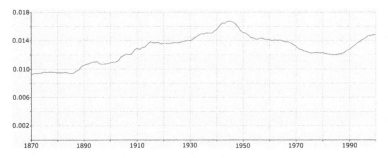

FIGURE 2.2 *Google's Ngram analysis of the word 'modern' – British English, Image Credit: http://books.google.com/ngrams.*

Several authors have considered Britain's engagement with modernity in the 1930s.[6] The most productive for this book is Bernhard Rieger's comparative history, *Technology and the Culture of Modernity*.[7] Here he examines how Britain and Germany dealt with technological developments, modern wonders, airmindedness, speed and their resultant accidents.[8] In 1938, the interwar obsession with speed and new technologies was changing in two ways. First, an admiration for technology was becoming more influenced by martial concerns, prompted by the increasingly likely future war. Second, it was moving away from the distanced observation of new things that characterized the 1920s and early 1930s to one where members of the public had direct experience of technology mediated through their own consumption. This was evident in, for example, the increasing ownership and use of motor cars and cameras, two fields that were predominantly male interests.

One of the characteristics of 1930s modernity was the gendered nature of its representation. This remained the position for many years, and to a certain extent still is, but in the years just before the war it is striking how different genders had modernity ascribed to them in different ways. For men and boys, modernity meant the impact of changing technologies in the world beyond the home, where speed and size were most important. For women and girls, public discourse on modernity revolved around their incursion into the workplace and the benefits of new domestic technologies. In reality, the impact of movies and women's writing throughout the decade meant that women both acted and thought in a different way from the previous decade. This topic has received a good deal of attention in academic writing and has revealed that women in the 1930s had a wider experience of modernity than might have been thought at the time.[9]

Being modern – speed and size

Speed was one of the great obsessions of the interwar period, particularly in its second decade. Humans have always had a fascination with speed. Horse riding provided excitement for millennia only to be supplanted relatively recently by bicycles and cars. In the first decade of the twentieth century, technological developments provided many new outlets for experiencing and worshipping the effects of speed. The Futurists saw the possibilities and built a mental connection between youth, speed and death.[10] The Great War cured the world of wishing for more death, but as Paul Virilio has explained, each new technology we develop is immediately associated with a new form of deadly accident.[11] Technological improvements in cars, ships, planes and trains provided the opportunity for daring individuals and competing nations to contest many different speed records.

For cars and motoring, the 1920s saw a change in emphasis. After the First World War, the world of motor sport was as concerned with endurance as much as it was with speed. *Autocar*, the magazine for elite drivers, featured rallies where distance achieved was the objective, reflecting the unreliability of cars on Britain's roads, when breakdowns and punctures were the norm for any long journey.[12] Within a few years, speed was the only thing. For racing enthusiasts, Brooklands in Surrey was the focal point for competing in and watching motor racing.[13] The image of huge cars barrelling around Brooklands' steeply banked tracks is an appropriate metonymic visual cliché for the period. This racing was fast and dangerous and attracted large numbers of spectators enticed by the danger and spectacle. In the 1930s, the general public, as opposed to the mixture of aristocrats and oily handed enthusiasts who raced at Brooklands, became after some encouragement from the newspapers and newsreel companies fascinated with the land speed record. Britain's domination of this contest in this decade was a source of national pride and famous drivers Malcolm Campbell, Henry Segrave and John Cobb were heroes to many.[14]

Flight had a rather different story. Air speed records were important in the 1930s, but Britain was less successful in the air than on the ground. Pilots and planes from the United States, Italy and Germany dominated this field. Britain's strongest contribution was in distance and endurance flying and Amy Johnson and her husband, Jim Mollison, were always in the public eye.[15] The focus for maritime speed records was on the Blue Riband (the fastest journey across the Atlantic Ocean). The launch of RMS Queen Mary in 1936 prompted an outpouring of national pride, and she held the prize for two short periods, competing with French and American ships.[16] With speed, there was a strong association between winning and the hero or heroine pilot or driver that emphasized individualism. For ocean liners, their great size was as remarked on as their speed. Because the public could not associate them with a celebrity, praise took on a more nationalistic tone.

Speed records were really about improved technologies, but where no hero was available, a different form of discourse occurred: the 'modern wonder or marvel'. Rieger notes that this idea, while prevalent in the 1930s, had much earlier antecedents: 'That Britons ... living between the 1890s and 1930s were not the first ones to conceive of technology as a "modern marvel," however, did not interfere with their belief in the exceptionality of their historical precedent.'[17] In fact, this term dates back at least to the Great Exhibition of 1851.[18] This sense of exceptionality was very present in 1938, as testified by the amount and variety of modern wonder material dating from that year. Historian David Nye has considered the American public experience of and discourse on new technologies. He uses the term 'technological sublimity' to describe how the speed and size of machine technology replaced the American landscape and works of nature as the focus for generating public awe in a modern world.[19] Rieger considers this a one-dimensional approach because it ignores the twin face of technology that Virilio noticed, that it is both fascinating and dangerous. There is little evidence in the material available from Britain in 1938 to suggest that popular writing presented these two ideas together. Its tone was almost always positive and was perhaps an unconscious avoidance of the anxieties that might have been provoked by discussing the efficiencies of modern warfare against a civilian population.

A wide variety of media in 1938 demonstrated a fascination with speed, size, technology and modern life. For example, it was seen in newsreel films and the topics covered in cigarette card series, which are an under-appreciated medium for historical analysis. It was very apparent in magazines and books aimed at young adults and older children and also featured in varying degrees in magazines aimed at those with technical interests, such as radio and photography.

Newsreels

Major newspapers and BBC radio broadcasts did not deliver much more than plain, factual reporting of developments in the modern world. Newsreel companies had a livelier, populist agenda and included modern wonders in their films. Newreels from the end of 1938, which reviewed the events of the year, showed this approach. British Pathé's 'Review of the Year' newsreel lasted fourteen minutes and had thirty separate items, which were focused on three main topics.[20] These were: war, actual abroad and feared at home (nine items), monarchy, mostly British (eight items) and sport of all sorts (seven items). Three items were about the exciting, modern world of 1938, featuring an innovative small aeroplane which took off in flight from the back of a larger plane, a new British land speed record achieved in America and the launch of the mammoth RMS Queen Elizabeth. Movietone, Pathé's chief rival, went further and recognized far more modern items in its summary of 1938.[21] As well as all the items covered by Pathé, they also featured material on a long-distance flight record achieved by British pilots, the launch of RMS Mauretania, RMS Queen Mary taking the Blue Riband and Malcolm Campbell gaining the world water speed record.

These news items were simple modern wonder material. The emphasis was on size, speed or duration. RMS Queen Elizabeth was huge and her launch was coupled with the new queen's first broadcast, so the launch had twice the interest. Newsreel companies' selection of this modern wonder material is intriguing. At a time of great national worry and fear, their inclusion could not just have been for light relief. Movietone included one item on 'The Lambeth Walk', the dance craze of 1938, so they could have used comedic material or light entertainment to lift the audiences' spirits if they wished. Instead, they turned to modern wonders, which shows the relative importance of such material in a year where there was much else that the newsreels could have included.

Cigarette cards

Most men and many women smoked cigarettes in the 1930s.[22] Competition between brands was intense and, to attract new customers, tobacco companies engaged in a variety of marketing techniques. One of the most persuasive was the inclusion of a small, illustrated card with each packet of cigarettes. Cigarette cards were first introduced in the United States in the 1870s and by the 1890s had found their way to Britain.[23] These promotional items consisted of a fixed number of illustrations on a particular theme, such as army uniforms or British birds. Tobacco firms wishing to stimulate a collection habit provided small albums for collectors so that they could keep their cards in an ordered and pristine condition. The desire to complete a collection before the tobacco company replaced the issue stimulated an intense brand loyalty. In their early years, at the height of the British Empire, cards promoted imperial, royal and military themes. By the 1930s, entertainment, film stars and representations of modern life had come to the fore.[24] As smoking became more popular between the wars, brand differentiation through cigarette cards became more important; thus enthusiasts now consider the 1930s as the leading decade for cartophilia (card collection).[25]

Cartophilists are keen to distance themselves from the idea that theirs was a hobby for schoolboys. One expert opined that 'cards were issued ... on subjects designed to attract the users of the product, who were of course adults'.[26] Collecting may have crossed several age groups of smokers and their children, but it seems to go without discussion in cartophilia literature that most collectors were and are men.[27] There seems to be something in the male psyche that attracts them to collecting and completeness, whether it is cigarette cards, football stickers or vinyl albums. Although books on

TABLE 2.1 British cigarette card sets issued in 1934 and 1938

Topics	Sets issued 1934	%	Sets issued 1938	%
Entertainment	16	41	10	18
Nature	3	8	10	18
Sport	7	18	9	16
Modernity/Technology	2	5	8	15
Military/ARP	–	–	7	13
Other	11	28	8	15
Travel	–	–	3	5
Total	39	100	55	100

FIGURE 2.3 *Wills Cigarettes, 'Speed #5' – De Havilland 'Comet' racer, Image Credit: Author's Collection.*

cigarette card history do not consider this point, it seems likely that most collectors came from working and lower-middle-class homes. In the 1930s, middle-class smokers often preferred pipes and could afford to read about the topics covered by cigarette card sets by buying a book.

1938 was a boon year in the history of British cartophilia. It was thriving due to the rearmament economy, and was the last full year before the war shut down such frivolities for the duration. An analysis of cards issued during 1938 shows coverage of a wide range of topics.[28] Table 2.1 shows how the types of card issued by British tobacco companies changed during the 1930s. Although the choice of starting year for this table is arbitrary, some broad trends are evident. Forty-one per cent of cards issued in 1934 were on an entertainment topic; typically, they featured film stars or pin-ups. The impact of talking movies could have prompted this excitement or it may have been a light-hearted response to the worries of the depression. By 1938, the emphasis had changed, with fun topics seen in only 18 per cent of issues. They had been supplanted by two interrelated topics: military subjects, such as fighter planes and the modern wonders of technology.

Two issues from 1938 typify how cigarette card publishers presented changing technologies. First, Wills' issue of 'Speed', a set of fifty cards. These cards were included in the well-known Gold Flake, Capstan, Woodbine and Star brands of cigarettes.[29] Gold Flake was by 1938 seeking to attract female smokers, advertising it as 'the man's cigarette that women like'.[30] Star and Woodbine were cheaper cigarettes directed towards poorer smokers, with Woodbine being the highest-selling brand in the country.[31] Second was Churchman's issue of a 'Modern Wonders' set of forty-eight cards, included in its 'No. 1' brand of cigarettes.

Figure 2.3 shows an example of the 'Speed' set of cards.[32] The illustrations, only 6.5 centimetres long, were finely rendered and in strong colours. The aesthetic appeal of the cards was very strong; eighty years after their issue the images are still striking. Each card portrayed the idea of speed very well and had a short explanation on the back, which was a model of good editing and clarity, telling the picture's story in just over a hundred words.

The 'Speed' series was conventional, with no hyperbole used in the descriptions, and no appeal made to modern wonders. It included cards on the following topics: racing planes, military planes, racing cars, racing motorbikes, liners, naval ships, speedboats and trains. British successes were the most celebrated, but the series was even-handed and not over-nationalistic and featured American, French and Italian successes. Although released in late 1938, a time when the danger posed by Germany's Nazi government was clear enough, the cards praised German efforts in building high-speed vehicles of various types. For example, card #13 showed the Heinkel He. 111 Bomber, soon to appear in real life over London. It recorded its 'two Daimler-Benz liquid-cooled motors each developing more than 1,000 h.p.'.[33] Overall, the tone of the descriptions of these cards was rational, factual and adult.

Churchman's 'Modern Wonders' set of cards contained three different themes. First, the set included several machines or devices because of their immense scale. For example, Card #27 showed a 'magnet that lifts 46 tons' which was 'of exceptional power'.[34] Second, there were representations of complex electronic and electric machines in production and doing a job of work in 1938. Finally, there was a smaller group of cards describing experimental ideas that gave a glimpse into the near future. These cards provide the most interest for present-day readers as they hint at future technologies that were not, perhaps, fully developed or understood at the end of the thirties.

The picture shown at the start of this chapter contains many of the themes considered central to the popular appreciation of technology in the interwar years. It is, first, an explicit part of a modern wonders series. Second, it reflects the series designer's obsession with enormity, and finally, the image echoes the ideas of technological sublimity. The image (see Figure 2.1) shows an American scientist gazing in profound and reverent awe at a gigantic tube blazing with a white light that proposes a clean and efficient future.[35] It is in fact an electronic relay, the building block for early computers. This is one example of a noticeable genuflection towards American technologies found in modern wonder material at the end of the 1930s.

Modern wonders for boys and young men

During the interwar years, publishers produced many books and magazines designed to attract the attention of younger readers. In the 1920s, imperial and natural themes led the way and were gradually superseded in the 1930s by a fascination with modern technology. One example of this was seen in a series of books by Ward Lock and Co. that described the 'wonders' of the world. The series began in 1915 with *The Wonder Book of Empire for Boys and Girls*.[36] Over the next two decades it covered general encyclopaedic topics, such as *The Wonder Book of*

Why and What and *The Wonder Book of Do You Know?*, together with books on military topics. By the early 1930s, technology provided much of the content, for example, in *The Wonder Book of Electricity* and *The Wonder Book of Inventions*.[37] As the decade progressed, the use of the term 'Modern' was becoming more prevalent, but Ward Lock did not distinguish its wonders in this way.

Two of the many magazines and story papers aimed at boys and young men available in the late 1930s specifically addressed modern life.[38] The first of these, *Modern Boy*, which was published from 1928 until the start of the Second World War, is very disappointing for those in search of public engagement with new technologies.[39] *Modern Boy* was, in reality, the home of conservative and imperialistic tales of daring-do redolent of a much earlier period and way of thinking.[40] An important contributor was Flying Officer W. E. Johns, the author of the popular 'Biggles' stories. *Modern Boy* contained much thwarting of foreigners' plans and straight punches to chins. A July 1938 issue contained several old-school stories, such as 'Head-hunters' Gold' and 'High-Speed Hideaway'. These stories usually featured planes, ships and cars, but the emphasis was on the hero rather than his vehicle.[41]

In 1937, Odhams Press launched a new magazine, *Modern Wonder*, aimed at younger readers in Britain and the Empire who were excited by the prospects of science and technology. As its name implies, it fully embraced a sense of wonder about the future. Each week it carried explanatory articles that aimed to intrigue and excite youthful enthusiasts. *Modern Wonder* was positioned directly at boys and young men. The magazine made it clear in its first issue that its readership would be male: 'The *Modern Wonder* League of Science aims to stimulate and encourage the great spirit of modern progress in the boy of today.'[42] It appealed to a sense of hope for the future that events in Czechoslovakia had not yet dimmed: 'For you the potential wonder-workers of the Future, are provided the opportunities by which you can realize your ambitions. Somewhere among you is a Marconi, a Malcolm Campbell, and Edison, a Henry Ford.'[43] This stirring call to technocracy was interesting in its appeal to all youngsters, who might rise from humble beginnings to become great men of science. The inclusion of British racing driver Malcolm Campbell, alongside an Italian and two Americans, seems rather forced compared to the real-world technological successes of Marconi, Edison and Ford. Once again the sense that the United States was the genuine home for a scientific or industrial prodigy is evident.

Modern Wonder was an odd mix of news, technical explanations, boys' adventure stories, colour centrespreads showing a new plane or car and a member's section. The edition for 14 May 1938 had on its cover a colour image of John Cobb's land speed record car, an idea that reflected on the obsessions of scale, speed and technology that typified modern wonder thinking (see Figure 2.4).[44]

FIGURE 2.4 Modern Wonder *magazine, 14 May 1938, Image Credit: Author's* collection.

This edition opens with a 'newsreel' section that has two main stories. Both were American in origin. First was a report on a Florida underwater film studio for photographing fish, which seems a spurious news item and second, an account on the Lincoln tunnel, a new route connecting New York City to New Jersey. The editorial gushed, 'As you can see from the picture … the tunnel is a very super affair.'[45]

Aviation played a key role in this issue. In 1938 because of the airmindedness campaign in Britain and the rapid development of passenger and military flying, this topic was a leading interest for boys and young men. Two main articles addressed the topic. The first was part of a course of flying lessons and its fourth instalment dealt with learning how to land a plane. The magazine described author Selby Lewis as 'our special air correspondent [who] initiates you into the secrets of making successful landings'. The article's primary aim was not only to indulge the fantasies of the magazine's adolescent readers but also to provide specific details that might have formed a part of a real flying lesson. The reader is brought into the fantasy, by being directly addressed. The lesson concludes 'All right, taxi her back to the tarmac. That's how it's done. We'll go up again and practice. You can do it yourself this time. Practice makes perfect in this part of flying.'[46] Unknown to the readers, most of whom thought they would never fly a plane in real life, it was possible that some got the opportunity in the RAF in the years to come.

The second article was found in the colour-printed centre pages. Under the title 'Giant American Air Liner', *Modern Wonder* provided a detailed exposition of Transcontinental and Western Airways' (TWA) new Douglas' DC3 air services. Eight small illustrations accompanied the central drawing of the DC3, showing the check-in at Kansas City airport, the plane's luxurious seating and overnight sleeping accommodation. The 'giant machine' was shown to be capable of a speed of 200 m.p.h. with a 1,000-mile range. Kansas City, Missouri was presented as the centre of a network of flights to all points of the North American continent, taking direct routes that were contrasted with the slow meanderings of the railway.[47] It is interesting, and a reflection of the level of everyday Americanization of interwar Britain, that young readers were not expected to need any briefing on the geography of the United States or the methods of travel employed there. The technical content of the issue was, though, brought closer to home by a short article on the 'Mechanical Marvels on the Manchester Ship Canal', which explained how tiny diesel tugs towed 'giant' liners up the canal. In 1938, diesel technology was making great headway over steam and was used in America and Germany to power its fast trains.[48] Even in the most unglamorous of settings, marvels of technology met with giant machines.

This edition of *Modern Wonder* provided an accurate sense of the usual contents of the magazine's output from 1938, but one issue from the following month showed a more regressive aspect. In among the usual subjects, such as 'Secrets of the Electric Train', 'G-Men of the GPO', and 'Mechanical Marvel Charts Storm-bound Ships', the magazine led with a full colour cover 'White Man's Magic in the Jungle'.[49] The article explained 'how science has found its way into the heart of the Dark Continent and how the natives react to the introduction of some of the marvels of the present'.[50] In this piece, the crudest aspects of British imperialist and racist attitudes that were seen forty years earlier in the novels of George Alfred Henty were applied to how Africans interacted with new technologies.[51] The author, Harold T. Wilkins, safe in his Fleet Street lair, trotted out banalities and mistruths that were totally out of place with the otherwise forward-looking aspects of the magazine:

> On arrival in the native village deep in the bush, men take the device out of the motor truck, and set a couple of delighted and grinning negroes astride on a tandem bicycle frame. 'Now, boys' says the white overseer 'you can pedal as fast as you like, but you must keep an eye on the needles of these two dials'.[52]

This article was unusual compared to *Modern Wonder*'s normal content in 1937 and 1938, but in expressing Britain's superiority to colonial Africa it indicated a wider theme. The magazine in its choice of material, its devotion to American scientific and industrial leadership and the occasional inclusion of imperialist material was unconsciously attempting a negotiation of Britain's role in the world just before the Second World War. Modern Britain, now a second-rate technological nation, but still ruler of hundreds of millions of 'natives' in the Empire, faced an uncertain future.

Material aimed at adults

Older readers were also interested in science and modern technologies, and publishers of modern wonder books and magazines tried to capture this large audience. One interesting 1938 book aimed at unsophisticated adults was *Marvels of the Modern World*. This was another Odhams Press publication, but written in a different style compared to its juvenile output. It was a straightforward and undemanding read and covered much of the usual material: transport, new technologies and science, but without the emphasis on the gigantic that featured in writing for the younger reader. One informative chapter, 'Miracles in Ferro-Concrete', might still interest the modern reader, and does not require the indulgences of nostalgia to do so. It covered the history of concrete and picked out notable recently constructed buildings that used this new building technique. The chapter identified the De la Warr pavilion in Bexhill, the Earl's Court Exhibition Centre and new workers' flats at Kensal House as good examples, which they were and are still thought so today. The chapters were anonymous and were probably written by jobbing journalists. This might explain the uneven nature of the chapter which concluded with a long and uncritical account of American skyscrapers, with no discussion of recent British office blocks (see Chapter 4).[53]

A chapter on railways, which began with a history of railway speed, continued the defensive tone towards the United States.[54] This topic was coming to something of a head in Britain in the late 1930s, with competition for the fastest run of a steam engine. Odhams published *Marvels of the Modern World* a little too early to catch Mallard's unbeaten run of 126 m.p.h. in July 1938, so it focused on Coronation, a fast new train of the London, Midland and Scottish Railway.[55] Coronation achieved its briefly held speed record in July 1937 and its sister engines pulled a luxurious scheduled service known as the 'Coronation Scot' from Euston station in London to Glasgow.[56] The chapter concluded in the same way as the discussion on concrete buildings with a breathless account of the distances covered and luxuries and innovations provided by railways in the United States and Canada: 'There is a valet who will sponge and press your suit while you sleep; and if you feel too lazy to shave in the morning the train barber will do it for you.'[57]

Also published in 1938 was a book that covered some of the same ground and used the same journalistic tone as *Marvels of the Modern World*, but took a wider view on what could be marvellous. In *The Modern Marvels Encyclopedia*, the writing was a little more serious than its rival, it was more British, with less genuflection towards the United States. As well as the usual wonder material on flying, cars, trains, science and engineering, this book also included short articles on anthropology, microbiology and stories of human endeavour.[58] It was far from being an encyclopaedia, but it covered a lot of ground without hyperbole or defensiveness.

One important, but now obscure, contributor to the modern wonders trope was Archibald Low who wrote many books on the theme. Low was a popularizing, well-published writer on science, technology and the future, who emphasized its potential for the transformation of everyday life.[59] After graduating from Imperial College in London and developing many inventions that were seldom realized as practical projects, he awarded himself the title of 'Professor'. This for his many academic critics added insult to injury. His friend, Lord Brabazon of Tara, wrote that he 'never really had any claim to the title'.[60] From 1924 until after the Second World War, Low produced a steady stream of books aimed at a non-specialist audience. From a long list of his publications, three titles draw the eye: *Our Wonderful World of Tomorrow* (1934), *Conquering Space and Time* (1937) and *What New Wonders! The Story of the Pasadena Telescope* (1938).[61] The first two of these books consist of Low's imaginative futurism, most of which did not come to fruition. More interesting is Low's *What New Wonders!*, which was a highly speculative book in which he cobbled together press cuttings on the construction of a new, American 200-inch reflecting telescope, which was not in fact completed until 1949, with his own insights into astronomy. Despite its flimsy premise, it provides us with two useful insights. First, it contained a justification for the modern wonder trope's obsession with what Low called 'bigness'. He explained, for instance, that doubling the length of a bridge involved squaring its weight, which often meant that engineers were nearing the limits of a material's capability.[62] Success in overcoming these problems was therefore a wonder. Second was the way the book engaged with this show of strength of American technology. Low downplayed this, and was keen to explain the significance of British and Canadian work with smaller telescopes.

Low was also the editor of the monthly *Armchair Science*, one of several magazines that catered for adults who wanted to understand the marvels of the world, know more about science or to better comprehend a new technology. *Armchair Science*, also from the Odhams' stable, ran from 1929 to 1941.[63] It advertised in *Modern Wonder*, perhaps trying to catch a father reading his son's paper. By 1938, Low's magazine had adopted a 'pocket' format using some original contributions, but for the most part depending on the republication of articles that had appeared in newspapers. Some of these articles were British, but most were from the United States. For example, the June 1938 edition featured articles from *America's Consumer's Digest*, *Christian Science Monitor*, *Telephone Review*, *General Electric Review* and *Sunday Mirror*. These 'special' articles were accompanied by regular features on topics such as astronomy, electricity and radio.[64]

'Those Hullo Bacteria', a condensed article from an American source, catches the style of the magazine. It posed a burning question of the age, 'Is the telephone a spreader of germs? Prominent scientists give the answer.' This human-interest question was answered by a quite serious account of studies carried out by Bell Telephone and two eminent American scientists. The answer was yes, but only in winter and spring. Another article in the same issue from a British source explained the wonders of television. 'Putting Pictures on the Air' explored a common journalistic theme of 1937 and 1938 which was to explain in simple terms how the BBC made television shows and how this technical process worked (see Chapter 4). The magazine used a photograph of a performer in his make-up chair to lead the article, inviting the reader into the story through Americanized, glib phrasing. 'Keeping up appearances is hard work when you're a television star, for the high-definition "emitron" camera has a critical eye. Here is Hugh Wakefield preparing to make a hit in the home set by putting himself in the hands of make-up expert Mary Allan.'[65] *Armchair Science*'s content was deliberately superficial, and aimed at those who wanted to understand the modern world of 1938, but did not have the inclination to dive deeper into its possibilities and problems. It had the same tone and the pocket size of *Reader's Digest*, first published in Britain that year.[66]

Picture Post (see Chapter 6) was a populist photojournalism magazine which began publishing in October 1938. It did not engage in modern wonder content, but did have a regular science column 'Science To-Day', written by journalist John Langdon-Davies, that presented 'the latest discoveries about animals, machines or medicine [which] are dealt with simply and vividly each week'.[67] The tone of the column was a little less chummy than *Armchair Science*, with one issue covering topics such as 'The Way to Measure a Tadpole', which was an introduction to the treatment of thyroid complaints and 'The Trouble About Pickles' as a way of explaining enzymes.[68]

Discovery was another late-1930s magazine that sought to explain the world of science and technology to ordinary readers. It was formed with much the same philosophy as the BBC, to inform and educate, but without, it seems, any need to entertain. Its approach was to provide space for eminent scientists and academics to explain their work based on what they thought would be interesting to the public.[69] Edited by Cambridge scientist C. P. Snow, later to become an influential novelist, the magazine had, at his instigation, increased its level of academic rigour, dropped its subtitle ('the popular journal of knowledge') and moved to Cambridge University Press, a publisher far removed from Odhams' Fleet Street ways.[70] *Discovery* under its new press was as dry and pedagogic as *Armchair Science* was reductive and glib. Its August 1938 edition gives a good impression of its content, situating itself some way below the scholarly level of a scientific journal, which its lay readers would find difficult to access, but a long way above the world of modern wonders. Articles included: 'Breeding Time in the Gull Colonies', 'Forty Years of Physics' by the late Lord Rutherford and a far from prurient explanation of the Hawaiian Hula Dance.[71]

The unrelenting direction of modern and scientific wonder material towards men and boys sits in direct contrast with the way most British publishers dealt with their female readers, who magazine editors almost always thought of as housewives and mothers.[72] *Modern Woman* was one magazine that made a specific call to modernity. It began its run in 1925 and, in 1938, was very typical of women's magazines of the time, featuring knitting, infant care, health and romantic fictions as its mainstays. The magazine also published occasional booklets on important topics for women. These implied that its readers were inexperienced, middle class and well-off and required explanations of how to show good manners, control their servants, undertake interior decoration and manage party games.[73] Odhams, publisher of *Modern Wonder* and *Armchair Science*, launched a competing magazine, *Woman,* into a crowded field in 1937. Based on Odhams' rather obsessive stance on modern life when addressing a male audience, one might have expected something distinctive from this magazine. In reality, *Woman* was a lighter read than *Modern Woman* with more romantic fiction and pitched a little down-market from its more established competitor. *Modern Woman* had one distinctive modern feature which appeared each month, a motoring page written by motoring editor, actress and former 'bright young thing', Sunday Wilshin.[74] Each month she answered readers' queries and in her column provided solid advice on car choices, and how to keep a car well maintained.[75]

It is noticeable that the advertising in these two magazines was rather more modern than their feature pages. An advertisement for a high-powered Ford V8 car placed next to Wilshin's column contended that 'until you have driven a Ford V8 you don't know what twentieth century motoring can mean'.[76] The assumption in both Wilshin's column and in the advertisement that women were influential in purchasing motor cars is intriguing, because even as late as 1938, most drivers were men. Two other advertisements explicitly recognized women's place in the modern world. Norwich Union proposed a pension for independent 'bachelor girls' which apparently would still have some value when the lucky bachelorette got married. There were also advertisements for 'Tampax' tampons, which in 1938 was a very new product competing with more old-fashioned arrangements for feminine hygiene.[77] It made a direct appeal to modern women and explained the product's features and advantages in straightforward language. This was also, along with Ford's V8, an example of an American company attempting to build a British customer base, which was a very direct form of Americanization.

Modern wonder books and magazines allowed for passive male readers to understand and then admire technologies from afar. Spotters at stations and airports who might have appeared to be more engaged with modernity were also, in effect, passive admirers. However, by the late 1930s, it was possible for Britons to directly engage with technology through their own consumption. This book records this phenomenon in, for example, the use of still and movie cameras to record everyday life (see Chapter 3) and in the acquisition of radio, radiogram and television sets (see Chapter 4). The first of these topics is interesting as it provoked the launch of several 'how to' photography magazines. This was also true of other domestic technologies, such as radios, but those magazines were very technical, based around wiring diagrams and a soldering iron, whereas photography was more creative and tellingly far less male.[78] One photography magazine stood out, the monthly *Kodak* magazine, subscribed to by owners of Kodak cameras. *Kodak* showed women controlling a machine and understanding its technical complexities. It also employed them as technical authors without any comment on their gender.

Kodak, a phenomenally successful American company with a worldwide market, had revolutionized cheap home photography in Britain and elsewhere with its 'Brownie' camera.[79] By 1938, it also offered 35-millimetre still and 8-millimetre movie cameras for the amateur market.[80] John Taylor has shown how, through their advertising, Kodak played its part in the interwar feminization of Britain and promoted gender equality. He explains that as early as the 1920s and throughout the interwar period 'Kodak advertisements rarely acknowledged that men used cameras'.[81] Taylor does not explain Kodak's reasons for this policy, but its marketing department may have either thought women controlled the decision to buy a camera, as they were thought to do with domestic goods, or it believed women projected a breezy modernity or perhaps both. In a marked contrast to the more fanciful magazines this chapter has discussed, *Kodak* downplayed the modern wonder style of discourse, emphasizing how easy, reliable and normal it was to use its machines. For example, an advert for the Ciné-Kodak Eight movie camera explained how 'you can make your own black-and-white films ... QUITE as easily as you take snaps!'.[82]

Kodak's promotion of women in its adverts for a technical, modern product was notable for the period, but putting them forward as technical experts was highly unusual at a time when almost all technical authors were men. *Kodak* magazine for April 1938 provides a good example featuring an article from Mrs M. Taylor who explains how to take good photos when visiting a farm: 'There are two things which I have found it wisest to never forget ... my gum boots and a colour filter ... with a Wratten K1 the exposure need only be increased half as much again.'[83]

The combination of women in its adverts with female technical writers explaining how to use filters and other technical considerations gave this magazine a distinctive attitude towards new technologies that emphasized their ease of operation, and a modernity based on an Americanized gender equality. These qualities were far from evident in the leading British enthusiast's magazine of the period, *Amateur Photographer and Cinematographer*. Its 1938 output suggests that all its writers and almost all its readers (judging by its letters page) were male.[84]

Conclusion

We have always been and will continue to be modern. Attempting a specific periodization that identifies one particular year as modern might be foolish, but without making any absolutist claims for the year, in 1938 there was an unusual emphasis on modernity in magazines, books and newsreels. It would be easy to assume that this was linked to the rise in militarism of the late 1930s, but a close examination of these sources finds that, although some military items featured in the magazines and cigarette card sets, most were civilian. This emphasis on modernity seems to be restricted to newsreel and literary sources, and nothing out of the ordinary can be found in movies or radio programmes of that year. That magazines were the source of most modern wonder material in 1938 is not that surprising as it was a format that lent itself to technical explanation and helpful illustrations. This was a medium that was affordable and attractive to older boys and young men who were the target audience for features of this type. As a result, reflecting late interwar society as a whole, most of the articles in these magazines were gendered and ignored the albeit limited role of women in scientific and technical discoveries at this time. The American camera company, Kodak, provided a glimpse of the future, featuring women writers and women photographers in its British camera user's magazine.

One of the key themes that emerges from this material is the attitude of British publishers to American technological leadership. A dialectic is woven into these magazines and cigarette cards, which praises British achievement, often in the form of speed records held by British heroes while recognizing that the United States was the home of most new technological achievements. This was written in two ways. First, it assumed that British readers knew and understood American life and geographies. They were, for example, expected to understand without explanation where Kansas City was and how it could work as an airline hub in such a large country. In effect, this made the reader American too.[85] Second, these articles reflected a rather apologetic pride, which proposed that people in the United States would be very impressed if only they could see what Britain had achieved. In effect, modern wonder magazines and books were negotiating a change in imperial leadership that was becoming, through technology, increasingly visible in

1938. The impact of the Second World War made this a much more one-sided competition, an advantage that continued until the early twenty-first century when American audiences needed Chinese achievements explained to them in the same way.[86]

* * *

The case studies that form the remaining chapters of this book describe and interpret aspects of technological, cultural and social change in the late 1930s. These cases are more than just modern wonder material but they reflect some aspects of this theme, such as the use of reinforced concrete as a building material, the rise of passenger airlines and the excitement generated by the introduction of television.

CHAPTER THREE

Glasgow's Empire Exhibition

*I cannot imagine any man or woman going away from this
Exhibition without a feeling of exultation that he or she
is a factor in the wonder of modern life.*[1]

The first of the case studies considers the Glasgow Empire Exhibition, one of the major public events of 1938, but now largely forgotten. Here were found displays of technology and engineering housed in buildings that exemplified British architectural modernism, but with, on occasion, a whimsical edge that looked forward to the more famous, but smaller, Festival of Britain on London's South Bank thirteen years later. This assembly of modern buildings also provided a preview of post-war industrial structures. Those attending the exhibition looked in awe at this modern world, which sat in marked contrast to the city that surrounded the exhibition site, Glasgow having suffered much in the years of depression. The experience of most visitors to the exhibition was, inevitably, passive, but the more privileged took an active interest by using their still and movie cameras to record their visits. Their self-mediated accounts provide pointed evidence of their experience of modernity.

FIGURE 3.1 *ICI Pavilion by Basil Spence, Image Credit: Architectural Press Archive/
RIBA Collections.*

In 1920, it was still possible to think of Glasgow as the second city of the Empire, such was its history in providing the leaders, engineers and functionaries that served Britain's imperial purpose. The knowledge that Glasgow had been the leading industrial city in the world, building the majority of the world's ships and providing much of Britain's coal and steel, supported this claim to greatness.[2] Ten years later, world events and economic crisis had destroyed Glasgow's prestige. Most of the Clyde's massive shipyards were silent, tens of thousands of skilled tradesmen were out of work or on short time, demand for coal and steel was minimal. Glasgow's dirty Victorian offices, factories, tenements and slums were a generation out of place. J. B. Priestley's third England, which identified an Americanized, secular modernity in parts of the midlands and the south-east of England definitely excluded Wales and Scotland. Nowhere was the modern world less embraced than in this proud city.

In 1934, the United Kingdom government was prepared to use Keynesian deficit financing to restart the country's regional economies. For Glasgow, this was evident in the resumption of the shipbuilding project that would, on its launch in 1936, become RMS Queen Mary and the rearmament programme that was breathing life back into an economy based around coal, steel and ships. In order to generate further growth in the Scottish economy, Sir James Lithgow and other Glaswegian industrialists prompted the Scottish Development Corporation to plan an exhibition that would put the city back on the world stage.[3] A world festival, such as Stockholm in 1930, Chicago in 1933 and Paris in 1937, was not a possibility as these were regulated by international agreement and Glasgow would have to wait many years for its turn.[4] It was, though, possible for the city to hold an Empire Exhibition. This idea was both feasible and appropriate for a city with such strong imperial credentials, Glasgow having been the site of successful exhibitions in 1888, 1901 and 1911.[5] Scotland's great and good mobilized to provide the sponsorship and leadership for this enterprise. Edinburgh set aside its traditional rivalry and agreed that the next Empire Exhibition would be held in Glasgow in 1938. After some discussion, the committee agreed that the most favourable location for the exhibition was Bellahouston Park, to the south of the city, near Rangers' Ibrox stadium. This had the advantage of being close to existing or potential public transport infrastructure and the disadvantage of being on a route from central Glasgow that led past some of the city's worst slums.

The 1938 Glasgow Empire Exhibition has received academic interest in recent years, but it is not anything like as well known to the general reader as the big British exhibitions that preceded and followed it, the 1924 Empire Exhibition at Wembley and the 1951 Festival of Britain.[6] I count myself as a fan of interwar modernism, but this exhibition had passed me by.

Design of the exhibition

The exhibition had five objectives, of which four had imperial interests at their heart, stressing the fellowship and possibility of progress provided by the British Empire. Its remaining objective had a modernizing theme: to 'stimulate Scottish work and production' although an appeal to 'Scotland's historical and scenic attractions' moderated its impact.[7] In effect, the exhibition had to engage with competing discourses on Scotland's past, its status as a nation, its imperial role and as an exemplar of modernity.[8]

One of the most significant decisions made by the Scottish Development Corporation was its appointing Thomas Tait, Scotland's leading architect, in charge of the design of the exhibition. His most well-known work at the time was St. Andrew's House (a government building in Edinburgh) and the pylons of Sydney Harbour Bridge. The latter project, completed in 1932, made news around the world and became a shorthand symbol for industrial modernity. Tait was, like many leading British architects of the 1930s, making the journey from a restrained classical approach to modernism, although he didn't care for the modernist title himself.[9] Despite this, he was an early advocate for this style of architecture. He was, for instance, the architect of an estate of flat-roofed, white-walled houses for Crittalls, the steel window company, as early as 1927.[10] Tait was responsible at Bellahouston Park for bringing together the largest assembly of modern architecture ever seen in Britain.

Tait exercised control over the design of the exhibition for both the layout of the site and the architecture of all its buildings. Bellahouston Park provided 175 acres of land for the project. This was a large site and compared favourably with the 1951 Festival of Britain site on the South Bank which only had twenty-seven acres to play with.[11] It was mostly flat, with a tree-clad hill at its centre.[12] Tait designed a 'C'-shaped layout comprising three long roadways, and proposed surmounting the hill with a 300-foot tower.[13] The three roadways provided access to the main exhibition pavilions. The largest had two parallel 'ways': Colonial Avenue and Dominions Avenue, with a flower-bed separating the pavilions of the white self-governing states from the other, blacker outposts of the as-yet undiminished empire.[14] At one end was the enormous Palace of Engineering, at the other, one of the two Palace of Industries.[15] A right turn here led down Kingsway, home to the huge United Kingdom Government Pavilion, another right turn found the exhibition visitor in Scottish Avenue flanked by two identical Scottish pavilions. Scattered among these principal buildings of the exhibition were many restaurants and smaller exhibition buildings provided by state and commercial enterprises.

The architectural press gave the exhibition a good reception. J. M. Richards, a leading modernist critic of the period wrote:

> An Empire Exhibition, in a country as architecturally backward as Britain, cannot expect to draw on the same richness of architectural talent as an

FIGURE 3.2 *Scottish Pavilion, architectural drawing by Basil Spence. Image Credit:* © *Historic Environment Scotland (Sir Basil Spence Archive).*

International Exhibition. We did not expect Glasgow to make the same active contributions to the sum of modern architectural experience as Paris did last year; in fact, with only the dismal memory of Wembley to guide us, we expected a great deal less; and the fact that the visitor to Glasgow finds himself in fact criticizing this exhibition by recent international standards, even if because of that his praise is sometimes qualified, is the greatest tribute Mr. Tait could wish for.[16]

Tait's insistence on standardization and prefabrication was one aspect of the exhibition singled out for praise. These ideals fitted into both a modernist and industrial sensibility through the use of the mass-production principles that had transformed manufacturing productivity in recent years. It was also a practical approach to solving the problem of building a sophisticated exhibition from scratch in about eighteen months. The key ingredient at Bellahouston Park was Tait's use of specially commissioned standard-sized asbestos cement panels in each palace and pavilion. The panels were spray-painted before leaving the factory, ensuring an efficient process and avoiding the difficulties of painting outdoors in Glasgow's unfavourable weather. He also commissioned long, low windows that fitted into the space left by omitting a panel.[17] As J. Neil Baxter comments, 'Tait's adoption of standard parts ensured order and unity: a plethora of different designs were give common scale.'[18]

Figure 3.2 shows a drawing of one of the more prominent components of the exhibition, the Scottish Pavilion. This building was officially attributed to Tait, but it is now accepted that Basil Spence was the architect. Spence, thirty years old in 1938, was to become one of Britain's most successful twentieth-

FIGURE 3.3 *The Tower of Empire by Thomas Tait, Image Credit: Architectural Press Archive/RIBA Collections.*

century architects, later famous for his designs for Coventry Cathedral and the University of Sussex.[19] The Scottish Pavilion exemplified a more relaxed approach than would have been the case in an exhibition held earlier in the decade. The designs had many of the typical features of modernist public buildings, but also had a lighter, more relaxed air achieved by using colour, blue in the case of this building. Spence deployed tall, slender towers to bear the Saltire, giving the building an elegant appearance.

The complete effect of Tait and Spence's efforts was evident in the final exhibition in a series of long, low buildings that produced a strong, coherent temporary cityscape that avoided strict modernism by adopting pastel colours, such as primrose, cerise, coral and poppy.[20] The approach to the main pavilions also avoided the clichéd Hollywoodism of many new commercial buildings of this decade, although this was not the case in the most famous structure in the exhibition, the Tower of Empire.

The Tower of Empire, soon popularly known as Tait's Tower, was a 300-foot steel structure anchored to the top of Bellahouston Hill, which gave it a commanding view over the exhibition site. The tower was a focal point for the exhibition and projected Glasgow as a forward-thinking futuristic city. The original idea was that the tower and some of the other more solid pavilions would be permanently situated in the park, but when the exhibition closed in October 1938, the organizers discarded this proposal as Britain began earnest preparation for a different and more serious future.[21]

Even from today's perspective, the tower presents a striking image. We are used to tall structures in Britain today, but in 1938 this was not the case; for example, people considered Senate House in London, at 210 feet, to be a skyscraper. The tower's purpose was reminiscent, albeit at a smaller scale, of the Eiffel Tower, which was the centrepiece of the Paris World's Fair of 1889 and its seaside tribute Blackpool Tower. The exhibition's organizers permitted themselves some hyperbole in their introduction: 'The Tower of Babel, the pyramids of ancient Egypt, the minarets of the East, the Gothic spires of Europe, and the sky-scrapers of Manhattan all testify to the constancy of man's aspiration towards the heavens. [It] is symbolic of all that is enterprising and is the crowning achievement of the imagination.'[22]

The tower consisted of a steel framework, clothed in pale blue corrugated steel panels.[23] It had three viewing platforms, picked out in a pale red, reached by two lifts. These platforms held up to 600 people at a time and on the occasional clear day in the rainy summer of 1938 provided a sixty-mile view of Glasgow and the Highlands beyond.[24] In total, about 1.3 million people went up the tower.[25] It was positioned above the Clachan, an exhibit of historical Scottish vernacular buildings and crafts; nowhere in the exhibition was there a greater contrast between the competing discourses of Scottishness and modernity. Colin McArthur describes this visual assault as though 'the Clachan and the Tower of Empire are polar points of the dialectic which threatens to render individual Scots schizoid'.[26] Scotland's cartoon-strip favourite 'Oor Wullie' also played with this idea, debating the merits of traditional vernacular Glaswegian versus 'correct' modern English when describing the exhibition to his teacher.[27]

Tait's tower received some gushing praise. Influential architectural critic John Summerson called it a 'noble piece of steel construction and a very proper ornament for a great engineering city'.[28] Even the diffident London press remarked that 'the tower dominates the exhibition and there is a certain melancholy in the thought that such a noble prospect will be lost to human eyes when ... the tower is brought low'.[29] The *Architectural Review*, 'the mouthpiece of British modernism' was less pleased:[30]

Though impressive from many angles it cannot be said to be an unqualified success; the use of modernistic clichés rather overwhelms its structural significance. On such a scale only complete sincerity succeeds. It is too self-consciously a monument; whereas in fact it is simply a lift-shaft. It might indeed have been more effective to have designed it in skeleton form so that the visible ascent of the lifts gave it a more characteristic interest and, incidentally, typify better the Exhibition's situation in the heart of an engineering world.[31]

More recent commentators have also found fault with the tower; Charles McKean compares the similarities of the tower's floodlight roaming the exhibition ground at night to the Nazi rallies held in Nuremburg in the same year.[32] More plausibly, Colin McArthur describes it as 'being inspired in equal measure by Le Corbusier, MGM and the Flash Gordon serials'.[33]

The thought that the exhibition, because of the problem of addressing the themes of Empire and Scotland's past and future simultaneously, had failed to fully engage with the possibilities of modern technology is interesting. Although Tait did not think of himself as a modernist, there was an explicit call to modernity provided by the architecture of the exhibition. The dramatic visual impact of the tower and the rapid construction and deployment of the main buildings using mass-production techniques demonstrated an aesthetic and practical response to the modern world.

These themes were also evident in the smaller pavilions that private corporations built to advertise their products and services. Tait was happy to allow these firms to appoint their own architects to work under his supervision, resulting in greater individualism than in the main pavilions. Of particular interest is the Imperial Chemical Industries' (ICI) pavilion. ICI was Britain's leading chemical company, formed from the merger of several companies working in different sectors, including chemicals, explosives, fertilizers, insecticides, dyestuffs, non-ferrous metals and paints. ICI also invented and marketed the early plastics, polythene and perspex; products that still have a place today.[34] In short, ICI was in 1938 a shining example of Britain's new industries.

Basil Spence also designed ICI's pavilion, a commission he won in a public competition on Tait's recommendation (see Figure 3.1). The outcome suggests that Tait allowed Spence a far longer rein for this project than he permitted for the twin Scottish pavilions. The resulting building was positioned below the Tower of Empire and next to the exclusive Garden Club restaurant, well situated for visiting dignitaries to notice it. Spence produced a small circular pavilion with three impressive towers that overlooked a small pool guarded by large frogs sculpted from sheet copper. He decorated each of the towers with sculptural panels to represent earth, air and water, which he considered were the elemental components of the chemical industry.[35] A new ICI non-ferrous product, cupro-nickel curved rods, tied the three towers together.[36] The interior of the pavilion was, apart from its steel pillars and wood frame, built entirely of ICI products.[37] Through this approach, Spence connected the exhibition to the modern world that Glasgow's industrialists wished for. He also introduced a whimsical element, welcome in a rather serious exhibition that mostly confined fun to its amusement park. Robert Hurd, a renowned Scottish conservationist architect, considered the ICI pavilion the best exhibit at Bellahouston.[38] After dark, floodlights illuminated the pavilion and a 200-foot coloured beam of light projected up from the pool.[39] The proprietor of the *Daily Record* considered that 'illuminated buildings such as this make Bellahouston a City of Brilliance by night'.[40]

In 1938, *Architectural Review* commissioned 27-year-old Hugh Casson to provide sketches for its special edition on the Empire Exhibition.[41] Thirteen years later he was to be the director of the Festival of Britain, where Spence was a member of his team. Spence could draw on his experience from the 1938 ICI pavilion by reusing the 'dramatic effects of exaggerated height and atmosphere' used there.[42] Some writers position the 1951 Festival of Britain as a signal post-war event; an exhibition that allowed Britain to find a new confidence that promulgated a new architectural style in Britain.[43] Casson's biographer thought that the 1951 festival drew on ideas from the 1930 Stockholm Exhibition: 'Cues were taken from ... exhibition designs from pre-war Europe for decorative effects ... including a prodigal use of colour and a preference for lightweight, nautically inspired buildings.'[44] Much of this applied to the Glasgow exhibition, which was also influenced by Stockholm.[45] The Atlantic Restaurant was the shape of an ocean liner, and Tait favoured coloured elevations, built from pre-fabricated lightweight panels. Some saw the 1951 festival as introducing a 'picturesque' element to 1950s design, modifying the strict modernism of the 1930s. Spence's ICI pavilion did this in spades. While the external face of much of the rest of the Glasgow exhibition was plain, there were some surprises in how the buildings interacted with each other, particularly the juxtapositions of the lower part of the park and the Tower of Empire and the Atlantic restaurant. Although John Gold concludes that the 'Festival [of Britain] brought the British public into intimate contact with modern architecture for the first time', one can't but help think that by British he means London.[46] While Casson's contribution to changing British architecture is still applauded, Tait was not so lucky and his work is now largely forgotten. A combination of metropolitan prejudice and disdain and, more importantly, very bad timing has deprived him of the status he deserves.[47]

The BBC, British Railways (BR) and the Post Office also delivered buildings and exhibits that connected with modern technologies. Of these three, the BBC and BR contained them within beautiful modern buildings, the latter by Joseph Emberton, one of Britain's leading interwar leisure architects.[48] The Post Office delivered a lump of a building that it inadvisably painted pillar-box red, putting it out of step with the pastels and white of the other buildings. The BBC demonstrated its services, including 'talks, television, musical and dramatic performances, news time signals, weather forecasts', and made several broadcasts from the exhibition site.[49] BR was able to show the latest in railway carriages from each of the 'Big Four' rail companies, together with a model railway exhibition, a hobby popular with both parents and children.[50] The Post Office building's ceiling housed a mysterious aeroplane flying across maps of the world, showing the routes of the Empire Air Mail, neatly connecting two key themes of the exhibition.[51] The Post Office also demonstrated 'TIM', its new speaking clock and showed a replica of a Coast Wireless Station that kept in touch with the Scottish shipping fleet in the North Sea and Artic Ocean. Live demonstrations of this modern technology were given from time to time.[52]

Visitors saw the latest developments in technology at the Palace of Engineering and the two Palaces of Industry. There were two buildings for 'industry' because the proposed initial design was too small and the exhibition thus needed a second building. Tait provided the additional building in rapid time using corrugated steel panels and his mass-production methods.[53] The *Architectural Review* appreciated the technologies involved in producing this structure, but did not approve of its contents. 'It is horrible to think what must be the impression of, say, a visitor from the Continent when he walks through the Palaces of Industry at Glasgow. [They] house an incredibly tasteless collection of tawdry and shoddy-looking goods – furniture, china, glass and fabrics.'[54]

Closer to home, visitors to the exhibition found the origins of some of the goods dismaying. A Glasgow man wrote, 'I'm beginning to wonder, if the show at Bellahouston is a British Empire Exhibition or a German and Japanese Exhibition judging by the goods used and sold.'[55]

Due to the power of eBay.com, it is still possible to appreciate what the sniffy architects from London were complaining about, as eighty years later, the souvenirs bought at the Palace of Industry and elsewhere in the exhibition are still for sale. Models of the Tower of Empire, spoons, plates, brooches, wallets and jigsaw puzzles commemorating the exhibition are available from about £5 to £40.[56]

The massive United Kingdom Government Pavilion, whose entrance was flanked by two marvellous Art Deco lions, housed a variety of exhibits that addressed the modern technological world. The 'Fitter Britain' exhibit tied into an important aspect of British life in the 1930s, the desire to move away from slum housing and dirty industries and to connect with the outdoors and sunlight. This exhibit featured a mechanical man with a naturalistic sculpture on one side. The other side displayed the inside of the human body as a machine with cameras for eyes and a petrol pump for a heart, accompanied by a spoken commentary explaining how he worked.[57] As Chapter 2 has shown, this reflected a common theme of the time: the rise of automation and the modern wonders of science here reaching an imagined pinnacle of a working robot. This mechanical man was designed by Welsh sculptor Richard Huws whose work was also later seen at the Festival of Britain.[58]

The United Kingdom pavilion had many other exhibits that portrayed Britain as technologically advanced, matching competing nations such as the United States and, more pertinently in 1938, Germany. To that end, the government provided the visitors to the exhibition with a working model of a mine and a blast furnace.[59] Some lowland Scots and visitors from the north of England would be well qualified to say whether the model was accurate or not as these areas were centres of production for both coal and steel. For middle-class visitors, it provided an insight into technologies they increasingly depended on, but of which they had no first-hand experience. The pavilion also presented a model of the world revolving in space. This sight is something that since the mid-1960s has been a commonplace image, but, here, intrigued a public who were, through science-fiction, increasingly aware of the possibilities of outer space. Nearer to home and the Clyde, this pavilion demonstrated a 'fully equipped bridge of a liner'.[60] This may well have been the first time Clydebank riveters were able to see one of the key components of a ship they worked on. Ocean liners were a symbol of national, technological prestige and a strong influence on 1930s design, their characteristics seen in *moderne* architecture for houses and public buildings.[61] The Atlantic restaurant, built as the prow of a ship on top of Bellahouston Hill, brought this idea to the exhibition.[62]

The Palace of Engineering was another site that paid tribute to the modern world of 1938. This huge building with a 465-foot frontage was divided into sections on building materials, electricity, engineering, metals, quarries, gas, hardware and shipbuilding.[63] It housed several wonders promoting domestic modernity with displays of luxurious fireplace suites in attractive enamel finishings, panel fires, gas and electric stoves, central heating and refrigerators. The palace showed innovations such as a 'mysterious door opened by invisible ray' and, on a much larger-scale, hydro-electric schemes on which Scotland led the way. Reflecting the times, a number of exhibits had military themes and showed the Armed Forces' use of Britain's latest technologies.

Visiting and experiencing the exhibition

The exhibition was open from 3 May to 29 October 1938, a year in which Glasgow had a rainy spring and summer. Admission was one shilling (5p) for adults and sixpence (2.5p) for children.[64] The total number of admissions for the whole run of the exhibition was 12.7 million people, which was somewhat fewer than the number needed to break even. The weather was a problem and some local commentators thought the festival had not been well promoted to English visitors.[65] Nevertheless, this was a huge number of people and about 50 per cent greater than the number of people who attended the much more acclaimed Festival of Britain at the South Bank in 1951. Almost all English visitors came by train, and for ordinary people who could only afford a day trip, the distances involved made attendance difficult. Even a day trip by train from as far north in England as Lancashire involved leaving at 7.30 am and returning at 3.00 am the following day. The total cost of 11 shillings (55p) per person excluded many who wanted to go.[66]

One journalist reported: 'Shrill Cockney voices, soft Highland accents, drawling Yorkshire dialects, staccato American phrases and foreign languages of all kinds can be heard. And here can be seen colourfully-garbed Japanese, Indians and Continentals.'[67] It is hard to be exact from this distance, but it would seem likely that most visitors were from northern England and Scotland within reach of the exhibition by train or coach, or if they were Glaswegian, by tram. It also seems plausible that most of the visitors were from prosperous working-class families and from the middle classes. The cost of entry deterred poorer families from attending, and Glasgow's slow economic recovery ensured that many Scots were in this position. That a Glasgow working-class newspaper, the *Sunday Post*, needed to run a competition for one of its readers to win a prize for a day out at the exhibition emphasized this.[68]

Oral history collection exercises or memoirs triggered by significant anniversaries have stimulated most of the personal accounts about the exhibition available to us today. The result is that they have generally been written by people recalling their experiences as small children. As a result, these accounts have their limitations. Artist James Morrison describes his visit to the exhibition on a Sunday and how his father enjoyed the Palace of Engineering. He also recalls that the site was muddy from continual rain, something that isn't noticeable in much of the boosterist material in the local press. Morrison was from a modest background but recalls his father enjoying it so much that, in a very unusual event for his family, he returned on his own to see all the scientific exhibits before the exhibition finally closed.[69]

Journalist Bob Crampsey describes his childhood visit to Bellahouston Park as part of a school party, which must have been a common way for many children to attend. Crampsey's account, 'One of the Thirteen Million' does not appear to have been rewritten by later experience as he emphasizes the typical schoolboy interest in larking about and getting bored by worthy stuff and wishing to get to the amusement park as soon as possible. He was, though, struck with the excitement of the exhibition after dark. 'In the evenings [the Tower] dominated everything. Even more wonderful were the fountains with the constantly changing coloured lights and the creeping neon signs which made visual poetry of the most prosaic advertisements.'[70]

The *Weekly News*, a newspaper that aimed itself at ordinary readers, produced a free souvenir of the exhibition. This provides us with an uncritical, but useful, summary of events written for its strictly Scottish audience. Alongside the patriotic material on the royal family and photographic records of the buildings, it shows how most visitors enjoyed the exhibition. It noted the fun to be had from dancing; it was popular to dance in the avenues between the exhibition buildings after dark, so popular at times that there was little room to do anything but watch. The souvenir explains that the military bands attracted little interest and public concerts only became well attended when the organizers added swing music to the programme. Elsewhere it notes the long queues for the exhibits, the good-humoured Scottish patience of the crowds and, in an era not known for its cuisine, the enthusiasm for trying out new treats such as open-air dining and toffee apples.[71]

The more distinguished middle-class visitor to the exhibition came by car, the organizers providing 10,000 daily car parking spaces.[72] Bearing in mind there were only about 70,000 cars in the central belt of Scotland, either this was a miscalculation or the organizers were expecting large numbers of English motorists to cross the border.[73] Author and broadcaster Magnus Magnusson, too young to go himself, recalled his parents driving to the exhibition in the 'faithful family Lanchester' returning home 'positively transfixed by pleasure and exhaustion'.[74] Middle-class experience of technology is telling because this group had the economic privileges that allowed for its early adoption. The wealthier section of the middle classes was usually the social group with the greatest opportunity to use new technologies rather than be used by them. There were exceptions. For example, cinema was a predominantly working-class and lower-middle-class phenomenon in the interwar period, so that this technology with its power to transmit American culture and modernity had a wide impact.

One important technology that transformed British culture in the late 1930s was the wide adoption of still film cameras and the much more exclusive and far more expensive hobby of amateur moviemaking. The Kodak 'Brownie' and other cheap cameras brought still photography to many lower-middle-class households between the wars, as evidenced by the large number of photograph albums from the period that still turn up at local auction houses. The photographs often feature the same topics: visits to the countryside, to the seaside, sitting in deckchairs, enjoying the garden, going on holiday. The limits of film and cameras at the time were such that amateur photographs were almost always taken out of doors. By 1938, for the wealthier photographer, the introduction of a 35-millimetre film had improved the quality and portability of cameras and this is seen in amateur photographs of the exhibition.

The exhibition was an opportunity for both camera makers and photographers. Kodak placed newspaper advertisements promoting its products as an ideal means of capturing a personal account of the exhibition.[75] I bought a collection of photos taken at the Glasgow exhibition that were available on eBay for a reasonable price. They were taken on a medium format camera, perhaps a folding, pocket Kodak that was popular at the time.[76] Each photograph in the collection is a landscape picture, most often showing the exterior of a pavilion, although occasionally a more picturesque approach was used. It seems this photographer went alone to the exhibition, or was interested in modern architecture, or perhaps both. Those visitors who did not own a camera could buy a small collection of postcards of the exhibition buildings to help take home the experience with them.[77]

Kodak, an enthusiasts' magazine, proposed:

Scotland's magnificent empire exhibition fully deserves the praise which has been so freely lavished upon it and offers an almost bewildering variety of subjects for your camera. … Whereas previous exhibitions have been predominantly white, the architects here have made full use of colour, and splendid opportunities abound for delightful Kodachrome pictures to the lucky possessors of Cine-Kodaks.[78]

The movies that amateur filmmakers took of the exhibition also reflected a preference for architecture over people. Home moviemaking was an elite hobby in the late 1930s. One broad estimate was that there were 250,000 Britons, mostly men, who had this as a hobby in this decade, compared to a mid-decade figure for the number of car owners of around 1.5 million.[79] If the estimate is reliable, then about 2.5 per cent of British households had access to a cine-camera.[80] This is not surprising; the prices of cine-cameras, film, developing and projection equipment prohibited all but the wealthiest section of society from participating in this interest. For example, a basic cine-camera cost £15 to £20 at the start of the 1930s, but as increasing levels of automation and sophistication became available, prices reached as high as £150 for a top of the range Kodak 16-millimetre colour cine-camera by the end of the decade.[81] To put this into context, a modern, suburban detached house in a smart area cost £1,000 or sometimes less. It is reasonable to assume that anybody taking a cine-camera to the exhibition was very well-off and had the leisure time needed to enjoy this pastime.

The National Library of Scotland has an extensive video archive, and one surprise of its catalogue is the large number of amateur films in its collection of the 1938 Empire Exhibition. Most of these were filmed in 16-millimetre colour, were silent and lasted from about 3 minutes to 15 minutes long. Reviewing these films provides much of interest. Of the six most complete films, four were, essentially, documentary films produced by amateur filmmakers; the remaining two share much similar footage but also contained shots of family members enjoying themselves at the exhibition.[82] These films do not capture the unconscious pleasure of home movies made to record family activities and events, which provide 'an ethnographic record, with the crucial difference that they are unmediated self-representations'.[83] There is little unmediated content in the exhibition films, which all show a directorial control. It is likely that film club members shot these movies intending their colleagues to see, review and criticize them.[84] The seriousness of their construction also explains an unpreventable bias towards this type of film being found in archives. It was the earnest amateur filmmakers who catalogued and preserved their films that were most likely to send them to an archive. The more unselfconscious, larking about filmmaker would have been far more likely to have thrown them away.

Many of these films used sophisticated techniques. They were all shot on expensive colour film stock; the most advanced were very thoughtfully edited and presented with carefully made introductory and interstitial titles. To my inexpert eye, the cinematography seems sophisticated, with steady panning shots of the exhibition, close-ups, sharp action sequences in the fairground, clever positioning of the camera and well-rendered interior shots and night-time views of the coloured lights of the fountains and neon advertisements. The films' amateur directors all chose similar subjects. Every film featured the Tower of Empire, either as a (I imagine) difficult vertical panning shot that emphasized its height and futuristic steel shell or, when taken from the viewing platform, a panoptical view of the whole exhibition. The exteriors of the exhibition palaces and pavilions got consistent coverage. Outdoor shots in summer sunlight were the best for providing a well-exposed, in-focus result, but there was more to it than that. Our modern eyes cannot expect to understand how thrilling it was to see such a grouping of modern structures in one location. In 1938, there were modernist buildings to see, if you knew where to look, but they were mostly one-offs; seeing them all in a panorama would intrigue any filmmaker.

Two of the films contain a small amount of personal, family life. For example, amateur filmmaker Don McLachlan cut a record of his family's visit to the exhibition into the more usual shots of the site. They seem to have had a very good time, smiling and parading for the camera.[85] They were a well-dressed, prosperous family with one lady sporting a mink stole. It is particularly enjoyable to see them eating Canadian soft ice creams. Several accounts of the exhibition mention this treat and it must have been unusual compared to Walls' more familiar 'stop me and buy one' hard ice cream brick. The film also makes much play of the family using a machine selling chocolate bars, which some visitors may have thought a novelty.

These films provide unusual colour images of the exhibition, but accidently offer more information than their makers intended. The trams whizzing about outside the exhibition show Glasgow's efficient public transport. Filming from the top of the Tower of Empire inadvertently reveals the drab council housing just beyond the boundary of the exhibition, providing a contrast between an imagined futuristic 'city' and the reality of post-depression Glasgow poverty. The smartly dressed people seen in the background of shots provide one surprising aspect. Everybody is in Sunday best, and enjoying themselves in a restrained fashion. It would seem that the admission fee of one shilling had prohibited the poorest Glaswegians from coming to the exhibition.

The exhibition reminds us that the experience of modernity is not spread thinly and evenly over the whole of society. Working at Ford's new factory in Dagenham was a modern experience, with the latest machinery, new technologies and work practices, but for the assembly line workers it was more of an 'iron cage' than it was exciting and liberating. Class and wealth were the determining factors providing the possibility for an individual to exercise his or her own agency in experiencing modernity. One shilling plus the tram fare was the price needed to get a passive reception of the exhibition. If you could afford a still film camera or, for the wealthy, a cine-camera, it became possible to interact with the exhibition to produce a curated, edited memory that conjoined two aspects of the modern world: camera technology and public modernist architecture. If it is true, as historian Norris Nicholson proposes, that 'film, of all kinds, has become a dominant narrative form of our time', then British amateur filmmakers in Glasgow saw this in full flow for the first time.[86]

Conclusion

The project to hold an exhibition in Glasgow in 1938 aimed to reintroduce a sense of pride and hope for the future that would help transform internal and external attitudes towards the city that had suffered so much over decades of decline. Known as the 'Second City of Empire', it is not surprising that Glasgow chose an imperial theme. Looking backwards from today's standpoint, this might seem to be a regressive move, but in the late 1930s the Empire and technological progress were compatible ideas in the quest to maintain Britain's position in an increasingly competitive world.

The popular success of the exhibition at the time and its continuing historical importance in architectural circles were due to the controlling influence of Thomas Tait. He provided two key qualities: first, his insistence that he controlled the general design and appearance of the exhibition and second, his sponsorship of bright young architects such as Basil Spence to work for him. The result was extraordinary. A leading expert on British modernist architecture, Alan Powers, describes it as 'a complete modernist environment'.[87] This was an idea new to Britain, where, in the 1930s, modernist buildings were constructed on a rather piecemeal basis. The exhibition showed Britain's future where new factories, offices and public buildings would be built in the modern manner. By insisting on standardization and prefabrication, Tait also embraced modern factory techniques, thus providing another glimpse into the years to come. The inside of the exhibition buildings produced, as we have seen, a more mixed picture. For every demonstration of new technology and modern art, there were also a hundred tartan tins of Scottish shortbread biscuits with an embossed image of the Tower of Empire. The negotiation between traditional Scottish themes, imperial pride and modernity produced an uneven sense of identity in the exhibition. There is little doubt that if this exhibition had been held in London it would now be renowned as an influential event that triggered a wider interest in modernism and the international style. The Festival of Britain of 1951, which was a much less visited event than Glasgow, and which employed some of the same names who worked on the Empire Exhibition thirteen years earlier, now claims this role.

Visitors to the exhibition were presented by state and private enterprises with a wide-ranging display of modern science and technology. What they saw emphasized how new developments were making the world a much smaller place through faster and more far-reaching means of transport or by advances in electronic communications. Middle-class visitors' self-representation and documentation of the exhibition provided an even greater sense of the modern world in progress. Amateur cine-photographers, using colour film, were present in surprising numbers in 1938. It would take two decades before this became commonplace, fuelled by rising incomes and the introduction of cheaper 8-millimetre cameras. This is a good example of a consumer technology on the rise in the late 1930s only for the wartime break to render it invisible, requiring it to be rediscovered as a modern, consumerist and American idea many years later.

CHAPTER FOUR

Big-screen televisions and push-button radios

The brilliance and definition of the picture were remarkable.[1]

This case study examines radio and television broadcasting and the acquisition and consumption of sets in 1938, focusing on that year's Radiolympia exhibition. In the late 1930s, the BBC broadcast worthy radio programmes, but continental stations offered an Americanized alternative for those who thought them too dull. Radios were a well-developed product and most homes had one. Meanwhile, Britain led the world with its high-definition television service. Much of the BBC's early television service was studio based, but it had already started making technically complex outside broadcasts. Televisions were in their first year as a genuine consumer product, most had small screens, but two companies offered large-screen televisions for wealthy customers. This case study reveals a surprisingly sophisticated state of play in broadcasting techniques and in the technical qualities, manufacture and distribution of receiving sets.

FIGURE 4.1 *Philips large-screen television, Image Credit: Daily Herald Archive/ National Media Museum/Science & Society Picture Library.*

'Radiolympia', the annual radio and television trade and consumer show, was held in August 1938, in what turned out to be the last such event before the Second World War. This popular meeting of the BBC, manufacturers, distributors and an excited public at the Olympia exhibition centre in Kensington provided the latest in electronic technology, entertainment and access to behind-the-scene displays that showed how programmes were brought to air. The exhibition dated back to 1922, a time when radio was still in its formative period and was not yet a consumer product.[2] In 1922, Radiolympia's audience mostly comprised male enthusiasts who liked constructing simple receiving sets using wiring diagrams and parts from electrical shops.[3] In complete contrast, by 1938, 72 per cent of households had bought wireless licences and were now listening to sophisticated, easy-to-operate radios.[4] When the number of illegal listeners and people dropping into friends' houses is added to this total, it can be understood why industry commentators thought radio acquisition had reached a saturation point.

Radiolympia 1938 marked the transition point where television was moving from its own enthusiast origins into a full-fledged consumer product. Radiolympia's visitors and national newspapers both noted this change. From 1932, enthusiasts had built homemade television receivers to pick up John Logie Baird's low-definition test broadcasts. Within five years, the BBC had rejected Baird's electro-mechanical invention in favour of the electronic Marconi-EMI system. This system's cathode ray tube technologies were to be used in television for a further seventy years. The BBC's removal of the uncertainty about British television broadcasting technologies prompted a rapid increase in the production of consumer receivers. Suppliers demonstrated a few sets at Radiolympia in 1937, but a year later, televisions dominated the exhibition.

Radio Pictorial, a popular radio magazine, was clear about the significance of Radiolympia 1938:

> When the history of television comes to be written it is certain that [this exhibition] will have to be written boldly as days that mark a turning point for this new art. ... The ordinary man in the street will no longer regard television as something outside his experience, but as a vital and living part of his entertainment.[5]

Histories of early broadcasting, of which there are many, provide a great deal of information on radio and television's development in the 1930s. As far as television is concerned, they tend to adopt a sharp periodization that emphasizes the shutdown of broadcasting in 1939 and its re-emergence after the war. They miss the arrival in 1938 of a genuine competitive market place for television receivers, where both technical enthusiasts and early adopters bought sets. General histories of the 1930s also perpetuate the idea that television sets available before the war were simplistic and had tiny screens, whereas, in reality, high-definition, that is 405 line, large-screen televisions came to the market in 1938.[6]

The story for radio is somewhat different. By 1938, radios were present in most homes, with high adoption rates in south, west and central England. Manufacturers had begun to differentiate their products by the addition of new features, such as push-button tuning, automatic frequency control and short-wave bands. Listeners were not as dependent on the BBC as might be first thought because commercial stations broadcasting from continental Europe provided Americanized English language programmes that were very popular in Britain.[7]

Stages in dissemination

Radios were a key ingredient in Britain's changing consumption patterns in the 1930s; their rapid adoption exemplified what Sue Bowden describes as 'The New Consumerism'.[8] Bowden, by analysing total household expenditure from 1910 to 1938, shows that, as real incomes rose over the period, families spent much of the increase on consumer durables such as cars, vacuum cleaners, electric irons and radios. In Britain, purchases of durable goods rose from 6.7 per cent of total expenditure in 1910–14 to 9 per cent in 1935–8.[9] Changes in spending for middle-class households, particularly those in London and the Home Counties, were proportionally higher.[10] This

TABLE 4.1 Percentage of British families with a wireless licence, 1924–38 and percentage of British families with a wireless licence by region in 1938

	British families with a wireless licence (percentage)		British families with a wireless licence in 1938 (percentage)
1924	10.7	Midlands	80
1926	20.0	West of England	80
1928	23.4	London and Home Counties	76
1930	29.6	North	69
1932	44.5	Wales	63
1934	56.1	Scotland	61
1936	64.4		
1938	71.4		

effect can be seen in motor cars, the most expensive of consumer durables, where purchasing propensities varied dramatically across Britain.[11]

Bowden identifies a three-stage process for the acquisition of consumer durables: first, when the most affluent in society buy unusual, desirable and expensive new products; second, when price reductions brought about by technological improvements allow an imitative middle class to share the cachet of ownership; and finally, when further technological changes (which in the 1930s often arose from the introduction of mass production) greatly reduce prices, allowing for widespread adoption.[12] Radio sets fit well into this structure and their adoption rates are shown in Table 4.1. In total, listeners held 8.9 million wireless licences in 1938.[13] In this year, only 65 per cent of homes had access to mains electricity, so many bought or rented batteries to power their sets.[14]

Compared to big purchases, such as motor cars and refrigerators, the simpler type of radio was cheap to acquire. The widespread availability of instalment credit, known as 'hire-purchase', which allowed poorer families to spread the cost of a radio over many months, was an important aid to consumption. For example, talent contest host Carroll Levis endorsed the KB 750 radio, available for 14 guineas (£14.70) cash, or on 'easy terms' of just over four shillings (21p) per week when average wages were £2.95 a week.[15]

Television first arrived at Radiolympia in 1936. Historian of British broadcasting, Asa Briggs, commented: 'The Radio Manufacturers' Association was felt to be somewhat "half hearted" about this – only seven manufacturers showed television receivers.'[16] However, it was at the 1938 show that television sets came to the fore as competitive consumer products. The *Observer*'s television correspondent (it is significant that it had such a role) reported:

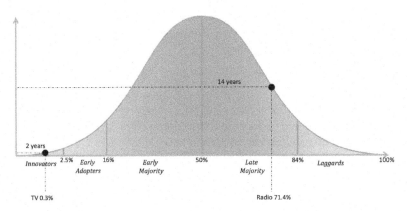

FIGURE 4.2 *Adoption rates for radio and television in 1938 using Ryan and Gross. Image Credit: the author.*

Ten thousand new television receivers will be installed in homes before Christmas if the confident expectations of those responsible for the wonderful show at Olympia are fulfilled. ... The stands showing television apparatus have been crowded. The interest has been real and the show has resulted in a large number of orders. Most of the firms making television receivers have sold all they can turn out between now and the middle of December.[17]

The BBC's television transmissions from Alexandra Palace had a limited geographical range before the Second World War. It promised good reception within a fifteen-mile radius, but viewers reported coverage from much further afield.[18] One estimate calculated that by the end of the decade, enthusiasts in south-east England had purchased about 30,000 sets.[19] This was a very small number, too few for it to belong to Bowden's first stage of diffusion described above. The people who bought these sets were even more refined than this. They fit better into the categories defined by Bryce Ryan and Neal Gross in 1943, which splits the first stage of consumer adoption into two categories, 'Innovators' and 'Early Adopters'.[20] Ryan and Gross typified innovators as the first 2.5 per cent of all customers, which would equate to 250,000 people, using the numbers who owned radios as a base. So, those who bought television sets in 1937 and 1938 were at the sharp end of 'innovator' purchasing (see Figure 4.2).

On the reopening of the television service after the Second World War, the BBC press officer Ernest Thomson commented on this period:

If you owned a television set before the war it was impossible to escape the feeling that you were a 'privileged person'. There was no snobbery about it, no sense of superiority; rather the reverse. It was like having a key to the pantry; you could, of course, throw scraps to the hungry – in other words, invite your neighbours round to see a particular programme – but that was being kind to be cruel. It gave them only a tantalizing taste of delights which were yours at any time, and left you more than ever with the sensation of getting the lion's share.[21]

Thomson suggests that owning a television in 1938 provided a lucky few with an almost magical means of travelling into a future world, which ordinary people would not experience for many years. As writer William Gibson may have remarked many decades later, 'The future has arrived, it's just not evenly distributed yet.'[22]

Radio in 1938

Radiolympia 1938 reflected the differing stages of the product life cycle for radios and televisions. Radio manufacturers, realizing that they were coming close to the point where most people who wanted a radio already owned one, started differentiating features on their sets to attract customers who wanted to upgrade to the latest technologies or to get greater ease of operation. Enthusiasts' magazine, *Wireless World*, noted this in an editorial:

> Wireless licences cannot possibly continue to increase in number at the same rate ... [as] the last dozen years or so. Consequently, the broadcast receiver industry has now to devote much of its energy to catering for the replacement market, and this tendency is particularly noticeable at the present Olympia Exhibition.[23]

In what was now a mature market, manufacturers offered a wide variety of radios with different features and prices. One type of basic radio was the small, battery-powered portable set. An example of this type was advertised as suitable for 'upstairs and downstairs, the garden, on the beach, in the car, in fact here, there and everywhere'.[24] This cheap £7 model weighed 18½ pounds (8.4 kilos), which was a lump by today's standards, and might have been too much for the little girl pictured in the advertisement to carry in real life. The cheapest mains radio shown at Radiolympia was the Belmont 'Midget' priced at £4, 4 shillings (£4.20) which bought a simple machine with no gimmicks and the minimum number of valves.[25] Generally, the greater the number of valves in a radio, the higher was the price, the extra electronics providing for more consistent volume, better tone and more stable tuning. By 1938, the better sets featured super-heterodyne valves, allowing clearer isolation of radio stations. The term 'super-het' was much used in advertising for radio sets, and although this technology was complicated, its naming proposed that you were buying a more advanced set. Radiolympia also saw the introduction of superior radios with Automatic Frequency Control (AFC) which solved the problem of weak radio stations appearing to drift in and out of tuning, requiring the user to make tiny adjustments to capture the broadcast.

Another innovation for 1938 was press-button tuning. Without this, listeners selected the band they required, either medium or long wave, and turned a knob to point a needle in the general direction of a station's name printed on the radio's dial. They then did a little more fine-tuning to get the best signal. 'Fine-tuning' is a term that has many uses today, but the Oxford English Dictionary traces its origins to 1924, just at the point when radios entered the consumer marketplace.[26] Push-button tuning provided electromechanical help to change the waveband and set the frequency of the station required. When coupled with AFC and super-het valves, this innovation made for a simpler and more reliable means of station selection. This was a significant step in radio's journey from an emergent technology in 1924 that only the proficient understood, to, in 1938, a consumer product that anyone could use. An advertisement from that year stated this idea clearly, 'Ecko motor controlled press-button radio ... Amazingly easy, gloriously lazy'.[27]

Wealthier consumers could buy larger, more sophisticated and expensive radios. Above £30, manufacturers often housed radios in decorative wooden cabinets known as 'console' sets, designed to fit with the tastes of most homeowners. This meant that rather than celebrating modernity, highly figured walnut veneers disguised the radio's modern function. Only the front-facing loudspeaker gave the game away that this was not a normal piece of furniture.[28] At the top end of this section of the market were a large variety of radiograms. A radiogram (for younger readers) was a combined radio and record player that shared the same amplifier and loudspeaker. This meant that the best electronics available in Britain provided high-fidelity reproduction of both recorded and broadcast sources. *Wireless World* described one of manufacturer RGD's most sophisticated models:

> Model 1295 is the most ambitious of the many highly developed sets shown by RGD. This model is an auto-changing radio-gramophone with an … amplifier giving an output of 12 watts. Four wavebands are covered, and among the refinements to be found are … improved bass reproduction and motor-driven push-button tuning in conjunction with AFC. The 14 button system … has been carried to its logical conclusion by making provision for remote control.[29]

This radiogram was priced at just a tad less than £100. That was quite a sum, about £6,000 in today's money, and is comparable to what a present-day hi-fi aficionado might wish to pay.[30] At the end of the 1930s, this machine represented the pinnacle of home audio in a single console. It prefigured the music centres that dominated listening to music from the 1970s to the 1990s and appealed to a very small market of wealthy consumers who wanted to have and to show off the best. This was much the same group of people as those who were first interested in television sets. Radiograms with automatic record changers enabled an 'album' set of classical music records to be played together so as to cover a whole symphony.[31] Cheaper radiograms were also available; for 20 guineas (£21) McMichael Radios offered 'a new radiogram at a very modest price'.[32] For those who wanted to make an even greater investment in their love of music, it was possible to extend radiograms with an extra set of speakers, providing multi-room sound. As one journalist predicted 'in future the modern house will have one good radio set with a loudspeaker in every room in the house'.[33] This prediction was not fulfilled, but it is intriguing to think that this modern approach to playing broadcast and recorded media was possible and desirable as early as 1938.

Radio broadcasting in 1938

The BBC had a monopoly control over radio broadcasting in Britain. Founding Director-General John Reith's puritan influence was such that the BBC exercised a strict control over broadcasting standards, promoting what it thought was good for its listeners rather than discovering and responding to what they wanted.[34] The result was that the broadcasts of the BBC's

National service comprised much worthy but dull material. Consequently, listeners tuned into alternative, jollier programmes provided by new stations broadcasting commercial, Americanized light entertainment shows in English from high-powered transmitters in continental Europe.[35]

The BBC and its most prominent competitor Radio Luxembourg offered very contrasting services. This was particularly true on Sundays when the BBC reflected the day's religious importance in its programming. The BBC broadcast in long time slots compared to its commercial competitors, with most programmes lasting from about 30 to 75 minutes. For example, on Sunday, 21 August 1938, it offered both a morning and evening religious service, and in between it transmitted popular light music that emphasized traditional interests and eschewed American material. Some examples for the day were: The Spa Orchestra (an outside broadcast from Scarborough), Luigi Voselli and his Hungarian Orchestra, The Park and Dare Workmen's Silver Band, an hour of classical music from gramophone records, and a talk – 'Is the Church worthwhile?'.[36] It is likely that it was.

Radio Luxembourg opened its Sunday broadcasts with fifteen minutes from gormless film star George Formby. Gracie Fields also contributed a quarter of an hour later in the day. At noon, Quaker Cornflakes sponsored radio set expert Carroll Levis and his 'Radio Discoveries'. This featured such luminaries as Ronald Bully (Crooner) and Patric Beddows (Musical Saw). At six in the evening, Ralph Reader presented the Radio Gang Show, followed by the Rinso (a soap powder) Radio Review starring Jack Hylton, one of the most popular bandleaders of the time.[37] This output was reminiscent of American commercial radio in the streamlined regularity of its scheduling, in the cheerful informality of presentation and in the ubiquitous hard-sell product advertising in between dance numbers.[38]

Radio Luxembourg began broadcasting in the early 1930s, and by 1938 was a well-established station. Radio Normandy, Radio Paris and Radio Lyons also broadcast to Britain in English. Radio Normandy was a sister station to Luxembourg and promoted itself with the strapline 'For Brighter Radio'. Its programme shared much of the same ideas and some of the same content as Radio Luxembourg but had more of an easy-listening feel to it.[39] Some idea of the influence of these stations can be seen in the popularity of Radio Luxembourg's children's programme 'The Ovaltineys' (sponsored by the makers of Ovaltine milky drink) that had a popular theme song and a membership of 1.2 million youngsters.[40]

Historian Paddy Scannell identifies 'The Band Waggon', a radio variety show which started in 1938, as exemplifying the influence of Americanized and commercial radio on the BBC. The broadcaster had become more relaxed in its approach to programme content by the end of the decade.[41] Scannell describes The Band Waggon's anarchic style, but does not dwell on one interesting aspect of this programme, which was its subversive, self-referential approach to broadcasting and the BBC. The programme's stars Arthur Askey and Richard Murdoch broke previous broadcasting conventions. They played with the roles of announcer and cast and created an imaginary world where the recording studio morphed into a flat above Broadcasting House, presaging an innovative approach to radio often ascribed to the Goon Show in the 1950s.

The historiography of British broadcasting has often downplayed or ignored the contributions of the continental commercial stations.[42] In 1938, particularly in southern England, tuning in to foreign stations was a normal part of everyday life. This practice was not part of the culture of exploration and experimentation that typified the very early years of radio; listeners accessed each station by pushing a button turning off a religious talk and turning on Jack Hylton. In this way, Britons had access to a far wider range of content than the BBC offered. The Americanized nature of the material they listened to prefigured the approach taken by pirate radio stations in the 1960s and much broadcasting in Britain in the years that followed.

By the end of the decade, listeners could spread their reach even further across the world. In the early 1920s, short-wave signals were the starting point for long distance transmission and reception of radio messages and early enthusiasts enjoyed eavesdropping on conversations from far afield (a phenomenon resulting from short-wave signals bouncing off the ionosphere allowing them to travel thousands of miles). The more sophisticated radio sets shown at Olympia in 1938 featured short-wave bands, the most expensive having three extra bands. For example, the Ferguson 773 AC Console radio offered 'a 5-band 12-valve receiver covering three short-wave bands, including television sound'.[43] This enabled an owner of the Ferguson

TABLE 4.2 Examples of foreign short-wave radio stations available in Britain in 1938. Information obtained from vintage 1930s Ultra 'Midget' radio from author's collection

Station	Location	Distance from London (km.)[44]
Boundbrook	New Jersey, USA	5,620
Chunking (Chongqing)	China	8,530
Delhi	India	6,720
Moscow	Soviet Union	2,500
Philadelphia	Pennsylvania, USA	5,700
Pittsburgh	Pennsylvania, USA	6,000
Schenectady	New York State, USA	5,400
Sydney	Australia	17,000
Tokio (Tokyo)	Japan	9,580
Wayne	Indiana, USA	6,270

773 to listen to transatlantic radio broadcasts, so gaining a direct experience of American radio rather than through the continental radio stations' hybridization of American and British sources. Short-wave radio provided direct, live, unmediated access to an American cultural source, which was very unusual in 1938.

Even mid-priced radios offered short-wave bands down to 16 metres, not enough to capture television sound on the 8-metre wavelength but good enough to listen to stations across the world. For example, a typical set of this type, the Ultra 'Midget', presented many foreign stations on its dial, but experimentation would offer a greater number than this, depending on atmospheric conditions (see Table 4.2).

This direct, if one-way, connection was a precursor to much that has become available through the internet. Getting excited today about listening to internet radio stations broadcasting in English from obscure American locations can be placed into a historical context, because the same experience was available eighty years ago.

Television in 1938

By 1938, the technologies enabling the capture and transmission of sound were at a mature stage. Changes to radio sets aimed at greater simplicity, improved fidelity and a wider choice of stations. In contrast, television was just emerging from its protean phase. One year earlier, the BBC had decided which camera technology it wished to pursue. It chose the 'Emitron' camera, an all-electronic solution, over an electro-mechanical alternative proposed by John Logie Baird. The Emitron camera had higher definition and a more frequent screen refresh rate than the Baird machine.[45] John Logie Baird's positioning in British popular history as the inventor of television ignores the role of other (foreign) pioneers and also ignores the inevitability of his poorly funded research into electro-mechanical television being superseded by cathode ray tube solutions, which, critically, did not need performers to use exaggerated make-up and worked well outdoors.[46]

EMI (originally Electrical and Musical Industries), a 1930s conglomerate formed from Britain's two leading gramophone record companies, developed this new camera.[47] Profits from the sale of recorded music thus provided the funding for British research into a workable television system. Technical author John Trenouth has scotched any suggestion that this was an American development:

> The Emitron tube is EMI's variation of the Iconoscope camera tube developed by Vladimir Zworkin at RCA. Both were developed during the early 1930s and the similarities between the two have led to suggestions that the EMI tube was a copy of the RCA [camera]. In fact, this was not

the case. The similarities exist because the technologies of the 1930s did not allow [alternatives to be deployed].[48]

The BBC's decisive choice of an electronic camera for its television service let it steal a march on other nations. As a 1938 brochure proclaimed, 'The Marconi EMI Emitron Camera – gave Britain supremacy in Television. ... This wonder of electrical ingenuity enables outdoor events to be televised with the same ease and clarity as studio scenes.'[49] For some observers, a camera with no moving parts was a strange innovation: 'Moving to and fro across the studio floor on their rubber-tyred trollies were the mysterious Emitron cameras – The "eyes" of television ... behind them trailed great snakes of cable leading to the control room.'[50] A starry-eyed journalist visiting the Alexandra Palace studios commented:

> At first the studio looked like a film studio except that the Emitron cameras seemed so small and unelaborate. Yet these electric eyes, no bigger than a hat box, cost £2,000 each! ... The cameramen might be robots. They sit at the Emitron cameras, wearing headphones, listening to the orders of the director ... whose voice cannot be heard by others.[51]

Television sets

Radiolympia was remarkable because of the wide variety of televisions on display. In total, twenty-three different manufacturers offered sets for sale. They included PYE, Philips, HMV and others who would be successful in the British market for decades afterwards.[52] Such was the excitement television created at this last Radiolympia before the Second World War that *Television and Short-Wave World*, a specialist magazine, dubbed the event 'Teleolympia', although this name didn't stick. It proclaimed: 'This year, television occupies a very prominent position at the Radio Exhibition. It is in fact, the newest and principal feature of the show and provides the first real attempt to show the public that the future home entertainment will be sound and vision.'[53] The conservative *Spectator* magazine, which was not much interested in technology, remarked: 'At the Radiolympia Exhibition this year the most noticeable thing is the marked progress of television. The sets are still dear, and reception imperfect, but it looks as if the corner towards full success has been turned.'[54]

Technology for television sets was changing as the 1930s drew to a close, with a wider range of screens becoming available. Some manufacturers offered very small screens. This was a rather desperate attempt to lower the price of televisions to attract more customers, increase volumes and thus further drive down prices to develop a mass market.[55] These small-screened sets provided a new lower entry point to the market, but families or groups could not view them with ease. For instance, the Invicta television had a tiny 12 centimetre × 10 centimetre viewing screen. It was a vision-only set,

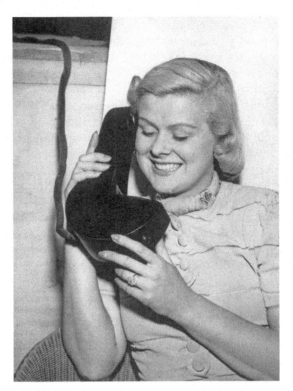

FIGURE 4.3 *Prototype handheld television, Image Credit: Imagno/Hulton Archive / Getty Images.*

the assumption being that the buyer would already have access to a short-wave radio that could provide the sound that went along with the pictures. This rather Heath-Robinson solution was priced at 21 guineas or £22.55.[56] This was a similar price to a cheaper radio set, so television could be yours if you wanted it, more as a demonstration than as home entertainment. One manufacturer tried to make a virtue of a necessity by taking a cheaper small-tube television screen and turning it into a prototype handheld personal television. It is reminiscent of the personal televisions that became available in the 1970s and after, but in 1938 battery technology was such that this set was powered via a long cable (see Figure 4.3).[57]

Most sets on display at Radiolympia had 25 centimetre × 20 centimetre screens, which became the standard size for televisions in the 1950s. This mid-range-sized cathode ray tube was about the size of a present-day tablet computer, so was suitable for family viewing in a smaller room.[58] As *Wireless World* noted, there was little commonality in the circuit design or valves deployed in these televisions, but a standard set of appearance and features was emerging: a mid-sized black-and-white screen set in a console cabinet. Viewers now almost always looked at screens directly, the practice of using a mirror and a sunken screen had become rather old fashioned.[59] A basic television set providing sound and vision started at around £40; if it included an all-band push-button radio, then the price rose to nearer £60. For those who wanted everything in one box, a combined television and radiogram cost between £120 and £175.[60] The higher sum is equivalent to about £10,000 today, which is the amount that people might pay for high-end televisions or hi-fi equipment. The very small number of people interested in a Dynatron television, all-wave radio and auto-radiogram at this price were engaged in conspicuous consumption to impress their friends, or perhaps they thought they were investing in the future of home entertainment for years to come. This television was a futuristic set, where all aspects of video and audio entertainment were available in a single place at the heart of the sitting room.

Although most manufacturers were heading down the mid-sized screen route, there were some developing bigger screen televisions that offered a picture size not seen again in Britain's sitting rooms until the early 1960s. Producing large-sized cathode ray tubes was not impossible in 1938, but was very difficult and expensive. For instance, RCA Laboratories in New Jersey had built a 45 centimetre × 60 centimetre screen, but its tube was 1.35 metres long, so it was hardly suitable for a domestic set.[61] As an alternative, there were two other ways to produce large-screen television images. The first and simplest was to connect an ordinary-sized cathode ray tube to a projector. This generated an image on a viewing screen attached to the television console as large as 45 centimetres × 55 centimetres (see Figure 4.1). Philips offered a set that projected a 'very brilliant' image onto a yellow/green screen.[62] It had a projection screen that 'automatically rises into its correct position when the lid of the cabinet is lifted'. A potentially deadly 25,000-volt supply, which required a special earthed steel case, provided the required level of brightness. Philips described its equipment as 'completely shock-proof', which was reassuring news.[63]

The *Times* reported this exciting development: 'A demonstration yesterday showed that the picture can be viewed in comfort by about 30 persons in an ordinary room. The brilliance and definition of the picture were remarkable.'[64] This demonstration to so many people indicated that pubs and clubs were the intended customers for big-screen televisions. In this way, a pub could host major sporting events and provide musical entertainment in the evenings, bringing in customers not able to afford a television of their own. This was a prescient idea; it has been common in recent years for pubs and clubs to show soccer and rugby games on big-screen televisions, an attractive prospect for those who don't have the pay-tv service required to watch the match and for those who just enjoy the camaraderie.

While Philips were pursuing the idea of large-screen television using optical magnification of a small, high-quality cathode ray tube, another manufacturer, Scophony, had even more ambitious plans using an entirely different technology. All other manufacturers used electronic cathode ray tubes to provide the image for their television sets, which was the same technology used in Emitron cameras, so for them television was electronic from end to end. In contrast, Scophony had invented a mechanical solution to the problem of big-screen television. This technology harked back to Baird's invention that used cameras with mechanical scanners. Scophony's alternative television set used a 'high-speed rotating polygonal stainless steel scanner' to produce its image from the BBC's transmitted signal.[65] The results were impressive. Scophony's domestic television had an image size of 60 centimetres × 50 centimetres. This set, the most expensive on the British market, cost £231 and Scophony demonstrated it in Derry and Toms' department store in Kensington throughout June 1938.[66] Scophony had ambitions that lay beyond the domestic market. Its directors had convinced themselves that the future of television was in relaying important events into Britain's cinemas for the huge audiences who attended these venues. As a result, it developed a set that projected a 180 centimetre × 150 centimetre image, which cinema owners could rent.[67] Scophony was mistaken in its belief that cinemas would continue to dominate visual entertainment and that television sets would remain prohibitively expensive. In fact, the box in the corner of our sitting rooms would, in the 1950s, dominate radio, supplant cinema and further reinforce domesticity.[68]

Programmes

In February 1938, Gerald Cock, the BBC's director of television, announced: 'I believe that set owners are getting value for their money now, and I am quite certain they will get more than value for their money before very long.'[69] In this year, the BBC broadcast about two hours of programmes per day. Although its marketing promised stars of the magnitude of Henry Hall, Tommy Handley, Gracie Fields and George Robey, this would not turn out to be an everyday occurrence.[70] For example, on Saturday, 6 August 1938, a day when the BBC offered the fullest programme of the week, it broadcast the following shows:[71]

3.00 pm	Health and Beauty
3.20 pm	Cartoon Film
3.25 pm	Starlight (Skating)
3.35 pm	British Movietone News
3.45 pm	Sweet Jam (Jazz) Intermission
9.00 pm	'Laburnum Grove' a play by J. B. Priestley starring Maurice Denham
10.30 pm	Close

Short programmes, cartoons and newsreels were relatively undemanding to produce. In contrast, the BBC broadcast Priestley's play, which lasted 75 minutes, live from the studio. One can only imagine the technical and practical problems involved in pulling off this production, demonstrating the BBC's commitment to this new medium.[72] During Radiolympia, the BBC extended broadcasting to a full afternoon and evening of transmissions, most of which came from the exhibition itself. This prefigured the hours of service that the BBC was to provide in the 1950s.[73]

The flexibility of the BBC's Emitron cameras allowed them to work well outdoors, and they were put to use at several public events in the first half of 1938. *On Television*, a brochure from that year, produced by manufacturers exhibiting at Radiolympia, placed great emphasis on this aspect of owning a television. 'If you have a television set, you can see many of the big national sporting events even better than many people who are on the spot. Armchair comfort, no waste of time travelling, best position in the place – a king could not want more!'[74] The brochure listed all the important outside broadcasts of the previous six months, suggesting that Radiolympia visitors had already missed much. The list included:

Oxford and Cambridge Boat Race

FA Cup Final [Soccer]

Trooping the Colour

The Derby [Horse racing]

Wimbledon Lawn Tennis

Test Match at Lords [Cricket]

'The Constant Nymph' – a play

'Broadway' – a gangster play[75]

On Television suggested that 100,000 people saw The Derby on television, which is probably correct if families and friends sitting around this unusual new attraction were taken into account.[76] Spectacular events of national interest were a far greater attraction than the BBC's often prosaic television studio output.

Outside broadcasts used several new techniques. For central London events, such as Trooping the Colour, the Lord's test match and the previous year's coronation, the BBC routed its transmissions via surface cables connected to the Post Office's West End underground circuit. Televising the Derby presented a more complex problem as Epsom Downs was well outside this area. The BBC solved the problem by devising a temporary short-wave transmitter positioned on top of Epsom's main stand, which transmitted the television signals to Alexandra Palace and from there to the viewers' televisions. High winds blew down their first attempt, so BBC engineers, using typical pioneer ingenuity, quickly fabricated another stronger transmitting tower. Three Emitron cameras covered the race, one positioned at the start with a telephoto lens, another at the finish line, and a third at the paddock using a standard lens. The signals from each camera went via a cable to the BBC's three mobile television vans; a Post Office telephone line sent the voice commentary to Alexandra Palace. A mobile generator provided power to the whole enterprise, as this countrified part of Surrey did not yet have access to the national grid.[77]

The Tatler News Theatre, which was a small newsreel cinema, presented the BBC's coverage of The Derby on a 2.5-square metre screen using a television connected to a projector. As the *Times* recorded:

> More than 200 persons were present in the theatre, and to many it seemed to be as thrilling as being in the grand stand at Epsom. ... We saw the [winning] horse come right through the crowd of runners to win in the most spectacular way, and the audience could not refrain from bursting into applause.[78]

Televising this important horse race moved the BBC a long way forward from 1936 and 1937's experimental broadcasting. Here was a sophisticated multi-camera transmission from a remote site requiring portable control vans, wireless transmission of television signals and a running commentary. In most respects this type of broadcast became a staple of BBC output for decades after the Second World War.

Conclusion

For most people in Britain in 1938, listening to the wireless was a routine, everyday practice. Its technology had stabilized in recent years and using a radio set had become simple and familiar. Most listeners tuned in to the BBC's National service and its regional variants and found programmes that had recently become less austere and more entertaining. But some Britons were already experiencing home entertainment in a way that would only become commonplace in the late 1950s and 1960s. There were large numbers of people in the South of England who habitually, and in particular, on Sundays, tuned into the continental radio stations that broadcast light entertainment programmes in English, using high-powered transmitters aimed at British shores. These stations provided Americanized production values and content with sponsored and commercialized programmes that made no appeal to the highbrow and traditional sentiments that informed the BBC's output.

For listeners with both a curious nature and a little extra to spend, radios equipped with short-wave bands allowed them to hear broadcasts from American radio stations. Although a version of American life was familiar to

British audiences through their regular consumption of Hollywood movies, this was unmediated access to the real thing with its aggressive advertising, soap operas and the latest music. This minority interest prefigured the Americanization of British radio in the 1960s and the easy access to world radio stations that the internet later brought about. Those with the most to spend bought radios that had completed the journey from obscure technical marvel to consumer necessity. As Sue Bowden points out, radio was an important example of the increased spending on durable products between the wars. By 1938, radios provided simplified and more stable tuning using push buttons, super-het valves and AFC.

In this year, Britain led the world in providing a television service, but only the wealthiest people living within the range of the Alexandra Palace transmitter could enjoy it in their homes. With the debate over technical standards completed in favour of Marconi-EMI, manufacturers responded by developing and offering for sale many different brands of television sets with screens just a little larger than today's tablet computers. Television was just about to make the jump from technical novelty to a luxury consumer durable that Britons would buy as soon as they could afford it. Some manufacturer's ambitions went beyond the limited cathode ray tube sizes of the time, building large-screen televisions for the home, pubs and clubs and cinemas. In the first two of these categories, they were prescient of television use over the next few decades, in their reliance on cinema audiences rather less so.

CHAPTER FIVE

The Adelphi Building

Another of those modern mammoth buildings of which some people think we already have more than enough.[1]

This case study examines the construction of a new office block in London in 1938. The Adelphi Building was a cause célèbre at the time because it required the destruction of a set of Georgian terraces, consequently exciting the concerns of a protean conservation movement for this type of architecture. The demolition eliminated a hidden, secretive, underground retreat of prostitutes, homosexuals and the homeless. This was all replaced by a new monumental building designed to house a head office of a large industrial concern. Conglomerate businesses, aided by improved communication networks, needed these new facilities to centralize control over their remote factories and branches. This building and others like it housed new office technologies that automated work previously done by hundreds of clerks. Women, who were thought to be more dexterous than their male counterparts, had a dominant role in operating these new machines.

FIGURE 5.1 *Executive floor, The Adelphi Building, Image Credit: Dell & Wainwright/RIBA Collections.*

In 1938, Hugh Casson, last encountered sketching the Glasgow Empire Exhibition for the *Architectural Review*, produced a guide to recent modern architecture in London.[2] The cover proudly claimed that all this modernity could be seen within a 25-mile radius of the Adelphi.[3] His identification of the central point of London seems askew to today's eyes, but at the time would have been more readily understood. If we need to describe a central point for London today, we think of Charing Cross; the Adelphi was located one hundred metres away. Perhaps the Adelphi was in Casson's mind for another reason. It was the location for the controversial demolition of one of the most important features of Georgian London and the recent erection of a set of modern offices that set a new standard for Britain that would not be matched for a further fifteen years. The new Adelphi Building was the latest in a series of monumental head offices established in London in the 1930s that made a dramatic impact on the capital's skyline.[4]

The original Adelphi

The Adelphi was one of the wonders of Georgian London and like so many buildings of that period was a speculative development.[5] In 1767, Robert Adams and his brother James were responsible for the construction of a hybrid building project overlooking the Thames near to Charing Cross. It comprised terraced houses for the middle classes and commercial and industrial premises directly underneath them on the sloping ground leading down to the river. The Adams misjudged the market, as fashion was moving ever westwards, and many of these new houses remained unsold. Close to bankruptcy, Robert Adam's clever use of a private lottery solved his money problems to enable completion of the project. The Adelphi comprised around forty family houses with, as was typical for the period, five storeys. The arched vaults below were not a total success, as the river intruded at high tides making them unsuitable for storage. Consequently, only those in the capital who had nowhere else to go would use them.[6] As architectural critic, Steen Eiler Rasmussen, put it:

> It is strange to see how the stratification of the community is plainly shown in the construction of Adelphi itself: the fine although plain houses for the upper classes built on two dark basements containing kitchens and rooms for servants and below these again the vaulted cellars where the poorest classes sought refuge.[7]

In Victorian times, the Adelphi lost its cachet and was, as Charles Dickens portrayed it in his semi-autobiographical *David Copperfield*, above ground the home of rented rooms for student lawyers and below ground the home of the dispossessed. David Pike has explained this connection between the physical nature of the Adelphi above and below street level and the

Victorian imaginary sense of the underworld and the underclass.[8] Public roads leading underneath the houses provided easy access to the commercial premises below the Adelphi. In the 1850s they lay adjacent to Hungerford Market and later, after the arrival of the railway in 1864, its replacement, Charing Cross station. Both the market and the railway station attracted the poor and rough elements and they found a damp and dangerous place to live below the Adelphi. Above ground, the upper part of the Adelphi became home to literary and theatrical types, attracted by its location close to London's theatres, who rented rooms in the now divided former family houses. Famous tenants included J. M. Barrie and John Galsworthy. The subdivision of Georgian houses into separate flats or sets of rooms was a common theme in Victorian London, which was only much later reversed when commercial development or gentrification converted them back into single occupation.

Rasmussen was too polite to spell it out, but the cellars below the Adelphi were not only a refuge for the poorest parts of London society, but also a site for casual prostitution. The Adelphi, so close to a major station and to the entertainments offered by the Strand, provided many willing customers for its furtive attractions. It was also a popular, if enormous, 'cottage' in the sense of providing an opportunity for queer sex at a time when this was illegal and strictly punished. Matt Houlbrook has shown that, in the 1920s, the Metropolitan Police, with encouragement from hard-line home secretary William Joynson-Hicks, was attempting to clean up central London and rid it of furtive places, such as urinals and undercrofts where 'persons of the sodomite class' could meet. The Adelphi was on Joynson-Hicks' hit list.[9]

In the early 1930s, Londoners with a few rooms to their names and a variety of small businesses occupied the houses sitting above this literal and metaphorical London underworld. The tenants of the rooms in 19 Adam Street, once one of the most prestigious addresses in the development, show the rather eccentric nature of its occupants in 1936. Each tenant occupied a room or two.[10] They included:

Martin Clifford (Advertising agents)
National Radium Commission
Fairchild Publications of New York
Arthur Godfree (Wine Merchants)[11]
Royal Statistical Society
Royal Economic Society
Adelphi Manufacturing Co.
Read Bros. (Builders)
Booth Steamship Co.
Lord Weir (Industrialist and Privy Councillor)[12]
Mrs Hardy.

By now, the Adelphi's scruffy but still elegant rooms were home to small businesses, individuals living alone or using the Adelphi as a London *pied à terre* and as administrative offices for learned societies without their own buildings. A large number of small rentals on varying leases were not the recipe for profit maximization; the whole site returned a modest £16,500 p.a.[13]

The intrusion of the modern world

Inadequate rental yields above ground and pressure from the authorities to clear its undercroft made the Adelphi ripe for redevelopment. The Drummond Estate, who owned the freehold, set about obtaining the Act of Parliament needed to overcome the legal complications of demolishing such a complex site.[14] This provoked a debate on whether such an important Georgian building should be demolished. Architectural conservationism had its origins in the Arts and Crafts movement whose members wished to protect medieval churches from garish Victorian improvements, and so formed the Society for the Protection of Ancient Buildings (SPAB). Their lobbying produced legislation that protected ancient monuments, but this was not designed to enforce the conservation of something so relatively new as eighteenth-century housing developments.[15] John A. Milne, chairman of the Royal Society of Arts, whose building lay next to the Adelphi, pessimistically and correctly forecast that the Adelphi's replacement would be a massive new single building.[16] SPAB supported the campaign; its secretary, A. R. Powys, pleading that the Adelphi was 'still beautiful in mass and fenestration'.[17]

The *Times* came out in support of conserving the existing buildings in an editorial proposing that the neighbourhood would be 'overpowered by some huge bully of a new building'. It suggested that the much criticized part of the Adelphi below street level was 'a fascinating and very useful underworld of streets, arches [and] cellars'. It concluded that the Adelphi was 'the most eighteenth-century thing left in London'.[18] There were also some protests from young architects who had noticed the connection between early Georgian design and architectural modernism, as both advocated order and eschewed unnecessary decoration.[19]

Their protests were to no avail. G. H. Drummond, one of the freeholders, responded to the pleas of the conservationists with a flat statement that they were within their legal rights to demolish the Adelphi without having secured approval from Parliament for a building to replace it.[20] Thus began the demolition of the old and construction of the new Adelphi. The future of the Adelphi Building became an important cause célèbre. Robert Byron, a young and provocative critic, made one of the most important contributions. He was one of the early members of the Georgian Group of the SPAB and the potential loss of the Adelphi was one of the key events pushing it forward.[21] Writing in the *New Statesman and Nation,* he coruscated the developers and their greed:

> Though the public – not just intelligentsia – is stirring at last, the parasites still hold revel before the dawn. It is the nature of these creatures, these landlords, speculators, house breakers, contractors and architects who have ruined the British capital, to work in the dark. The transactions by which they live, compel it, … they are corporations … whose deals are done in private. Who put up the money to buy the Adelphi from its original owner, for instance, and made the first profit on it?[22]

The Adelphi Building was an early example of the later battles fought out in the 1960s and 1970s between property developers wishing to create new large-scale offices and conservationists who had a quite different view of London's future.

The demolition site was of such scale and in such a central location that it could have served a variety of commercial purposes. Some thought it would be the site for a mammoth block of flats, similar perhaps to the 1,250-apartment Dolphin Square further upstream from the Adelphi that also opened in 1938.[23] It could also have been the location for a new hotel, like its near neighbour, The Strand Palace Hotel, that reopened in Art Deco style in 1929.[24] It is possible that the Adelphi's developers shied away from either of these two options because of the neighbourhood's poor reputation. It is more likely that the presence next door of the mammoth office headquarters for Shell-Mex influenced their final choice, which was a large-scale and modern head office building designed to attract a big-name client.

The development of head offices in Britain

Offices made a slow transition from their mercantile origins. As late as the mid-nineteenth century, companies had their counting houses near to where they undertook their business. In order for this to change, some enabling technologies needed to be introduced into the business world to provide rapid communication over long distances. A reliable postal service was the first version of this idea. The example of the eighteenth-century East India Company shows us that its slow but reliable method of sending instructions and information over thousands of miles allowed a head office to control distant operations successfully without the use of any mechanization.[25]

As far as domestic operations were concerned, the arrival of the railways in the 1830s achieved the most dramatic time/space compression ever seen in Britain, allowing metropolitan businessmen to make day trips to industrial areas and vice versa.[26] Railways also sped up the postal services leading to a fast and reliable letter delivery service, which was a vital ingredient in the transfer of detailed written information. The Post Office established this in Britain by 1840, the year it introduced the first Penny Post. From the 1850s, telegraph wires were installed along the railway tracks which provided the possibility of near real-time communication. The introduction of the telephone in the early 1900s was the final element of changes to communication technologies that enabled businesses to exercise greater control over their remote branches, factories and warehouses. Improvements to the postal service, railways, telegraph and telephone were all made in the years up to 1938 that increased their efficiency and reach.[27]

As the nineteenth century progressed, Britain experienced a period of intense capitalist activity, where competition for market dominance eliminated inefficient players. The result was an increased concentration of economic activity into the hands of larger and larger corporations. National organizations, such as the big railway companies, the joint stock banks, the Civil Service and the Post Office, all with geographically dispersed networks, needed a single point of coordination, thus driving increased centralization. Like the East India Company of a century earlier, they relied on a command and control structure, with local bookkeeping and administration.[28]

Traditionally, clerks were male, well educated and able to turn their skills to a wide variety of tasks. The most proficient and reliable could look forward to elevation to head clerk or even perhaps to partnership. The late-Victorian head office changed how they worked, so that administrative duties were centralized, with each clerk only responsible for a single task. This involved splitting a clerk's duties into its components, so separate teams of clerks opened the mail, wrote a reply or a minute, and filed the correspondence. Messengers moved documents between departments, in the same way as parts moved along an assembly line.[29] As a result, clerks lost their previous close relationship with the business owner, which was replaced by a layer of remote management.[30] These practices, established in the late nineteenth century, produced large productivity gains over the older system and were the basis for the organization of head offices in the 1930s that underpinned the architectural design for the Adelphi Building. This development was analogous to the experience of skilled artisans, who instead of assembling a whole product worked on a single part. These deskilled workers and clerks produced good-quality results at a much lower cost per item. In factories, this required a scale-up in size, from many small workshops to a single large factory, for office work it meant a move from local administration to centralized administration at a head office.[31]

At the same time, the management of these large businesses became more sophisticated with management accounting and statistical analysis techniques replacing traditional ways of managing business knowledge. The invention of punched cards, sorting machines and printers led to the idea that head offices could also be centres for data processing, producing financial statements for customers and management information that could increase a company's efficiency and profitability. This required a great change in the quality of information available to the new managerial classes and a large increase in the volume of data that clerks collected, interpreted and filed, resulting in a rapid rise in their number.[32] This notion was first taken up in the insurance industry, and, specifically, in industrial insurance. These were simple low-cost life policies sold to families across the industrial centres of Britain, with payments collected door-to-door every week. Prudential was the leading provider of this service and achieved its success by giving better value for money than its competitors, providing a better funeral for the same weekly cost. It stole a march on its rivals by lowering its costs of administration through job specialization, centralization and standardization.[33]

The possibilities of the new technologies that became available in the 1930s encouraged the next wave of head offices. London was the site for several prominent new headquarter buildings aiming to accommodate businesses that had recently and rapidly grown by merger and acquisition. A selection of large head office buildings constructed in London between the wars is shown in Table 5.1.

The Shell-Mex Building, which was fully occupied in 1935, just three years before the completion of the Adelphi Building, provides useful insights into how a headquarters organization conducted its activities. A publicity booklet promoting oil giant Shell-Mex (which at the time embraced both the Shell and British Petroleum brands) set out detailed floor plans for the building. Each floor offered, outside a central core of lift shafts and toilet blocks, a large open configurable space which could accommodate

TABLE 5.1 Large London head office buildings constructed between the wars

Building	Location	Architect	Date
Adelaide House[34]	London Bridge	Sir John Burnet, Tait and Partners	1925
Britannic House	Finsbury Square	Edwin Lutyens	1927
Midland Bank	City of London	Edwin Lutyens	1924–1939
ICI House	Millbank	Sir Frank Baines	1928
London Transport HQ	St. James' Park	Charles Holden	1929
Unilever House	Blackfriars	Sir John Burnet, Tait and Partners	1931
Shell-Mex House[35]	Embankment	Ernest Joseph	1935
Adelphi Building	Embankment	Hamp and Collcutt	1938

high numbers of specialist clerks.[36] Centralized corporate departments such as marketing and sales demanded their own sets of offices. The accounts department occupied a whole floor, with its cashiers secure in a separate locked room. Other head office functions such as secretarial, publicity, staff management and wages also shared a floor. Product engineering and sales departments such as the motor oils department and the fuel and general oils department had their own floor. A staff restaurant, a parking garage and an air conditioning plant occupied the lower part of the building.[37]

The Adelphi Building

The Adelphi freeholders held a competition in 1934 to find the most attractive design for the new Adelphi Building. Two firms competed for the brief: Architect J. J. Joas put forward a design that was influenced by the Adelphi's mammoth neighbour Shell-Mex House. Its appearance was a mix of a 'super-cinema and a town hall' with a big tower.[38] Despite this type of architectural design being at the height of fashion in 1934, it was, along with a competing, more traditional alternative, rejected. The competition's organizers then offered the project to the architectural practice of Collcutt and Hamp, chosen because their design maximized the amount of lettable floor space.[39] Stanley Hamp took responsibility for the building's design. This was a surprising choice as Hamp had no previous experience of building

FIGURE 5.2 *The Adelphi Building by Stanley Hamp, Image Credit: Architectural Press Archive/RIBA Collections.*

an office, but had recently designed two hospitals.[40] Hamp was fifty-nine years old when he won the commission for the new Adelphi Building and was a far cry from the bold European modernists that *Architectural Review* admired.[41] Hamp had a much more Edwardian story; his father was head waiter at a restaurant where Collcutt lunched each day, so he asked Collcutt if he would take on Stanley as his assistant.[42]

The newly formed Adelphi Estate Company did not have a tenant signed up, so like its eighteenth-century predecessor the project proceeded as a speculative development, with the strong prospect of attracting a big name to the building. The company's agents produced a marketing brochure that presented the Adelphi as glamorous and prestigious.[43] Britain's economy was recovering in 1938 through increased international confidence and the effects of rearmament. As the completion date neared, the building's agents took out advertising space in the commercial property pages of leading newspapers, placing great emphasis on the commanding views of the Thames available from the building's top floor. One advert proposed that 'you may enjoy the views [of The Thames] if you tenant the Building and so, moreover, may your Colonial and Foreign customers'.[44] In this way the Adelphi Building was marketed as a new commercial landmark that dominated central London.

Hamp designed the Adelphi Building as a massive new office block of some 335,000 square feet that conformed to the specifications of much that followed in the mid-1950s in the reconstruction period after the Second World War (see Figure 5.2).[45] It was a multistorey office block, built on a rectangular footprint, with open plan floors that could house large numbers of clerks. It opened in late 1938 comprising eight floors above ground level, two floors below ground, and a parking garage, which held up to five hundred cars.[46] The capacity of the garage indicates the scale of the operations envisaged in this building and the anticipation of it being filled with the vehicles of directors and senior managers who expected to commute by car. By 1938 it had become reasonably common for executives to travel in this way, as it provided the privacy and flexibility not afforded when travelling by train. At a time when more and more people in London and the Home Counties owned cars, an executive garage offered a level of distinction that put a driver one-up on the mere weekend motorist. Rising car usage and increased restrictions were making parking in London much harder than it had been five years earlier, hence the need for large office blocks to provide such a big garage.[47]

The next two floors, both below ground level, contained boiler rooms and support services for the great building. On the ground floor on either side of the main entrance was space set aside for two small shops, a bank and for licenced premises. Providing retail space on the ground floor was, and still is, a good way of improving rental income for office blocks, and was popular in American offices of the same period. The licenced premises, intended for a large public house, were carried over from the old Adelphi, the licence maintained throughout the rebuild by keeping the pub in a shed. On arrival in the grand entrance hall, its floors and walls decorated in a rather austere travertine marble, workers sped up to the upper levels in a set of six high-speed lifts travelling at 450 feet per minute. A further two lifts were provided for service workers.[48] The upper part of the building comprised seven floors for administrative staff and one floor for executives.

The plan for an administrative staff floor of the Adelphi Building is very instructive in showing how the world of work had changed by 1938. It was an open space configurable to a variety of different formats for office work. What is striking is the fixed infrastructure shown in its architectural plans. The eight lifts noted earlier are present and correct; the only other component shown is the toilets. On each floor there were four toilets, of which three were for female use.[49] The number of toilet cubicles and urinals would suggest today a workforce for each floor of around 280 women and 115 men.[50] It seems likely that, with the reduced emphasis on personal comfort prevalent in the 1930s compared to today, the total number of employees could have been as many as 500 people per floor. Two conclusions follow from these most quotidian of observations. First, this design expected the building's tenant to employ a large number of head office clerks, sitting in big open rooms, an idea that suggests them sharing a high-volume but common process. Second, the high number of women workers reflects the changing world of the clerk. It is worth remembering that this layout was not a response to the specialist needs of a particular customer, but a speculative one aimed to attract the widest number of potential tenants.

The introduction of female clerks to the labour force in Britain dates back to the late nineteenth century and was consequent on changing social attitudes, lower wage rates for women, improved female literacy and numeracy and new technologies. For the same wage, a female clerk was better educated, from a higher social class, less bothered by promotion and more adept at using mechanization than her male equivalent.[51] The market responded to these advantages by recruiting female clerks in large numbers. By as early as 1921, 46 per cent of all administrative clerks in Britain were women, their main tasks were associated with communication technologies, the typewriter, telegraph and telephone.[52] Typing, in particular, was a gendered task. In 1931, the census identified 217,000 typists working in the United Kingdom; of these 97.6 per cent were women.[53] This demarcation by gender was long-lasting and was not overturned until personal computers replaced typewriters. My own experience of work at a large head office in the mid-1970s coincided with the introduction of typewriters with tiny amounts of their own memory, soon to be displaced by word-processing terminals. Here, all the secretaries and typists, without exception, were women.[54]

In the 1930s, at head offices like the Adelphi Building, managers were also highly likely to choose female clerks to operate mechanized adding and bookkeeping machinery.[55] The repetitive and delicate nature of the work involved suggested to male managers that women were best equipped to undertake this work. The Civil Service of 1938 understood this:

> In the first place, they have in an eminent degree the quickness of an eye and ear, the delicacy of touch which are essential qualifications of a good operator. In the second place, they take more kindly than men or boys do to sedentary employment and are more patient during the long confinement to one place.[56]

Managers did not expect women to take their job too seriously. British society saw women's work as an intermediate step from school to marriage.[57] In 1938, it was expected that women would leave work just before they wed; employers and trade unions both accepted this idea as desirable and normal.[58] Management, which was staffed almost entirely by men, completed this gender divide in head offices. In the Adelphi Building, the male 'high-ups' were just that, occupying the top floor of the building. But, despite all this and because there were few more favourable positions in the late 1930s, women working in prestigious London head offices thought it a desirable and pleasant job. For those educated women who would never contemplate working as a domestic servant, it was better paid and classier than working in a factory or shop.[59] In London, the Adelphi Building's designers expected that a tenant could attract two thousand qualified, young, single women to work on the floors laid out for administrative tasks. These women were part of a workforce from the lower-middle-class families that lived in the capital's burgeoning suburbia, which in total grew by 1.9 million people between the wars.[60] Commuting into Charing Cross from the suburbs by tram, bus, railway and underground, they were an example of modern women in modern jobs in very modern buildings. The Adelphi Building's architects designed the administrative floors so that women could hold over three-quarters of the clerical jobs. It was, in this way, a precursor to modern office life in the 1950s and beyond, when by 1961, 64 per cent of all clerical staff were women.[61]

In 1938, head offices were now factories for the processing, interpretation and storage of data, undertaken by clerks, each working on a single part of a complex process. The mechanization of office administration reinforced the idea of a clerk as being like a factory worker. As Adrian Forty has pointed out, the utilitarian nature of office furniture in the 1930s, such as steel desks, chairs and filing cabinets, coupled with the extensive use of office machines, added to the air of industrial design that typified modern offices of the period.[62]

Introducing technology into the office began with improved distant communication using the telegraph and telephone. It was a common practice for large firms in the 1930s to include a telegraph address on their stationery and in advertisements, encouraging their correspondents to communicate in this way if a message needed to be sent with speed and accuracy. The more advanced head offices had their own teleprinters, which were machines that could print off telegrams, avoiding the need for a messenger to run the message round on a bicycle or motorcycle. By 1938, large firms were installing telex machines, which were teleprinters connected on a point-to-point basis with an equivalent located elsewhere in Britain. Using this technology, a head office could send instructions or a branch could send data on an almost instantaneous basis. In this way, they obtained a simple version of the extensive telex networks Britain enjoyed in the 1950s and beyond.[63]

Head offices also depended on telephones. As late as the 1920s, letters formed the majority of office communications, which if formality was required were typed, but if not, a handwritten note just as easily sufficed. By the late 1930s, telephones were used for more informal queries or discussions; the number of telephones used by businesses roughly doubling between 1925 and 1938.[64] It was also common for companies to include their telephone numbers in their literature and to show their level of sophistication by showing how many external lines were available at their switchboard, that is, the number of simultaneous outside calls they could handle. In large head offices where various departments were on separate floors, conversations were made on internal telephones. For example, Shell-Mex, the Adelphi Building's next-door neighbour, proudly announced in 1935 that it had an internal, automatic telephone room with 300 lines and capability to expand to 900 lines.[65]

Many other mechanical aids supported the modern office of 1938.[66] A detailed catalogue produced by International Office Machines Research Limited in that year has recorded them for posterity. It explains the features of the very varied types of equipment available in Britain just before the Second World War.[67]

Its comprehensive index included the following types of machine:

Accounting

Adding

Calculating

Card systems

Dictating

Duplication/Copying

Letter opening

Pneumatic tubes

Telephones

Teleprinters

Typewriters.[68]

Telephones and teleprinters have already been discussed. The catalogue shows two main types of typewriter: an electric version from the American equipment company International Business Machines, later IBM, and a manually operated machine from the Imperial Typewriting Company, a British company. The American typewriter was slicker and less awkward than the domestic offering. American businesses were far more automated than their British equivalent and they led the way in modern design, an advantage that increased in the 1940s and 1950s.[69] The American typewriter was a technology that remained essentially unchanged until the mid-1960s and beyond.

By 1938, accounting machines were being introduced into forward-thinking large offices. They replaced handwritten ledgers which had been the method in use for centuries. As businesses grew and dealt with greater and greater volumes of accounting data, it became less feasible to maintain a manual ledger. This old technique required a steady pen, accurate transcription and copperplate handwriting in the manner that Dickens' Bob Cratchit might have recognized. Adding machines had removed some of the difficulties of manual bookkeeping but a more automated solution was needed. Accounting machines combined typewriters with adding machines and could automate the transcription and calculations required and write the result onto pre-printed cards. This approach continued in use as late as the 1970s.[70]

Various machines using punched cards catered for head office data analysis. Acting together they provided systems that would eventually be replaced by electronic computers. In fact, punched cards linked this technology of the late 1930s to the early electronic computers of the 1950s and 1960s, as both used them for input. In Britain, punched cards were in use as early as the 1890s. The innovative Prudential was an early adopter because it had a simple single product bought by millions of customers that was ripe for standardization. If an insurer could record all the customer and policy details on an identical single card then it became possible for it to gain a massive cost advantage in processing, storing and interpreting the data it contained.[71]

By the late 1930s, tabulating machines could provide sophisticated automatic data analysis from punched cards.[72] It required demystification for its potential customers: 'The principle of the Punched Card system, as applied to accounting and statistical work, is quite simple and not a thing of mystery.'[73] The system required three machines: first, an operator used a card punching machine to transcribe, for example, sales invoice data onto a card, each hole in the card representing a letter or number; second, a clerk fed the collated punched cards into a sorting machine; finally, another clerk fed the sorted cards into a tabulator printer which produced the customer statements or cost analysis as required. This standardization through machines applied factory techniques into the head office, reducing costs and increasing the accuracy and timeliness of management information.[74]

The Adelphi Building did not quickly realize all these possibilities. As 1939 drew on, it had failed to find its anchor tenant. By then, the level of uncertainty brought about by events in Europe had introduced a short-term, wait-and-see attitude in Britain's businesses. A tenant had, though, been found for part of the building. Aluminium Union Limited (AUL), which did not require an army of clerks, took over the top floor of the building. AUL fitted it out in the most modern and lavish style (see Figure 5.1).[75] The executive offices had thick, luxurious carpets and beautiful wood-panelled walls and were equipped with modernist furniture, the whole far more reminiscent of the 1950s than the 1930s. AUL's offices were gained through an eccentric, if very modern, entrance door that featured exciting technical products made from aluminium. It is interesting to note such a conspicuous note of progress and luxury three months into the Second World War, a time when one might have thought priorities lay elsewhere.

Conclusion

By 1938, London had become the location for many of the new headquarter buildings established since the First World War. These offices were a response to a wave of mergers and acquisitions that had established new mammoth corporations such as ICI. They were enabled by changes in management and administration practices mimicking the specialization, separation of duties and de-skilling seen in manufacturing concerns, powered, as in the factories, by new technologies. For offices, automation that improved communication networks and accounting was the most important. New head offices required thousands of clerks to operate the machines that provided the information needed to control such large businesses. Large amounts of floor space accommodated them. On the top floor, executives supervised their departments, all many miles from the factories that generated their income.

The centralization of administration in major cities, a distance away from the factories and warehouses where the physical work was done, came into full effect in the late 1930s. The rise of head office sales, marketing, planning and personnel departments encouraged a new type of manager with very specific technical knowledge and expertise. Located in Britain's major cities, he (they were almost all men) commuted from the suburbs by train and then increasingly by car and lived a distinctly different life from his provincial predecessor. They occupied the higher floors of office blocks that were developed with a square, open plan to accommodate large numbers of clerks, many using office automation machines. This type of centralization and mechanization of business continued as a way of life into the 1960s and, for some companies, into the 1970s.

The Adelphi Building was the latest and most modern of all these interwar head offices and its design was repeated in the decades after the war. The construction and demolition of its Georgian predecessor was also one of the driving forces behind the establishment of conservation groups that were in the 1970s ready to defend Britain's cities from large-scale property development intended to turn eighteenth-century houses into sites for new offices.

CHAPTER SIX

Picture Post – The modernity of everyday life

We firmly believe in the ordinary man or woman.[1]

This case study examines the introduction in 1938 of an important magazine, *Picture Post*, which provided a preview of the future of post-war popular photojournalism. Influenced by eastern European magazines, *Picture Post* adopted a style new to Britain and which proved almost immediately popular. One particular aspect positioned this magazine as modern and significant, which was how it portrayed ordinary people; in fact, it distinguished itself by even portraying them at all. *Picture Post* took an unpatronizing interest in the common people just when many commentators thought them an undistinguished, Americanized mass in the thrall of secular consumerism. This case study argues that there was a strong connection between *Picture Post*'s pre-war presentation of the importance of the ordinary and the increased interest in everyday life seen in the 1950s that was not necessarily dependent of the democratizing impact of the Second World War.

FIGURE 6.1 *Picture Post's first cover, 1 October 1938. Image Credit: IPC Magazines/ Picture Post/Getty Images.*

1938 saw the launch of a new weekly magazine that quickly attracted a large readership because of its modern photographic style and intelligent and accessible journalism. *Picture Post* was an important publication in the Second World War, and was influential in championing an agenda that would result, in 1945, in a new Labour government and a programme of social change. This wartime claim to fame, which cultural theorist Stuart Hall described as 'indelibly identified in the collective imagination' would be enough to ensure that its reputation lived on long after a rather premature demise in 1957.[2]

Although *Picture Post* became famous for its commitment to social justice and in its breaking boundaries in Britain for how news magazines might look, this chapter examines how it prompted a growing interest and validation of ordinary people and ordinary life that was a modern way of seeing the world. This emphasis in *Picture Post*'s photographs and journalism was evident in other changes in British society in the late 1930s that reflected a turn towards the ordinary and everyday.[3] For example, there was widespread popular interest in literature examining working-class life and in the everyday appeal of British actors, such as Gracie Fields and George Formby.

The origins of *Picture Post*

Both those directly involved and later commentators have written about *Picture Post*'s origins. Its history is, therefore, well known and does not need repeating in full here, but to provide some background to this chapter, its key features are described below.[4]

Three men, Stefan Lorant, Tom Hopkinson and Edward Hulton, were central to how *Picture Post* came together. First and foremost was Stefan Lorant, who emigrated from Hungary to Germany after the First World War 'because [he] found its political climate oppressive and Hungary too small to give scope to [his] talents'.[5] While resident in Germany, he worked in its emerging film industry and then became, using the skills he had learned in the movies, editor of the *Münchner Illustrierte Presse* (Munich Illustrated Press). This was a great success; Lorant considered 'the magazine a vehicle for his personal expressions and interests in the social and political environment'.[6] Munich in the early 1930s was a dangerous place to run a liberal magazine, and Lorant spent six months in jail for his stance on National Socialism. On his release, he moved back to Budapest and became the editor of *Pesti Napló* (Budapest Diary), which was a move forward from his work in Munich and was *Picture Post* in protean form.[7] In April 1934, Lorant, like many other artistic and intellectual Jews, moved to Britain where he set about producing British versions of his previous work. The first was the influential *Weekly Illustrated*, which was an important staging post in the development of British photojournalism. *Weekly Illustrated* contained many of the themes that later typified *Picture Post*, although it was a little lighter, more populist and had less dramatic photographs than its eventual successor. It was followed in 1937 by *Lilliput*, a pocket-sized magazine that took an irreverent look at British life, often juxtaposing comedic and pompous images for surreal and humorous effect.[8] A year later, due to lack of advertising, *Lilliput* was losing money; Lorant needed access to capital to allow it to continue in print. He found it from Edward Hulton, who bought *Lilliput* and agreed to provide funding for a new 'picture' magazine.[9]

Edward Hulton was the only son of Sir Edward Hulton, once owner of the *Daily Sketch* and the *Evening Standard*, having sold them to Lord Beaverbrook in 1923. In 1937, the younger Edward was thirty-one years old, a failed Conservative political candidate who had inherited his father's fortune. Using his new wealth, he founded The Hulton Press. His meeting with Lorant paved the way for the development of *Picture Post*. [10] As Robert Key, a journalist on the magazine, recalled:

> Hulton does not seem to have been clear what he was getting from Lorant with the new magazine, thinking he admitted later, in terms of some reforming Conservative political review to give expression to the new ideas with which he, in his own fashion as a young man of the thirties, was increasingly preoccupied. What in fact he was buying was a gleam in Lorant's eye.[11]

Lorant, with his background in cinema and photojournalism, needed a British editor to manage the written aspects of *Picture Post*, which ranged from small captions to full articles. Tom Hopkinson, who had collaborated with Lorant as an assistant editor at *Weekly Illustrated* was the obvious choice. Lorant was the dominant influence in the formative period of *Picture Post*, Hopkinson was key to its longer role in campaigning for social justice. His biographer thought Hopkinson wished to contrast 'the lives of the rich with the reality of poverty and deprivation, picturing, he hoped, the lives of ordinary people with the eye of a Rembrandt. Hopkinson was an excellent caption writer and always stressed the need for words to reinforce the message of his pictures.'[12]

The first issue of *Picture Post* on 1 October 1938 was the product of three young men's imagination; Lorant was thirty-seven, Hulton thirty-one and Hopkinson thirty-three years old. *Picture Post* was, it turned out, the very thing the British public wanted. Within a few months, its circulation had risen to well over one million and its place as a centrepiece of late 1930s and 1940s popular culture was assured.

The look and content of *Picture Post*

Picture Post was a highly innovative magazine for Britain, but Stefan Lorant's involvement ensured that it was not just a British imitation of a foreign original. Lorant, who left Britain for the United States in 1940 is now regarded as the leading name in twentieth-century photojournalism.[13] *Picture Post*'s style seems both familiar and understated today, but was a revelation to British readers when compared to the staid material that had preceded it.

For example, in its issue for 1 October 1938, the cover of the longstanding and worthy *Illustrated London News* presented a page of advertisements that looked like it was printed in 1908 rather than 1938. One advertiser's claim that there was no need to worry, 'you can safely enjoy The Doctor's China Tea' seems Edwardian and was perhaps targeting wealthy, elderly readers. This issue led with seven pages on Chamberlain's latest meeting with Hitler, the copy accompanied by unremarkable full page photos of the prime minister's visit. Much of the rest of the issue contained material on Air Raid Precautions and the politics of *lebensraum*. In sum, it dealt with the pressing political issues of the day. More populist, but just as old fashioned, was *John Bull* magazine, which comprised articles on general interest topics broken up by the occasional unremarkable photograph.[14] *Picture Post*'s famous first front cover is a good example of the way it advertised itself as something new and different on the newsstands. Hopkinson recalled that Hulton, as proprietor, wanted a battleship on the first front cover reflecting an understandable interest in British rearmament in late 1938. Hopkinson suggested a girl for the cover only for Lorant to overrule him, demanding two girls (see Figure 6.1).[15]

In marked contrast to its competitors, *Picture Post*'s first cover had a very clean look, prominently showing its price of three pence, a quarter of the price of the *Illustrated London News*. As expected from a photojournalism-led approach, one image dominated a page designed to share the proportions of a 35-millimetre film.[16] It was not a conventional photo. Instead of Neville Chamberlain, it showed two young acrobatic women dressed as cowgirls caught in mid-air. The use of fast shutter speed to freeze them in time suggests a shot taken with a handheld camera using one of the new faster 'Selo HP2' 35-millimetre films.[17] This was an example of Lorant's experience of 35-millimetre cameras in Germany having a direct influence on his photojournalism. The other aspect of the cover was the sexuality of its subject. Although this seems very restrained by today's standards, the amount of leg on view was unusual for the time in a mass-market publication. Throughout 1938, *Picture Post* had a tendency towards a prurient objectification of women through the, at the time, supposedly legitimate practice of showing underdressed women as long as they were 'natives' or artist's models.[18]

An inside page from *Picture Post* in December demonstrated its innovative layout. First, instead of a photograph supporting the journalism, here the photo *was* the point and the writing provided background for the image. Three different fonts appeared on the page, the headline in a huge font size for a magazine of this period. Second, the photographs were of greatly differing sizes and set in a montage. Although their proportions were pleasing, one can't help but wonder if the relative sizes of the photographs and text reflected Lorant and Hopkinson's status in the magazine or, perhaps, the size of their egos. Finally, the topic was unusual, and to use a twenty-first-century idea, a little 'meta' in that it described how *Picture Post* produced its news stories.[19]

By its fourth issue, in late October 1938, *Picture Post* had got into its stride, presenting material that would typify its output for the next few years.[20] Its contents were in five main categories: personalities, news, travel, information and stories and features on ordinary people. The issue for 22 October 1938 provides a good example of how this worked. For the personality category, Lorant's choice demonstrated what he wanted *Picture Post* to represent. In most British popular magazines of the period, an article about a famous personality would have been about a film star, say Joan Crawford, or a bandleader like Jack Hylton, names famous throughout the country and guaranteed to get readers' attention on a bookstall display. *Picture Post* led its issue with a cover showing young women flirting with a guardsman and a report on *Evening Standard* cartoonist David Low.[21] In 1938, featuring a leading critic of appeasement such as Low was a political statement, a radical line Lorant pursued during his editorship and that his successor Hopkinson continued. Putting aside the politics of this choice, Lorant assumed that ordinary readers were intelligent and inquiring and would respond positively to an approach that recognized this. He was proved right in his confidence because as 1938 wore on, sales increased steadily.

In the news category, the issue included straightforward material on the deployment of barrage balloons in London as part of Air Raid Precautions, cute photos of a new gorilla at London Zoo and a feature on the Cossack choir formed by escapees from the Soviet Union. *Picture Post* dealt with the important and topical item of the large-scale evacuation of children from Britain's big cities as news, but showed it through the lens of a personal account and photographs from a teacher who led one of the evacuated parties. Closer examination of this personal account shows it to be disingenuous. A professional photographer had taken all the images, but the page was made up as if the readers were sharing a teacher's photograph album, a rather stylized handwritten script serves as her diary entries.[22]

There were travel articles on Sark, Japan, Piccadilly Circus and a house at Land's End in Cornwall. This last item combined candid photography of visitors and of the rather scruffy tea house that formed the focus of this tourist trap. This anonymous article took an all-too-common late-1930s *de haut en bas* view of this type of holidaymaking and followed the line of the Council for the Protection of Rural England and early conservationists, such as Patrick Abercrombie and Clough Williams-Ellis.[23] One example: 'There is no view of the country so good as that from a high carriage or the back of a horse. There is no view worse than that from a saloon car.'[24] For this magazine's typical readership, which was urban and working or lower middle class, this was a misdirected conclusion, because by 1938 it had become clear that these people bought a car as soon as they could afford

FIGURE 6.2 *Speedway Spectators, Picture Post, 22 October 1938, Image Credit: Felix Man/Picture Post/Getty Images.*

to.[25] This article was off message for *Picture Post* and showed that it had not yet found a consistent authoritative voice.

In this same issue, Lorant's choice of features provided an early example of his intentions for the magazine. There was a short piece on speedway, an Australian import second only to football as a spectator sport in the late 1930s and especially popular in London.[26] The article was topped with a photograph, not of a glamorous speedway rider, but of his audience. The photograph showed a young woman carrying a child both rapt in their interest in this fast and dangerous sport (see Figure 6.2).[27] This was a beautiful photograph, taken at night with a flashgun to produce a *chiaroscuro* effect. Lorant retained the services of two German photographers Hans Baumann (known as Felix Man) and Kurt Hubschmann (known as Kurt Hutton) who worked with him on his earlier magazines. Like Lorant they were both refugees and shared his knowledge of European photojournalism.[28] Felix Man's picture presented this ordinary young woman in Renaissance style, Madonna and child at the speedway. The intent here was clear; the spectator was more interesting than the star rider.

The next feature emphasizing ordinary people was about a club for grandmothers. This club, based in London's Victoria Dock, catered for women over sixty who met every Monday to listen to a talk, a gramophone recital and to have a cup of tea and play checkers.[29] There was a single editorializing sentence that proposed that if other grandmothers knew that a club like this was possible, then they would form one, otherwise the article confined itself to rather light-hearted reportage. The article did not reveal its intentions to its readers. It was a study of the workaday lives of elderly poor women who seem to have more fun that might be expected at the club.

It was a further celebration of the ordinary and virtuous, but done in a way that didn't hit it home with a sledgehammer.

A third article, 'A Glamour Girl's Day' maintains this theme.[30] This seems, based on its title, much closer to the prurient showbiz articles common to many magazines in the 1930s. Putting aside the contradictions involved with the magazine's own occasional use of this type of material, the article takes a surprising view of the topic. The feature had a subheading setting out its theme: 'Glamour girls, one might suppose, live only on champagne and oysters, wear nothing but frills and ostrich feathers, [and] come home the next morning. How different is the reality!'[31] The article did not explain much about what being a glamour girl meant, it seems that the term would be easily understood by the magazine's readership. The subheading alluded to the idea that if you were a glamour girl, people expected you to be a stripper or worse. Here it referred to a troupe of American dancers visiting London to appear at the Dorchester Hotel, which was an icon of Americanized modernity in London's West End. The visiting dancers were young, some of them only sixteen years old; they had 'perfect figures and heights'. These young women were, according to the article, having a dull time in London, chaperoned by their relatives, spending time between performances doing their washing and visiting museums. Their chaperones allowed them out for the evening to dance for fun, if it was with young men they approved of. It is hard to see the point of this article unless it was the news that not all dancers were strippers. It pushed the idea home that these young women, despite their age, occupation and nationality were just ordinary people doing a job that had its routines and *longeurs*. In this way, the intention was perhaps to distinguish *Picture Post* from film magazines, which proposed that American entertainers were always glamorous. *Picture Post* suggested the opposite; these glamour girls were just like us.

The final article selected from this issue returns to this theme to examine the world of young women training to be pilots in the National Women's Air Reserve.[32] This article typified the magazine's approach to the possibility of the impending war; it didn't address the topic directly, but looked at its consequences from a human-interest point of view. It explained the women's ordinary backgrounds to the reader. 'One or two may be going by car. Most will be going on bus, on bicycles, or on foot. These girls [are] typists, telephone operators, nurses, dressmakers, shop assistants for six days of the week.'[33] These women were to become pilots in the Second World War, ferrying and delivering planes for the RAF. *Picture Post*'s attitude towards them and its emphasis on their bravery and steadfast approach foreshadows much wartime reportage and propaganda. To complete this account, this issue also contained articles on how the Foreign Office worked, a page on modern science (see Chapter 2), two short stories and a four-page colour supplement on British artists. This last item was for readers to cut out and pin up on their walls.

By the end of 1938, *Picture Post* had introduced two extra features: readers' photographs and letters. The first of these shows how far cheap cameras, films and processing had penetrated into British society by the end of the 1930s. Readers from all parts of the country, often from modest houses in modest streets, submitted amusing or surprising photographs on many topics.[34] Letters were a common feature in most magazines of the period. In a key difference, *Picture Post* would publish critical letters as well as those reflecting its increasing popularity. One pompous letter stands out, which stated: 'I am moved to astonishment at the presentation of week after week of pages of totally unknown, totally undistinguished and, worst of all, totally uninteresting people.' A reply came via an editorial rebuttal, placed immediately below the letter, that either Lorant or Hopkinson could have written:

This is a vital point at issue. PICTURE POST firmly believes in the ordinary man and woman; thinks they have had no fair share in picture journalism: believes their faces are more striking, their lives and doings more full of interest than those of the people whose faces and activities cram the ordinary picture papers.[35]

Celebrity culture in 1930s Britain

Although *Picture Post*'s rebuttal picked out 'debutantes and dictators' as examples of the type of celebrities featured in other magazines, it is likely that the appeal of this phrase was its alliteration. The doings of debutantes and bright young things may have propped up gossip columns, but in the 1930s it was the royal family that received most coverage in newspapers and magazines. The nation had respected King George V and his austere consort but they did little to inspire popular journalism. In contrast, his sons, Edward, Prince of Wales and Bertie, Duke of York were central to popular journalism. By 1938, the new king and queen and their young daughters offered much of interest to readers with families. After the royals, film stars were the most common object of magazine celebrity worship. As D. L. LeMahieu has noted, 'Why British audiences displayed such intense interest in film stars remains an open question.'[36] Nevertheless, in the 1930s there was a celebrity culture just as pervasive and foolish as today, which fan magazines such as *Picturegoer* and *Girls' Cinema* and the popular press fuelled.

Going to the cinema was the most popular cultural activity in Britain in the 1930s and was a habit that women, the young and working and lower-middle-class audiences were keen on.[37] Many of the stars that British audiences admired were Americans seen in Hollywood films. For example, *Picturegoer* magazine's list of top stars for 1938 included Charles Boyer, Spencer Tracy, Robert Taylor, Margaret Sullavan, Greta Garbo and Bette

Davis.[38] Britain also produced some first rank Hollywood stars such as Robert Donat, Ronald Colman, Leslie Howard and Vivienne Leigh, all resident in the United States. Once in Los Angeles, they became as remote and exotic to British audiences as their American colleagues. As Mark Glancy explains, film magazines described movie stars' lives featuring their often-humble origins and original names, but showed that they led lives that British readers would think unimaginably glamorous.[39] It may be that revealing a star's humble origins proposed a possible upward mobility for British readers.[40]

By the late 1930s, British cinema had made a comeback from the domination that American productions had held since the silent era. It had its own homegrown stars such as Michael Redgrave, Anna Neagle and Jessie Matthews. These names were also remote and glamorous, but the most popular British stars of all were much more down to earth. In 1938, the British trade paper *Kinematograph Weekly* identified that the most 'winning' stars of the year were George Formby and Gracie Fields, both of whom promoted a particular, heightened form of ordinariness.[41]

Formby and Fields had much in common with each other, both were from Lancashire and neither fitted the normal requirements for film star beauty. George Formby presented himself as toothy and gormless, physically inept, but somehow always getting the girl and winning through.[42] After starring in a series of formulaic comedies, Formby was at the peak of his career in 1938, headlining two films: *I See Ice* and *It's in the Air*.[43] Gracie Fields specialized in patriotic, upbeat films that promoted self-reliance and community spirit. These themes were central to her most famous film *Sing as We Go* (1934) where Field's *joi de vivre* could open closed mills and overcome the slump. Jeffrey Richards describes Fields, perhaps a little unkindly, as 'neither beautiful, nor, in her film heyday, young'.[44] Both actors had different qualities than conventional film stars. It wasn't their Britishness, as Jessie Matthews, a big star, also appeared in British films but was never thought ordinary. For both, combining their ordinary appearance with their presentation as working-class heroes who upset the strict hierarchies of 1930s Britain struck a chord that was reflected in later decades in an increasing interest in the lives of ordinary people.

Picture Post provided little coverage of celebrities. In October 1938, its take on a member of the royal family arriving at a public event was to show a photograph of the waiting crowd.[45] In the same issue, Gracie Fields featured in a six-page article to mark the occasion of her forthcoming concert at the Royal Albert Hall in front of Queen Mary. Fields was forty years old at this point, and this concert was intended to be the ultimate triumph of her career.[46] In its early months, *Picture Post* was finding its editorial stance and this long article on Fields displayed some reaching about for a consistent line. The main tone of the article was hagiographic, setting out Field's rise to stardom from her humble origins in Rochdale. Fields received praise for her interest in children and her charitable work; a hyperbolic description of her ordinariness reinforced her saintliness. At this point in her career

Fields was extremely wealthy. The article in fact praised her ability to attract £50,000 for each film she made, which in today's terms would be equivalent to £16 million.[47] *Picture Post*'s photographer showed her living in some style in Hampstead, but, throughout, the article and its photograph captions disabled the idea that Fields was anything but a very ordinary person, living in unusual circumstances. Various examples of this were:

- Grace's nature is unlike that of a film star as can be. She likes old clothes, would as soon travel into town by bus as in her own smart coupé.
- 'My biggest treat is to have a job of building started. They say I must have been born with a brick in my hand.'
- On the swing together [Fields is pictured with her nephew]. Imagine any other film star being pictured like this.

Fields may well have been, as Jeffrey Richards thought, 'generous, affectionate and unpretentious throughout her life', but *Picture Post*'s need to gild the lily by presenting her as the most famous ordinary woman in the country reveals its agenda.[48] Later in 1938, it featured an article on Jessie Matthews, almost as big a star as Gracie Fields, but on this occasion, Matthews was, it would seem, too starry, so a six-page feature was devoted to her film stand-in. In this way, *Picture Post* could reference a glamorous star, but position her in the world of ordinary people.[49]

The massive popular success of Formby and Fields evidences the wide attraction of ordinariness in the 1930s. In reality, these two actors were extraordinary in their abilities and in their careers and success. However, there was a great gap between their appeal to audiences and the style of conventional good-looking British film actors such as Michael Redgrave and Margaret Lockwood who both starred in Alfred Hitchcock's *The Lady Vanishes* in 1938.[50]

Other 1930s ordinariness

For amateur performers, there was a remote possibility of stardom; as we have seen, film magazines often mentioned a star's ordinary and humble beginnings. One way of achieving national fame was to take part in a talent contest, which was a common feature on the interwar music hall circuit and a cheap way of producing a popular radio programme. By 1935, Carroll Levis, a Canadian impresario, had taken his music hall 'Discoveries' talent show into a new medium, by having it broadcast on Radio Luxembourg, a jollier alternative to listening to the staid content put out by the BBC. It was a precursor to the wide range of musical and variety talent contests shown on television today.[51] Ralph Reader, an actor and manager active in the scout movement, produced amateur entertainments featuring his scouts, which then became the popular Gang Shows that played to large audiences in British theatres. In 1937, he starred in a movie *The Gang Show*.[52] Both these shows evidenced that the British public was interested in entertainment provided by ordinary people, perhaps because they were seeing themselves on stage, in complete contrast to the world of Hollywood films.

One area of life that, in the 1930s, combined celebrity and ordinariness was sport. Two of Britain's favourite sports of the decade were cricket and football. Many cricketers of this period were amateurs from a public school background, so were difficult for the man in the street to identify with. Len Hutton, who scored 364 runs against Australia in 1938, was England's most famous cricketer and its most successful professional. Working-class professionals took part in the same cricket teams as amateurs but dressed in separate changing rooms and had to address their amateur teammates with a 'Mister' or 'Sir'.[53] In contrast, working-class sportsmen dominated football. At the highest level, football was an all-professional sport, players were subject to a maximum wage and their contracts were unlimited and owned by their clubs. In this way, even the most successful football players of the period, such as Alex James and Ted Drake, earned a maximum of £9 a week.[54] Sport in 1930s Britain thus provided the means for celebrity while remaining in other ways ordinary. It was a commonplace event for football fans to share a tram home with the star footballers they had just watched at the match.

Ordinariness and democratization

Historians have seen *Picture Post* as one of the elements that in the amplified context of the Second World War led to an increased democratization of Britain, which led to Labour's victory in 1945. In the 1930s, these elements formed part of 'an oppositional social democratic consensus [that] gradually evolved across Britain'.[55] The other elements that are most commonly cited alongside *Picture Post* are the British Documentary Film Movement, Mass-Observation (M-O) and best-selling social conscience novels. Each of these was up and running by 1938, but each one's interest in ordinary people differed from that of *Picture Post*.

The British Documentary Film Movement refers to a loose collection of film directors and production companies. Influenced by Russian and German cinema and by the general leftist stance of most intellectuals in the 1930s, they produced striking short films that documented the life of working-class people in Britain. Under the leadership of figures such as John Grierson, teams of young directors, writers and cameramen turned their attention to real-life topics that were a world away from the representation of the working classes in conventional movies and newsreels. These films were produced and released by government agencies such as the Post Office and by well-intentioned industrial concerns such as the British Commercial Gas Association and Daimler.[56]

Eighty years later, their results still catch the eye. One well-known example of the genre is *Housing Problems* (1935).[57] This film examined slum housing conditions in London and proposed modern blocks of flats as a clean and humane solution to the intractable problem of Britain's broken Victorian housing stock. The unusual aspect of this film was that it featured 'real' working-class slum dwellers who spoke on camera describing the conditions they lived in. This approach was in stark contrast to public information films of the period that featured eminent men explaining why a particular problem needed solving. This method provided a voice to the most unheard section of society, which was a less mediated version of working-class experience than *Picture Post* achieved with its articles on Grandmother's clubs. But, in terms of impact, *Picture Post* was a far more important vehicle for the portrayal of ordinary life. Generations of history, sociology and media students are now familiar with British documentary films but, at the time, they had a very limited circulation at film clubs and international film festivals, and were not seen by a wide audience in Britain.[58]

Tom Harrisson, an anthropologist, and Charles Madge, who was an artist, founded M-O in 1937. M-O was another contributor to the rise in interest in the world of ordinary people just before the Second World War. Both these men were in their twenties, younger even than the founders of *Picture Post*. Victor Gollanz of Left Book Club fame funded this odd combination of social science and situationist art, which worked by combining observation, enquiry and survey. Ben Highmore aptly describes M-O as being 'on the fault-line between science and art, objectivity and subjectivity, rationalism and irrationalism'.[59] Through these means it obtained a feeling for what ordinary people thought about their lives, work and leisure and their views of the politics of the day.[60] M-O's investigation of Bolton provides much interesting material about working-class life just before the war.

M-O's correspondents wrote diaries that provided a direct insight into their thoughts and feelings. These reports produced surprises, revealing, for example, the commonplace anti-Semitism of the period. They suffer from the problem of response bias in that the reports were completed by the sort of people who were prepared to fill in reports.[61] As a consequence, some academic writers have criticized M-O's observations of ordinary life as being unscientific. The M-O approach provokes the thought of a superior race examining the everyday life of aboriginals, reflecting Harrison's previous work with Pacific islanders.[62] M-O's influence on the promotion of the lives of ordinary people is probably greater today as a historical archive than it was at the time.

The impact of the slump and deprivations of the late 1920s and early 1930s in many of Britain's outer regions encouraged the return of a genre of British fiction, largely dormant since the Victorian period, the social conscience novel. Its most well-known examples were Walter Greenwood's *Love on the Dole* (1933) and A. J. Cronin's The *Stars Look Down* (1936) and *The Citadel* (1937). The reading public leapt upon these bestsellers, which explored social conditions in the cotton and mining industries at a time when book reading was at an all-time high in Britain.[63] Public and cheap private libraries ensured that these books had a wide circulation in ordinary households. To these books might be added J. B. Priestley's *Let the People Sing* (1939), which stressed the importance of community, and Orwell's non-fiction *The Road to Wigan Pier* (1937), which had a similar intent to the documentary film movement. Orwell was, though, mostly read at the time by members of the Left Book Club, and was, because of this, less influential on mainstream culture than the author of a bestseller.

Both the documentary film movement and M-O took a keen interest in ordinary people. Their emphasis was on the poor and on working-class life; both were earnest and well meaning in their wish to inform Britain on the realities of its class structure. They did this with little warmth or empathy. Social conscience novels had plenty of these qualities, but being fiction had a diluted impact. *Picture Post* was more attuned to working-class and lower-middle-class life and was a magazine that thought its readers both intelligent and enquiring. *Picture Post*'s celebration of ordinary life, together with other forces of social change such as documentary films and M-O, was instrumental in promoting the ideas that came together at the end of Second World War in a dramatic shift towards social democracy.

The promotion of ordinary values was also seen in elements of popular culture just after the war. One such was the long-running radio programme *Have a Go*, which started in 1946, hosted by the northern wartime newsreader Wilfred Pickles.[64] This was an early instance of BBC radio featuring ordinary people. It started out as a simple quiz show and turned into an opportunity for contestants to perform a party piece or to tell an anecdote.[65] In the same year the BBC introduced a programme *Down Your Way* which visited a new part of Britain each week and interviewed 'Mr John and Mrs John Citizen' and played a record request for them.[66] The first show from Lambeth featured guests such as a rabbit seller, a Covent Garden porter, a herbalist, a director of The Young Vic and Monty Modlyn, a local character, later to become a popular broadcaster.[67] Both of these two shows were long running, lasting until 1967 and 1992, respectively. After the war, films, literature, plays and television increasingly featured stories of ordinary lives.[68]

Conclusion

It is difficult to decide whether *Picture Post* directly influenced this post-war presentation of ordinary people or whether it was a product of the 'people's war' or both. It is possible to say that *Picture Post* presented a singular way of viewing the ordinary world before the start of the Second World War, well before the Blitz spirit and other wartime effects promoted a less class-bound

British society. In this way, it prefigured post-war radio programmes that took ordinary people as their subject and a gradual unpicking of class and culture in the 1950s.

The launch and immediate success of *Picture Post* in 1938 produced an unusual form of modernity in Britain, which was a revaluation of the way public discourse presented ordinary people. Rather than being a vehicle for middle-class humour, it presented ordinary people as powerful actors in their own lives. 'Ordinary' in this sense was not equivalent to 'working class' as much of *Picture Post*'s readership and content revolved around lower-middle-class life just as much as working-class life. As Su Holmes puts it, 'The association of "real" and "ordinary" people with the working-class ... has a long history in British popular culture, with some of the most famous examples being the British Documentary Film Movement, "kitchen sink" drama ... and television soap opera.'[69] *Picture Post* in this way took a rather unusual approach to ordinariness.

Picture Post's inclusive sense of ordinariness was both a reflection and promotion of social and cultural changes in Britain in 1938. Two years later, George Orwell saw the same thing in his identification of a classless new Britain based in the suburbs. Wartime conditions provoked his response, praising what J. B. Priestley had condemned when he observed the same symptoms in 1933. If *Picture Post* had existed at the time, Priestley might well have added it to his list of things that contributed to his new England. Britain's wartime experiences were the most important generator of its new inclusive, democratic leanings given full voice in the 1945 General Election, but the influence of *Picture Post* and other democratic sources had started this process long before war became inevitable.

Picture Post brought about a small revolution in magazine production in Britain. For once, this was not a reproduction or adaptation of an American source, but was the result, like many other new ideas of the time, of the recent immigration of an East European Jew to Britain. Like other Jewish intellectuals, Britain was, for Lorant, a European staging post for a final move to the United States. Lorant's artistic sensibility combined with new technologies to great effect in *Picture Post*. His combination of sharply reproduced photographs taken with 35-millimetre handheld cameras produced a result that was worlds away from its British rivals. Placing *Picture Post* and *John Bull* side-by-side shows how the new drove out an old and tired predecessor.

CHAPTER SEVEN

Cars, coaches and charabancs at the Prospect Inn

Charabanc parties from the large manufacturing towns, playing cornets on village greens and behaving with a barbaric lack of manners.[1]

This case study focuses on the relationship between increased working-class mobility and the construction in 1938 of a small roadside public house, the Prospect Inn, an obscure example of British interwar architecture. The Prospect Inn was a radical departure from most new pubs of the 1930s, which would be enough to merit its inclusion as an example of 1938 modernity, but its architect's intentions reveal more. In the 1930s, segregation of leisure by class of customer was the norm, with pubs providing a simple public bar for the working classes and a more sophisticated lounge or saloon bar for the well-off. Increased mobility among working-class holidaymakers, via cars, motorcycles, motor coaches and charabancs destabilized the arrangements in traditional country pubs. Rather than dissuading poorer customers, the Prospect Inn welcomed charabanc trippers into a public bar that was as beautiful and sophisticated as the lounge next door, reflecting an increasing democratization of leisure that would take full effect in the 1950s and 1960s.

FIGURE 7.1 *The Prospect Inn, car park. Image Credit: RIBA Collections.*

In the 1930s, there was a sense in intellectual circles, and not always an approving one, of a growing democratization and classlessness in British life.[2] As discussed in the previous chapter, the social consequences of the Second World War amplified this idea leading to widespread changes in the rigidity of the class system in the years that followed.[3] In 1938, the loosening of class hierarchies was apparent in leisure activities such as the frequent and large-scale attendance at luxurious super-cinemas and in many private and municipal facilities that welcomed customers from both the working and lower middle classes.[4]

The charabanc and its smarter sibling, the motor coach, were one ingredient in the development of greater classlessness in interwar British society.[5] In contrast to railway carriages, which segregated passengers into three classes of travel that were as much a social structuring as a pricing policy, charabancs and motor coaches offered a single, sometimes luxurious, offering.[6] J. B. Priestley, a man who was familiar with expensive cars, commented: 'I doubt if even the most expensive private motor [cars] ... are as determinedly and ruthlessly comfortable as these new motor coaches. ... They have annihilated the old distinction between rich and poor passengers.'[7]

The growing popularity and luxury of charabancs and motor coaches

By 1938, many middle-class families owned cars; in total, there were just less than two million of them in Britain.[8] There was a strong regional dimension to this acquisition, with households in the suburbanized south of England being most likely to have one on their drive. In some smarter suburbs, one house in two had access to a car. A smaller, but significant, number of working-class drivers also owned cars, aided by an active second-hand market and by sharing costs with friends.[9] Cars provided working-class motorists and their families with a spontaneous, autonomous, motorized mobility.

Long before 1938, poorer members of society had achieved some of these benefits through the charabanc. This disconnected them from the more controlled and directed forms of public transport that used to take the working classes to the seaside such as the train and the steamer. The *char-à-banc*, formed (as its French name suggests) from a simple combination of lorry and bench, made its first appearance in motorized form as early as 1900.[10] After the First World War, ex-military lorries were transformed into charabancs to meet the demand for working-class leisure encouraged by shorter working hours and higher wages. As Priestley noted, motor coaches superseded these unpretentious vehicles as the interwar years progressed. A fictional account described this transition: '[This charabanc] was a box-like vehicle capable of seating twelve people besides

FIGURE 7.2 *A streamlined charabanc/motor coach. Image Credit: Photo by Chris Sampson. Creative Commons Attribution 2.0 Generic licence. Converted to monochrome, cropped and edited.*

the driver. Originally she had been the property of a motor coach owner but competition in size and luxury of motor coaches had made her out of date for his purposes.'[11] One example of the later type of coach produced by the English Electric Company boasted 'luxurious seating, good ventilation and roominess, sunshine roof, lavatory and ample luggage space'.[12] Figure 7.2 shows a typical design.

Britons used the term 'charabanc' throughout the interwar period to describe both types of vehicles. One commentator thought it a degraded term: 'What ought we to call the motor-coach? Call it that. And cease talking of charabanc – resolved by common utterance into cheerybank.'[13] Distinguishing between motor coaches and charabancs is sometimes problematic, but it is possible to say that, together, they were a popular form of transport for most families who did not have cars between the wars. In 1937, there were approximately forty million passenger journeys by motor coach and charabanc, split equally between the two categories. There had been an increase in usage of 17 per cent over the previous four years. By 1951, this had more than doubled to ninety million passenger journeys.[14]

By the start of the 1930s, motor coaches were providing regular services throughout Britain. Priestley's trip from London to Southampton, on which he based his observations, was one of several scheduled coach journeys each day between these two cities. The fare for this route was eight shillings (40p) return.[15] An equivalent rail fare was thirteen shillings and threepence (66p) for a third-class ticket.[16] Journey times also differed; the motor coach took four hours to make the journey, while the train completed it in two hours. For the working-class passenger, if not on an urgent journey, the choice of coach was a natural one. At the cost of two extra hours of their time, they could exchange a draughty and uncomfortable third-class railway carriage for a seat in a luxurious coach. This offered what Richard Hoggart, in his examination of interwar working-class culture, *The Uses of Literacy*, considered to be the same level of comfort as a super-cinema, all coupled with a 40 per cent cost saving.[17] Hoggart's connection of these two forms of leisure is intriguing, as super-cinemas provided everyday glamour and luxury to working-class cinemagoers for the first time, and were a dramatic improvement on the flea-pits that preceded them. The move from rail to road did not please those who believed in a planned economy. The 1937 documentary film, *Roadways*, showed the motor coach as being part of a chaotic unregulated system of transport that made Britain's roads inefficient and dangerous, although the film acknowledged that motor coaches provided links to parts of the country that the train could not reach.[18]

Motor coaches also provided scheduled services from urban areas to holiday towns such as Ramsgate and Margate. A flyer for summer excursions from Croydon provides an example of this type of journey. It showed a wide variety of possible seaside destinations on the south coast, with coaches leaving every day at 9.15 am returning at 5.00 pm from Brighton, Worthing, Eastbourne, Littlehampton, Clacton, Margate and Ramsgate among other resorts. Priced at eight shillings (40p) for a day return, these journeys were one shilling and sixpence (7½p) cheaper than the train.[19] Excursions to Whipsnade Open Air Zoo and to the Navy Day at Portsmouth were also offered.[20]

Economist C. T. Brunner, in an analysis of road transport published in 1928, proposed that charabanc customers fell into two distinct types:

> There is first of all the seaside charabanc traffic. This consists in the main of visitors of a relatively wealthy class who are spending a fairly long holiday at a particular seaside town. The seaside weekend tripper of the poorer class does not patronize these charabancs to any extent.[21] … The second class of charabanc traffic consists of joy-riders from the industrial towns. The class catered for is much lower one than the seaside charabanc passengers and is usually referred to as 'trippers'.[22]

Brunner suggests that passengers in this supposedly classless vehicle observed a self-electing class distinction by choosing different destinations depending on the cultural content on offer. In 1937, Skinners of Hastings advertised a typical example of the first type of charabanc outing: 'To Battle Abbey, Fare 1/6d …. Historic interest is the chief note of this tour but it is immediately combined with delight in pleasant scenery. On the return journey, we have to surmount Blackhorse hill, which has an elevation of 500 feet.'[23] One shilling and sixpence (7½p) was well within the budget of many working-class families in the relatively prosperous south-east of England in the late 1930s, but these same families may well have thought of the opportunity to see nature and history at first hand as unattractive. Hoggart supports this notion, describing how working-class culture was, in general, directed towards excitement and immediate gratification rather than contemplative enjoyment.[24]

The juxtaposition of middle-class charabanc customers and working-class 'trippers' might well have caused unease and confused class relations. For example, writer Eric Newby recalled a childhood seaside charabanc trip that had attracted, what his middle-class parents considered, the 'wrong' sort of customers:

> I began dimly to apprehend some of the reasons that might have contributed to my parents' apparent lack of keenness for this outing. The other passengers were trippers. In spite of their appearance they were both jolly and friendly, much more so than some of our neighbours at the 'better end'. They called my father 'governor', my mother 'mum' and the charabanc a 'sharrer'.[25]

As Brunner proposes, urban groups centred around a place of work, a pub, a church or a particular street travelling to the seaside characterized the second form of charabanc trip. These varied in composition from rowdy groups looking forward to drinking and fighting, to respectable groups who made a more dignified progress to the seaside. This type of charabanc had a lower price than a scheduled motor coach, reflecting its simpler facilities and economies of scale.

Rowdy charabanc parties were the subject of much disdain from both intellectual and conservative commentators in the 1930s and formed one of that decade's pet highbrow hates, along with bungalows, suburbia and electricity pylons.[26] For instance, historian Norah Richardson wrote: 'Many of us have … regretted [the countryside's] desecration by ribbon development, the motor charabanc and the bungaloid growth.'[27] The *Midland Daily Telegraph* complained of 'charabanc parties which passed in a blur of horns, musical instruments and singing through peaceful towns and villages, scattering streamers, balloons, bottles and banana skins'.[28] Best-selling travel writer, H. V. Morton, wrote: 'I have seen charabanc parties from the large manufacturing towns, playing cornets on village greens and behaving with a barbaric lack of manners which might have been outrageous had it not been unconscious, and therefore only pathetic.'[29]

Morton and Richardson were writing about working-class groups making incursions into the countryside, and this seems to have been the locus of most criticism. The charabanc party's autonomous mobility provided working-class access to areas of the countryside that were distant from railway stations and to roadside pubs for the first time. These places were previously only available to middle-class drivers and to locals, and so this new mobility had become a problem.[30]

Documented examples of bad behaviour on interwar charabancs are hard to trace as oral histories of charabanc journeys were recorded long after the event by the better-behaved type of tripper. One book that otherwise contains jolly memories describes one negative incident:

> We were all happily sauntering back to our coaches when somebody shouted 'A FIGHT' and 220 of us made a grand audience to two or three Maltby lads who were sailing in to one another. ... I didn't see much of the actual fight but I did see them carry a woman off with a bleeding nose (I think it was one of the lad's mothers).[31]

All-women parties could also exceed the bounds of appropriate public behaviour:

> That's the day the laundry girls have off. Yesterday one of my mates took a coach-ful of them down. There were thirty-two of them and they had twenty-four crates of beer on board. Well, when they got to Southend, it was decided that they had perhaps best not get out, so they stopped at Billericay and ended up with whiskey and port.[32]

Oral history accounts show that charabanc parties could also be well behaved. For example, the same respondent who recorded the brawl noted above recorded how respectable some charabanc trips were:

> For many, this was the only seaside outing of the year. Everyone would try to look their best, the women in dresses and hats and fur stoles – can you imagine wearing a fur stole to the seaside? We were very conscious of our appearance – and the men would also be in hats and smart suits.[33]

The more progressive interwar commentators agreed with this sentiment. George Bernard Shaw, in considering the changed circumstances of working-class women in the late 1920s, proposed that 'dances and charabanc excursions and whist drives and dressing and wire-less concerts stimulate and cultivate them'.[34] C. D. Burns concluded optimistically that 'a modern crowd at leisure keeps spontaneous order, and it may easily "bring out" what is best in a man, rather than what is worst. Community singing indicates what is possible.'[35]

Although it is tempting to imagine a binary of 'good' and 'bad' charabanc trippers, a record from a M-O study of a pub's charabanc trip taken from Bolton to Southport in 1943 shows that mixed levels of behaviour were possible within one charabanc: 'The party arrived home about midnight. My informant described them as some very nice people, and some lowlife folk. The very nice people kept together and held aloof from the fights and brawls.'[36] Businesses had to be careful when accommodating charabancs.

They had a choice of whether to admit them or not. If they said yes, then they could expect some troublesome customers among the respectable parties.

Entertaining the charabanc tripper

1938 saw one distinct change in working-class leisure, which was the government's introduction of a week's paid holiday.[37] This provided more opportunity for an extended stay at the seaside using a motor coach. Before 1938, day trips to the seaside were the most affordable and fun holiday for the urban working classes. At the seaside, a wide variety of leisure possibilities was available ranging from a day on the beach, or if the weather was less than perfect, concert halls, amusement arcades, parks, pubs and cafés provided alternatives.[38]

Interwar intellectuals proposed that Americanization and an inauthentic consumerist culture brought about by increased, but indiscriminate, spending by working-class holidaymakers had debased seaside resorts. J. B. Priestley noted this in his well-known observations on Blackpool.[39] C. E. M. Joad took this idea one step further suggesting that many seaside resorts comprised 'shops with buckets and spades, with ghastly imitation jewellery, with unusual pottery, dusty archaic purses, pincushions made of shells … nothing real and everything pretending to be something else … tawdry finery, sticky sweets, fly-blown cakes and a general air of hot dustiness.'[40]

This idea of debasement accompanied a suggestion that these same forces were producing a more homogenized British culture. For example, one observer, Yvonne Cloud, thought that Britain's seaside resorts had become largely identical, providing a flattened experience of modernity. This was quite a common reaction in the 1930s, and was a thought that disdainful intellectuals also applied to suburbia and to the high street:

> All seaside places of any polarity are equally 'modern'. When they all have their cinemas and bars and pin-tables, their automatic machines and bars; their swimming-pools, their tennis-courts their golf-links and their dance-halls. When their beaches are all equally crowded, their bandstands packed, their piers alive, their hotels a-hum, their boarding-house parties debouching on to the steps …. Every place provides the same fare to-day.[41]

In reality, seaside resorts offered a wide variety of experiences to different visitors depending on their preferences and budgets, often within a few miles of each other. For example, the Fylde coast had raucous Blackpool but also offered more sedate fare at Cleveleys and genteel entertainment at Lytham St. Annes.[42]

In the south, Margate, Ramsgate and Broadstairs presented quite different experiences for the different sorts of charabanc parties. Ramsgate was a traditional Victorian seaside resort and channel port, whose attractions were, perhaps, more suited to older visitors. Broadstairs was, despite being surrounded by its more democratically minded sister resorts, an oasis of middle-class values, more attractive to private cars than charabancs. Cloud made an exception to her conclusion about the similarity of holiday resorts for Margate, writing that the 'the smell of the air is different here'.[43] Margate, although originating like its neighbours as a Victorian holiday resort, had adopted a more modern personality with the reconstruction, after a fire, of the Dreamland amusement park in 1935.[44]

The relative attraction of seaside resorts to working-class and lower-middle-class trippers resulted from a century-old history of negotiations with the impact of new transport technologies. The arrival of steamer day-trippers at Gravesend and Margate brought about a contestation between Lord's Day observation campaigners and local businessmen, which the latter won. Gravesend, for example, received a dramatic rise from 292,000 trippers per annum in 1830 to 1.1 million ten years later, leading it to become less popular with wealthier holidaymakers.[45] The arrival of the railways amplified this process. In 1851, an influx of poorer day-trippers at Blackpool caused concern from those who wished to maintain the status quo, in one example protesting that 'unless immediate steps are taken ... Blackpool as a resort for respectable visitors will be ruined'.[46] Bournemouth's improvement commissioners resisted the railway for many years, allowing the town to maintain its exclusivity until as late as 1888.[47]

Charabanc trippers were, in effect, choosing a class of resort where they could feel comfortable and have fun. Genteel holidaymakers chose particular towns or parts of towns where they only encountered people of their own 'caste'.[48] A degree of class segregation was thus achieved. One town, Frinton, refused to allow coach trips or charabancs into their resort at all during the interwar years, reflecting the resistance to the railways of the previous century. Within a particular resort, a similar self-elected segregation allowed working-class, lower-middle-class and middle-class patrons to experience separate forms of entertainment. A wide choice of cinemas, from fleapit to super-cinema, enabled the different audiences to enjoy themselves in different ways at different prices. Brad Beavan has described the raucous way that a working-class audience responded to films that contrasted with the more discriminating but passive manner of the middle classes.[49] In another example, the distinction in titling between restaurants and cafés provided for a simple class separation. There were exceptions. As the 1930s progressed, seaside resorts offered facilities that attracted a broader class of customers. For example, lidos, swimming pools and municipal pavilions did not distinguish by class or by differential pricing policies.[50]

The halfway house

On a lively charabanc trip, visiting a pub to break the journey to and from the seaside was as important a contributor to the success of the outing as the choice of holiday resort.[51] Pubs on the main highways between urban centres and coastal resorts were likely to attract the interest of charabanc parties. Brewers sometimes described them as halfway houses or, if aiming at the more middle-class customer, as roadhouses. Landlords had a choice to make with charabancs: They either made it clear that they were not welcome or they went out of their way to attract charabanc customers by providing parking, large public bars and toilet facilities. Alan Delgado suggests in *The Annual Outing* that pubs that wanted to attract charabanc customers were, in effect, making a Faustian pact that exchanged cash for tolerating depraved behaviour: 'A party would arrive and, like locusts, descend on a public house. As suddenly as they arrived the locusts left, leaving behind a legacy of dirty glasses, spilled beer, insanitary lavatories and stubbed cigarette ends on the floor of the bar.'[52]

Delgado's reductive conclusion does not sit well when one considers the wide variety of charabanc outings that ranged from the very respectable to the rowdy. Brewers were, in fact, keen to encourage charabanc traffic in their public houses. David Gutzke has described the scale of the brewers' response to the charabanc phenomenon and cites the example of Ind Coope's Fortune of War pub on the Southend Road. This huge mock-Tudor pub at the halfway point between Southend and London attracted regular motor-coach services and, after two enlargements, could serve 'an astonishing 250 charabancs daily during the summer'. Gutzke cites many other examples of pubs that were pleased to serve charabanc customers.[53]

By considering in detail the Prospect Inn, a pub that was built in 1938 specifically to attract and serve charabanc customers, it is possible to show that progressive brewers recognized that respectable charabanc customers deserved a more sophisticated place to drink, which was equal to that provided to middle-class motorists.

New arterial roads and the Prospect Inn

The Prospect Inn, shown in Figure 7.3, was located at Minster, a small village in Kent, a few miles from Ramsgate. In the 1930s, Minster was a country village that had little to distinguish it from hundreds of similar spots in the county, but for one feature: it was close to the main road from Ramsgate to London.[54] From a drinking point of view, it fell within the purview of Ramsgate brewer, Tomson and Wotton and, in 1933, it purchased an existing pub together with four acres of land. The intention was to demolish this pub and replace it with one that was both progressive and modern.[55]

Progressiveness was a key theme in the brewing industry in the 1930s, which had resulted from concerns over widespread drunkenness during the First World War. At the end of the war, brewers responded to the threat of potential government intervention with self-regulation and proposed that pubs should, in future, change their atmosphere by providing non-alcoholic

FIGURE 7.3 *The Prospect Inn, Minster, Kent, by Oliver Hill Image Credit: RIBA Collections.*

beverages and areas for recreation and games. One key provision was the need to reduce the amount of perpendicular drinking (i.e. the tradition of standing at the bar, buying rounds and drinking to excess).[56] In a progressive pub, most customers were seated and drank in a respectable manner. These proposals to change the nature of the pub were, in effect, a concerted attempt by brewers in Britain to change the pub's role as a centre of unrespectable male working-class life into something with a much broader class appeal.[57]

Road traffic to the Kent coast increased rapidly throughout the 1930s. This was prompted by the strong growth in car ownership in the south-east of England that was accompanied, as has been shown, by substantial numbers of charabancs and motor coaches.[58] The construction of new arterial roads that allowed for much higher speeds also encouraged travel from London to the coast. The Southend Arterial Road, site of the Fortune of War, was one example. On the other side of the Thames Estuary, the Thanet Way arterial road sped traffic from London to Margate and Ramsgate. It had two well-known halfway houses, The King's Head and The Roman Galley. The former was an olde-worlde nineteenth-century pub that was 'a busy house of call for the numerous motor-coaches', the latter was a new, brewer's Georgian building next to the arterial road that was a 'regular halting-place of the numerous motor-coaches which now follow this road to the Kentish coast'.[59] A 1938 survey of road traffic shows that these two routes were among the busiest in the south-east, and, given the predominance of cars in that area, perhaps among the busiest in Britain.[60]

It was not Tomson and Wotton's intention to build a large, mock-Tudor or neo-Georgian pub. They wished to commission a modern design for this roadhouse pub, a bold choice for a firm that had its fair share of traditional pubs.[61] This led to the search for an architect who could design a pub that was modern but not too modernist. The brewery chose Oliver Hill, best known today for his Midland Hotel in Morecambe, a modernist railway hotel in a Lancashire seaside resort, which he had recently completed.[62]

The London, Midland and Scottish railway built The Midland Hotel against its own hotel committee's objections that Morecambe was not the place for 'a first-class hotel operation'. They reached a compromise by building a large separate café for 'traditional' (i.e. working and lower-middle-class) customers.[63] It is intriguing that Hill was the architect of two successive designs that dealt with the problems of separating different classes of travellers. Hill wrote to Tomson and Wotton accepting the commission for the Prospect Inn: 'I shall be delighted to do your roadhouse, provided of course that it may be modern as distinct from imitative period.'[64]

The years between 1933 and 1938 were important in the introduction of roadside pubs and clubs. Often referred to as roadhouses, these buildings ranged from small pubs like the Prospect Inn, through to pub/hotels like The Comet at Hatfield to enormous Americanized country club establishments such as the Ace of Spades on the Kingston Bypass and the Thatched Barn on the Barnet Bypass.[65] The success of these larger establishments reflected their targeting of increasing numbers of middle-class motorists. They rarely admitted working-class customers and would have 'turned up their noses' to coach parties.[66] In an unusual move, the Prospect Inn deliberately set out to attract charabanc customers.

Charabancs and class separation

Hill took a while to realize his project and it was not until the end of 1938 that he completed the Prospect Inn. By that time the original budget of £3,000 had increased to just less than £8,000, making it an expensive small pub, about £2 million in today's money.[67] The result was striking in appearance. The new inn was deliberately made visible to motoring traffic on the nearby arterial road. Hill recorded that 'on the roof, visible for a considerable distance is a whitened reinforced concrete pylon, floodlit at night and surmounted by a red star' to advertise the inn's presence.[68] He also specified that the pub's name be spelled out in 18-inch high 'intense red' neon lights.[69]

Hill wished to name the pub the 'HMS Prospect'. This idea did not find approval with Tomson and Wotton who wished to retain the previous pub's name.[70] In this idea, Hill was referencing an important theme of 1930s architecture, which was the softening of modernist edges with American streamline influences that became known as *moderne*. This, as has been shown in Chapter 3 at the Empire Exhibition's Atlantic restaurant, was often connected with maritime influences from, for example, the new transatlantic

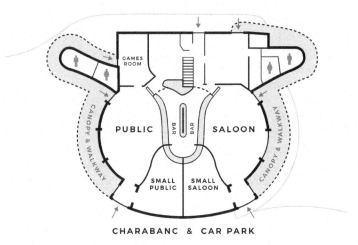

FIGURE 7.4 *The Prospect Inn, plan. Image Credit:* © *the author, prepared by TheBr&newstudio.*

liners of the period. As seen in Figure 7.3, the executed building retained some of these influences in its porthole windows, pylon mast and the decked feel of the design. Conservationist organization, Heritage England refers to these features in its listing details for the Prospect Inn as being in the 'International Modern Cunard' style.[71]

The spatial ordering of the car park and inn was clear. The parking arrangements shown in its architectural plans, specifically allowing for both charabancs and cars, demonstrated an openness to a wide variety of customers (see Figure 7.4).[72] Charabancs were to park on the left of the inn where their customers could access the two public bars. Hill, in an unusual design for a modern pub, placed access to the toilets from the car park rather from inside the bar. This suggests that he was aware that one of the 'well-known' proclivities of charabanc customers was the need for an immediate use of the facilities due to passengers drinking excessively on the journey. Car drivers parked their cars on the right-hand side of the building and made a beeline for the two saloon bars, where they could expect to be part of the 'right' crowd, where the men dressed correctly in a sports jacket and tie. In this way, the Prospect Inn supported class segregation.

Basil Oliver, in his thorough review of the interwar pub scene, thought 'Saloon Bar has a faint suggestion of superiority, and is the haunt of the "toffs" (or would-be toffs)'.[73] Pubs that Oliver considered the leading exemplars of progressive design in the 1930s all maintained a social apartheid in this way.[74] For example, one of the most important roadhouse pubs of the period, the enormous Berkeley Arms in Cranford that resembled 'a palatial French Chateau', attempted to cater for both upmarket motorists and local workers.[75] This huge pub had 'the delicate sophistication of a Mayfair restaurant, complete with jazz band, skilful chef and noiseless long-tailed waiters'.[76] Turning into the side road away from the junction with the main road would bring you to one of two public bars available to working-class customers 'where one may play darts in the company of the local lads'.[77] From today's perspective this sounds optimistic, but perhaps in the 1930s the customers of public bars were tolerant of sports car drivers with pencil moustaches offering them a game of darts. A brusquely named 'Meal Room' that provided simple fare for the wealthier customers' chauffeurs completed the class separation.[78] The Prospect Inn accentuated its segregation by its ordering of the amusements on offer. The Games Room, with a built-in darts board and a shove ha'penny table, was only accessible through the public bar, which would have been a step too far for middle-class customers.

In maintaining class separation in his design, Hill was reflecting a norm in pub design that lasted for many decades after the Second World War. It is unlikely that Tomson and Wotton would have contemplated building a pub with a single large bar whatever Hill's intentions. Throughout the interwar years, public houses and railway carriages had this class-based separation but charabancs or motor coaches did not. Some roadside places may have had both restaurants and cafés to allow for different classes, but many did not. Here, rather than a formal division, customers made a choice of an establishment where they were comfortable, electing their own class segregation.

Tomson and Wotton commissioned the Prospect Inn at a time of rapid change in middle-class mobilities. For much of the interwar period drivers most often used their cars for special outings for leisure and pleasure.[79] Top on the list were trips to the countryside and to the seaside.[80] The columns of *Autocar*, which was the leading motoring magazine of the period, featured suggestions for places to visit in the countryside and the experience of seeing England anew from the car was quite common in interwar literature.[81] Trips to the seaside were also incredibly popular, although frequent traffic jams were its inevitable result.[82]

For most middle-class motorists, respectability was the key to their enjoyment. *Autocar* provided an example of this when it published correspondence from motorists who welcomed the new closed-bodied cars because they allowed them to dress in smart clothes and to distinguish themselves from mere mechanics.[83] Drivers like this could only enjoy motoring leisure at hotels or tea rooms that served 'people like us'. As the 1930s progressed, and car ownership spread even further into the lower middle and working classes, the problem of class mixing through increased mobility became more apparent. This was a trend noted by one motorist who recalled that 'when you got cars in hands of the sort of chap who would go to the seaside in braces with mum and the kids in the back and so on, I think the standards of road behaviour probably dropped a bit, if you see what I mean'.[84]

This separation worked, but there were exceptions. For example, in 1938 not all car owners were middle class. By this time, the reduction in car prices and the rise in real incomes had led to working-class drivers contributing between 5 and 10 per cent of the total driving population.[85] How would this type of driver behave when parking at the Prospect Inn for the first time? Only speculation is possible, but one could imagine that the aspirant, quite well-off working-class driver might try his hand at the saloon bar, behaviour which in the 1930s would lead to social anxiety. Middle-class customers would be sensitive to a 'counter-jumper' who would betray his origins by his accents and manners. He might fall into the category of Basil Oliver's 'would-be toff'. Other working-class drivers might have felt more at home in the atmosphere of the public bar.

Providing for the respectable working-class drinker

At the start of the interwar period, pubs were simple affairs, most having two bars, a saloon bar for the more respectable, seated, male customer and a public bar or tap room for working-class customers, most of whom stood. In the late 1920s and throughout the 1930s, through the influence of the progressive brewers and the rise of suburban living, pubs changed in their design, appearance and social standing. Most new pubs of the period had carpeted saloon bars with quite elaborate furnishings and decorations, whereas their public bars, although moved on from the spit and sawdust of earlier years, were much plainer in execution, reflecting the distinct separation of classes and tastes of that time.[86] The new, larger pubs' introduction of an exclusive 'lounge' bar often accompanied by waiter service, encouraged respectable drinking where middle-class men and women could socialize together.[87] One consequence of the move to build more respectable pubs was an upgraded public bar. One brewery reluctantly recognized this change and commented that 'even the public bars should not be furnished for a really rough public bar trade'.[88] David Gutzke records such a public bar, built in 1937, which was 'palatial and had oak seats upholstered in crimson leather, silver-plated fittings and rubber flooring'.[89] Gutzke summarizes the position:

> When improving existing premises, brewers might alter public bars, but really spent the most money on the lounge and other features. Rebuilding old or building new premises were altogether different. Brewers here could modify the architecture of the all bars, though again public bars meant masculine drinkers who wanted beer not flowers, prints and improved decor.[90]

The detailed design of the Prospect Inn reveals a great deal about Hill's intentions. Despite his background as a society architect, Hill was active in progressive circles and had a social conscience. This is revealed by his membership of the Council for Art and Industry, which promoted good modern design and his pro-bono work on several state primary schools in the late 1930s.[91]

Hill subverted the usual class-based separation in his detailed plans for the Prospect Inn by producing a design that did not disadvantage working-class charabanc customers. The public and saloon areas of the pub were identical in size. This was unusual, as progressive interwar pub designs usually showed a domination of the saloon bar over the public.[92] Hill moved beyond these ideas to construct a democratic public house, achieved through equality of design for each bar, which received comprehensive and well-illustrated coverage in architectural and building journals.[93] Photographs show that the saloon and public bars were almost identical. They both incorporated walls in buttercup yellow and bar fronts in natural silver-grey oak. The saloon bar had a linoleum floor decorated with stylized plants and had what appears to be a cocktail cabinet behind the bar. The lino of the small public bar pictured bricklaying implements and, in the large public bar, husbandry and wheatsheaves. The bar stools provided one distinction. The saloon bar had stools with modern tubular steel legs, and the public bar had stools with more traditional wooden legs.[94] So, the public bar of the Prospect Inn provided an equal, if separate, space for the respectable working-class charabanc drinker to enjoy.

The Prospect Inn's *moderne* architectural styling reflected a wider democratic influence in interwar public buildings. Bruce Peter in his book, *Form Follows Fun*, identifies the strong connections between *moderne* styling and municipal or public buildings. He notes that seaside pavilions, lidos, and holiday camps (whose juxtaposition with the sea allowed for nautical metaphor), cinemas, greyhound stadia, zoos and commercial exhibitions often used this design.[95] To these might be added municipal airports (see Chapter 8) and many of the public libraries built in the expanding suburbia of the 1930s.[96] *Moderne*, as a hybrid style that softened the rigidity of modernism with American cultural sources, was looked down on by purists. As Peter puts it, 'Buildings exemplifying fusions of American and European design ideologies have usually been taken to be terminally inferior, particularly in comparison with their supposedly "purer" Continental counterparts.'[97]

Many seaside and suburban lidos adopted a *moderne* style. In one example at Saltdean, also constructed in 1938, the democratic nature of the lido's 'single pool for everybody' design extended to a café and a library.[98] Intriguingly, Tomson and Wotton built a *moderne*-style lido at Ramsgate, which included a large single-class café called The Aero that it decorated with murals featuring the interior of a 'contemporary pub'.[99] Hill's design for the Prospect Inn suggests a deliberate attempt to create a public building that welcomed respectable working-class charabanc customers and one that reflected the democratic nature of similar buildings in that style in the late 1930s.

Conclusion

At the start of the interwar period, the joint efforts of brewers, publicans, charabanc owners and coach companies presented day-trippers with simple propositions. The charabanc was, for many working-class holidaymakers, their first experience of independent powered mobility in a vehicle free to travel where its customers wished it. They did so in uncomplicated style, in a converted lorry with some wooden benches fitted to it, covered by a tarpaulin against Britain's variable summer weather. Charabanc journeys were, often, but not always, accompanied by one or more stops at roadside pubs. These offered primitive public bar facilities that could quickly become overcrowded by the arrival of a charabanc party.

Throughout the 1930s, charabanc parties' visits to the countryside crossed the invisible lines of interwar moral geographies and were consequently a focus of concern for intellectuals and other commentators. Poorly educated, badly behaved townies did not, it would seem, understand how to behave in rural areas. Much boorish behaviour may have taken place, but the concern over charabancs suggested a wider worry about the effects on a highly stratified society of the increased mobility of the poor, who had previously been confined to specific sections of the city with occasional visits to the seaside. Working-class charabanc trips to certain types of seaside resorts were, through historical precedent, acceptable, Margate but not Broadstairs, Blackpool but not Lytham. Charabanc parties agreed with this separation, not through politeness or by accepting a class-based apartheid but because they found genteel resorts dull and expensive.

As the 1930s progressed, the provision of better facilities benefited charabanc customers. As J. B. Priestley noted, the coaches they travelled in had become much more sophisticated and luxurious, particularly on scheduled journeys to the seaside. It would be unwise to think that this applied to all charabanc trips; it is likely that large numbers of basic, functional coaches plied their trade throughout the decade. Many of the pubs that welcomed charabanc customers upgraded their facilities. Often, this was connected to the progressive movement for the development of improved public houses. This meant that clean toilets and smart, if plain, interiors replaced spit and sawdust. By 1938, at the Prospect Inn, this reached an apogee where modern architecture and progressiveness combined to deliver a public bar for the charabanc customer that was the equal of its adjacent saloon bar.

Putting aside this separation, motor coaches and charabancs contributed to the process of social convergence in the late 1930s. Public houses either forbade or encouraged these vehicles, depending on how they saw themselves. Progressive brewers such as Tomson and Wotton came closest to being able to emulate other modern leisure facilities such as the lido where customers were not separated by their class. For pub drinkers, class separation would be the norm for many more years. It took until the 1960s before most working- and lower-middle-class people had the disposable income to enjoy 'luxurious' surroundings. By this time, they had the money to spend on more sophisticated holidays and looked further afield than Ramsgate for their fun, and thus began the inevitable decline of the Prospect Inn.[100]

CHAPTER EIGHT

Britain's new airports

*The rising generation will accept air travel as a purely
normal activity of daily life.*[1]

The final case study examines the developing world of British domestic
airports and flight in 1938. In this year, the spirit of 1930's airmindedness
reached a peak not only because of the build-up for war, but also because
this year saw the opening of several new airport terminal buildings, the
largest at Manchester Airport. Britain's first airport at Croydon was
now thoroughly old fashioned, so these new buildings showed the way
for future post-war developments. These modern terminals, designed to
attract businessmen and the wealthy, were the result of a long campaign
to encourage local councils to build airports. Britain's domestic flight
network needed rationalization in 1938 so it could offer a viable
alternative to the elderly, inefficient railways. A government committee,
noting the inefficiencies of an unregulated network, proposed that a hub
and spoke system be introduced to make domestic flights simpler and
more popular. The case study contrasts flying for pleasure and business
in 1938 with an earlier form of airmindedness that was based around
distant observation of planes and hero worship.

FIGURE 8.1 *Birmingham Airport by Nigel Norman, Image Credit: English Heritage/ Heritage Images/Getty Images.*

The association between changing mobilities and modernity is both strong and causal. This was especially so in the late 1930s, where, for example, rapid increases in car ownership transformed family life.[2] On water, when RMS Queen Mary crossed the Atlantic in August 1938 in just less than four days, British interests in the transatlantic route and in winning the Blue Riband for the fastest journey were realized.[3] Train enthusiasts could distract themselves from the inefficiencies of the British railway system by following speed record attempts such as when Mallard achieved a speed of 125 miles per hour in July 1938.[4] As far as aviation in Britain in the interwar years was concerned, it comprised two overlapping phases. The first phase, which lasted from 1919 to the mid-1930s, was one of exploration and admiration, pioneer flyers, air displays and 'five-bob flips' for a short flight around the aerodrome. The second phase, which began in the late 1920s with the opening of Croydon Airport's new terminal building, saw foreign and domestic airlines forming new transport networks, and for the wealthier middle classes, flying becoming a more accepted means of transport.

This chapter is largely interested in the second phase, which reinforces one of this book's themes that sees Britain in 1938 as the epitome of a modern, pre-war consumerist world. That is not to say that interesting developments in British aviation were confined to this year. The period from 1936 to 1939 saw the construction of many new modern airport terminals that made London's first airport at Croydon, with its short runway, nearby housing estates and cramped terminal building, seem outdated. In 1938, Manchester, Luton, Exeter and Ipswich municipal airports opened for business. Ramsgate Airport opened in late 1937 and Birmingham Airport, which was planned for 1938, in early 1939. Although it would be foolish to conflate the ideas of architectural modernism and modernity, the new terminal buildings excited the architectural community and a wider public with their deployment of functional, elegant structures.

One further idea that characterized the second phase of interwar aviation was airmindedness, which, in Britain, was a campaign managed by the Air Ministry and influential aviators such as Sir Alan Cobham to proselytize the benefits of aviation. Airmindedness was an influential force in developing both airports and the airline networks that used them. Geographer Peter Adey defines it as 'an organizing and educational tool to promote the economic and social prosperity that could be afforded by flight, and to combat the problems of industrial decline and unemployment'.[5] By 1938, airmindedness had taken on a military hue as Britain prepared for a future war that airpower would dominate. For example, in 1935, an advertisement in *Aeroplane* magazine celebrating the Royal Air Force (RAF) Display Day showed an aircraftman holding up two small children 'helping to bring British children up in the way they should go, for the good of our race and our people'.[6]

Interwar aviation and public admiration

The end of the First World War resulted in a surplus of young pilots and engineers from the Royal Flying Corps (RFC) who now sought employment in a new and exciting industry. A culture of speed and endurance that so typified the 1920s powered advances in technical knowledge of flight and developments in aircraft manufacture. For instance, a competition to find the first aviators to cross the Atlantic non-stop stirred public interest. The failure and presumed death of Harry Hawker and his navigator in an unsuccessful attempt in 1919 received much public attention. Their unexpected return to Britain after being rescued by a trawler met with an outpouring of public joy and acclaim.[7] Allcock and Brown's successful attempt later that year led to similar acclaim and immediate knighthoods for the two airmen.[8] Over the next few years, aviators set long-distance records across the Atlantic and to South Africa and Australia. Of the famous pilots who undertook these perilous journeys, three are of particular interest: Sir Alan Cobham, Charles Lindbergh and Amy Johnson.

Sir Alan Cobham was a wartime flyer who made a living as a commercial pilot after hostilities ceased. After some time spent as an air taxi pilot, Cobham made return flights to South Africa and Australia in 1925–6, reinforcing a growing sense of imperial airmindedness in Britain. He became a new public hero and was knighted at the age of thirty-two.[9] In 1927, Cobham's fame was overtaken by the exploits of Charles Lindbergh who made the first successful solo transatlantic flight from the United States to France, and became one of the most famous men in the world. As Janet Daly Bednarek reports in relation to the more sophisticated American experience: 'In the 1920s and 1930s, aviation was a mass phenomenon of a different sort, a recreational activity. Most people experienced flying as spectators, not participants.'[10] This was evidenced on Lindbergh's arrival in Britain. On his landing at Croydon, enormous crowds mobbed his plane. 'From an early hour on Sunday, large numbers of people arrived at the aerodrome so as to be in good time. … Many came by car, but trains, trams and "buses from all points leading or near to Croydon were packed throughout the afternoon".'[11]

Over 100,000 people came to Croydon on this unusual day.[12] 'Motor cars and what few police could be spared were at once rushed to meet them. … It was obvious to many that there was going to be trouble.'[13] Even before Lindbergh's arrival, a section of the crowd broke into the central part of the airfield, making it difficult for Lindbergh to land, and when he did so, surrounded him and his plane.

Amy Johnson provided a new domestic heroine for the British public. In 1930 she began an unheralded solo flight to Australia; the *Daily Mail*'s exclusive promotion of her journey generating great interest in her flight. By the time she returned to Britain she was a national celebrity, one of the most famous people in the country. Her publicity portrayed Johnson as an ordinary person, when in fact she came from a well-off family, with her father financing her flying. The combination of gender, ordinariness and heroism made Amy an object of popular worship. Her journey from Croydon to London took the form of an almost regal procession.[14]

> Miss Johnson was driven round the aerodrome in a car, while the mobile floodlight showed her to the waiting crowd. ... Then she drove at little more than a foot pace. ... It was drizzling on and off, and the car was an open tourer. But the patient waiting thousands along the 12 miles of route certainly deserved a glimpse of her whom they had come out to see. So Miss Johnson stood up in the car and bowed to the people.[15]

The interwar period provided many other diversions for those who wanted to observe aviation at close quarters. They came in two main forms: First, through air displays held in an organized way at leading aerodromes such as Hendon or in convenient local farmer's fields by travelling flying circuses; second, by visiting aerodromes and airports to watch the planes.

Hendon became the leading aerodrome for hosting public air displays from as early as 1912, which was only six years after the first powered flight in Britain. Initially, the exciting and daring air displays attracted the wealthiest section of London society, with tickets at two guineas (£2 10p), which was a considerable sum. A year later, Hendon announced a night-flying display that was more widely attended, spectators numbering in tens of thousands. Experience gained in the First World War professionalized flying and led to the formation of the RFC. From 1925 onwards, the RAF (successor to the RFC) held a display day at Hendon that met with great acclaim. This annual charitable event lasted until the late 1930s and regularly had over a hundred thousand spectators.[16] When demobbed pilots sought work after the war, they formed flying circuses that gave small-scale air displays using cheap and available ex-RFC planes. They moved from town to town, staying in each place for a day or two. It was at these events that many people saw flight for the first time, and the braver took to the air in a quick tour around the airfield. These flights often cost five shillings (25p), giving the name to 'five-bob flips'. Cobham, needing to earn a living after his long-distance heroics, operated a professional flying circus from the late 1920s into the early 1930s.[17] At one event in 1933 he promised '20 Thrilling Events and 15 Aircraft, Bombing Exhibitions, Parachute Descents, Flying Lessons and Aerobatics'.[18]

Across London from Hendon, Croydon Airport became the most important centre of international flying in the country, as Imperial Airways introduced services to Paris and other nearby European cities. The Blue Riband service to Paris cut journey times by many hours and provided a glamorous and luxurious service for the rich. Imperial Airways' planes departing and arriving at Croydon's airport terminal building were, for a few years, an epitome of interwar modernity.[19] Croydon Airport catered for sightseers in two ways. It offered a tour of the terminal building to groups and the technically minded and provided a simple spectator viewing area at one end of the airfield, which gave a great view of the planes as they taxied before take-off and after landing.[20] In this way many thousands of airminded spectators could enjoy the thrill of flight from a distance.

Interwar aviation and passenger travel

The leaders of the airmindedness project were aware that in continental Europe and, in particular, Germany, flying as a means of public transport was further ahead than it was in Britain. For example, in 1927, German planes carried 150,000 passengers compared to 19,000 by British airlines.[21] Air Minister Sefton Brancker, unable to win Treasury support for a national initiative, turned his attention to Britain's municipal authorities as possible sponsors of a network of local airports. He proposed in a letter to all local authorities with populations over 10,000 that they build their own aerodrome. It read, 'It is the opinion of the [Air] Council that every town of any importance will sooner or later, find it just as essential to possess well sited aerodromes as it does to-day to possess railway stations, roads, [and] garages.'[22]

Cobham was quick off the mark and launched his own 'Municipal Aerodrome Campaign'. In his autobiography, he disarmingly explained his expectation that, along with promoting airmindedness, he might win valuable consultancy contracts from local authorities who would need his expertise in establishing an aerodrome. He could also make money from five-bob flips: 'I should be taking up the civic dignitaries in the morning ... giving them my full educational treatment ... but in the afternoon, I should be free to take up the general public, for payment.'[23] A meeting of the many interested local authorities at a conference in London on the 'Necessity for Municipal Airports' gave the campaign a boost. One speaker imagined a not too distant future 'when every home would have its aircraft shed'.[24] Although this prediction now seems fanciful, the conference and the campaign were important steps forward. Rather than universal private use, Cobham envisaged a network of internal air routes feeding the international hub at Croydon.[25] National figures such as Brancker and Cobham, each with their different motivations, were sufficiently far-minded to see how aviation would be a key element in commercial and military power.

The years that followed saw Britain experience the worst of the slump, and local authorities throughout Britain had more pressing problems than setting up aerodromes. By late 1933, economic conditions had improved a little, and the debate over municipal airports restarted at a second conference. The London Chamber of Commerce and the Royal Aeronautical Society organized this meeting, held at the Mansion House in the City of London. The Prince of Wales, an aviator himself and at the height of his fame and esteem in the United Kingdom, was its star speaker.[26] His message was that British aviation needed to speed up so as not to be left behind. It was becoming clear by this date that American-built monoplane airliners were faster and technically superior to the large British biplane designs that made their way steadily across Europe. For example, the groundbreaking Boeing 247 plane was just coming into service in the United States.[27] The prince advocated a similar plane for Britain: 'It was necessary to realize that in some countries machines were being built with cruising speeds nearly twice as ours. We must now think in terms of cruising speeds of 250 miles an hour.'[28] His point was that achieving this level of speed would allow airlines an important competitive advantage over trains, making local airports viable. At a dinner at the Savoy Hotel that evening, Sir Alan Cobham responded to a speech by the secretary of state for air, Lord Londonderry, in his customary unrestrained style.

> It was a simple fact that the municipal airport movement was an utter failure. They had been striving for years to persuade the municipalities to go ahead. They knew all about the facts but nothing was done, and nothing would happen in civil aviation until every town had an airport, so that everyone could fly from anywhere to anywhere else.[29]

It was difficult to see the way forward for British airports. As an article in the *Aeroplane* put it: 'As a commercial speculation aerodromes are not yet tempting … is the country to be supplied with aerodromes as a National undertaking? In other words, are we to have landing-grounds as the result of Capitalistic Enterprise, or of Municipal Trading, or of pure National Socialism?'[30]

The response to these pleas was, in the end, municipal. Over the next five years, nineteen local authorities acquired licences for a local aerodrome.[31] This was not enough to promote a realistic network of domestic flying routes, and the facilities available were often simple and crude. In 1937, looking back on the progress made since the conference, one commentator, reviewing how domestic airlines had fared in this period, concluded:

> [Their] history has on the whole been a sad one, many were under-capitalized; the personnel were lacking in experience, the aircraft used were unsuitable, the complete lack of navigational aids made regularity or punctuality impossible. The travelling public was not 'ready' and in the majority of cases the methods of airline operation did little to create confidence in this new method of travel.[32]

Things were about to change. The period from 1936 to 1939 was one of intense development of new airport buildings and a comprehensive network of domestic air routes. In 1936, one airport provided a fleeting glimpse of what might be possible. This was the development of a passenger terminal at Gatwick of radical design. This new building at an established aerodrome on the Surrey/Sussex border was privately financed and not part of the municipal airports project. Its owner Morris Jackaman planned to attract airlines to a new modern airport that could compete with Croydon and Heston. Jackaman promoted it as being outside of London's fog belt, but within easy reach of town: 'A main line station on the airport … No farther than crossing to the tube'.[33]

London's first airport, Croydon, had failed to increase the scale of its terminal building in response to the greater numbers of passengers it now served. Most of its passengers arrived by coach from central London, a journey that was prey to increasing levels of traffic jams, a situation that was difficult to improve on without building a new railway line.[34] On arrival, after completing the cursory formalities, passengers walked across to their airliner without any protection from the elements. In February 1938, *Popular Flying* magazine described Croydon as 'an airport fit for a second-rate Balkan state'.[35] In contrast, Gatwick offered its passengers a modern experience. As advertised, it had its own station that provided services to Victoria or London Bridge, so it was easy to get to and from both the West End and the City. On arrival at Gatwick railway station, passengers walked through a tunnel into the terminal building. They then reached their plane using a gate via an electrically powered covered gangway, just as we expect today.[36] Unusually, the terminal was circular in plan, allowing planes to move around the building in an ordered manner. It became known because of its round shape and tiered upper floors as 'The Beehive'. Jackaman described it as an 'island on an aerodrome' with the terminal in the middle of the airfield.[37] One critic thought terminals should not use a rotunda design as it made expansion more difficult.[38]

On the ground floor of the terminal, passengers could sit in a lounge and bar, or, if they needed to eat before flying, try the restaurant on the first floor of the building. The terminal was built in reinforced concrete and finished in artificial stone and wood. It was fully air-conditioned. The Beehive was, in effect, Britain's first modern airport terminal.[39] Although

FIGURE 8.2 *Ramsgate Airport by David Pleydell-Bouverie, Image Credit: Dell & Wainwright/RIBA Collections.*

Jackaman was thorough in his design for his building, he paid less attention to airfield drainage, which made aeroplane movement impossible in very bad weather. This resulted in cancelled flights and then a complete halt in scheduled services from the airport.[40]

Britain's modernist architects were very interested and excited about new airport terminals in the late 1930s, as these buildings captured the possibilities of new technologies, superfast travel and the thought of everyone flying a plane or flying in a plane.[41] According to Wolfgang Voigt, 'Some of the most striking airport buildings [of the late 1930s] were created in Great Britain which worked successfully to make good its earlier shortcomings in this field.'[42] The Royal Institute of British Architects (RIBA) held an exhibition of the best modern airport architecture in 1937.[43] One of the terminal buildings that attracted the most attention was at Ramsgate Municipal Airport. This was a beautiful building in a modernist style in the shape of a giant wing (see Figure 8.2). It was later described in a selection of the best British interwar architecture:

> A curved plan enables more aeroplanes to park in relation to the building than a straight one, and is appropriate to the apex of the field, as is the concave form of the entrance front. There is expressive lightness and grace about this handling of a problem still new to architecture in Britain.[44]

The terminal was to be a local social centre and club as well as in the future the hub of an airport offering regular scheduled services:

> All the main rooms open directly on to the terrace through folding glass doors. It is the object of the operators to serve good food, indoors or out, and thus attract even those who are not particularly interested in the *raison d'etre* of an airport. Here they are very sensibly following what has been general rule on the Continent for a number of years.[45]

An interesting and enterprising American, Whitney Straight, owner of the Straight Corporation, ran Ramsgate on behalf of the council, as he did several other small municipal airports. Born to a wealthy family, Straight attended Dartington Hall, an experimental liberal school, where he learned to drive a car and fly a plane, winning his pilot's licence at seventeen years old. He raced cars at Brooklands, and in 1935, at twenty-three years old, formed his aviation company, which manufactured planes as well as running airports.[46] His company's annual report for 1938 described Ramsgate Airport as 'a work of imagination and utility'.[47] Ramsgate distinguished itself by being the location of an annual holiday 'Aviation Camp' where keen would-be amateur pilots learned how to fly during their summer break, staying at tents on the airfield often with their wives and children.[48] The camp advertised: 'Living right on the airport in comfortable little marquees, for only £5, 5s a week, which includes your free flying lesson, lots of flying as a passenger, and ground instruction in many aviation subjects'.[49]

In 1938, municipal authorities completed three important British airport terminal buildings at Liverpool, Manchester and Birmingham.[50] Although commercial flying preceded the buildings, the opening of a terminal was significant because it was the point when councils expected large-scale passenger use at their airports. Passengers became as important as planes and pilots for the first time. This chapter will now focus its attention on activities at Manchester's Ringway Airport. Ringway was Manchester's second attempt at an aerodrome. Its first at Barton was substandard; Dutch airline KLM thought it unsuitable and dangerous.[51] Manchester's council members decided that developing Barton was not achievable at a reasonable cost and so a search for a new site began. The decision to go forward with Ringway was controversial, with a council meeting approving it by a single vote. Such was the controversy that a public enquiry into the decision was held in October 1935 at which Sir Alan Cobham stated that he was strongly in favour of improving Barton rather than going ahead with the £300,000 Ringway project. Cobham's opinion notwithstanding, Ringway was approved as the site of the new Manchester Airport.[52]

At the same time as this debate was playing out, less than thirty miles to the west in Liverpool, Speke Airport was in the course of development. One of the municipal airport campaign's consequences was that it reignited old civic rivalries. For Manchester and Liverpool this had been in play since their industrialization. In 1934, Liverpool's local grandee Lord Derby signalled the city's desires: 'I want to see Speke as the Clapham Junction of the air. I want to see it develop into a centre from which shall go out to all parts of the world aeroplanes. … Let Liverpool be so to speak, the nerve centre of the world.'[53]

Lord Derby was promoting the continuance of Liverpool's status as a major maritime city, with an airport alongside a seaport. In this respect, Liverpool, despite the Manchester Ship Canal, had a strong geographical advantage. As far as railways were concerned, Manchester was more favoured. It was inevitable, because of the rivalry between the two cities, that Manchester would want its own airport. Its more central position in relation to major northern population centres was a distinct advantage. Local sentiments were evident in an article in the *Manchester Guardian*: 'It is proposed to take the KLM planes through to Liverpool which has been the terminus in recent years, but the Dutch firm make no secret of the fact that Manchester, with its regional population of four and a half millions, is their main objective in preference to a largely transporting city like Liverpool.'[54]

Not everybody on Manchester Council saw the point. Shortly before it opened, Councillor J. Watts suggested that the Council sell the airport, proposing that 'there is no justification for calling upon poor people and small shopkeepers to subsidise the travelling expenses of industrialists'.[55] Watts had accurately summed up the intentions of the municipal airports campaign and the Ringway project. Their sponsors did not envisage that new airports would transform leisure travel, but that they would provide a new conduit for conducting business.

The new airport provided a service from Manchester to Croydon to connect with Britain's international air hub.[56] Manchester had a good connection by rail to London's Euston Station, a journey that took about 3½ to 4 hours.[57] It was hard for airlines to compete with these city-centre-to-city-centre timings; they had a greater advantage when travelling to destinations that required a change of train, and an overwhelming advantage when travelling over water. For example, one of the first services Ringway offered was Railway Air Services' route from Manchester to the south-west of Britain.[58] This was, in essence, a stopping service calling at Liverpool, Birmingham, Cheltenham, Bristol (reached in just under 2 hours), Southampton, Isle of Wight and then Brighton, arriving 3½ hours after leaving Manchester. A new service to Northern Ireland transformed journey times; Belfast was now only 1¾ hours away.[59] Businessmen wishing to fly to Europe could take the KLM service to Amsterdam and, because of Dutch airmindedness, connect to Berlin, Copenhagen, Vienna and Budapest, the latter being reached in 7½ hours, transforming a journey that had required many days of rail travel.[60] Connections to forty different European cities were available via Amsterdam and to a lesser extent Croydon. A single fare to Vienna was £14, which is around £800 today. This provides compelling evidence that customers were either wealthy or businessmen.[61]

Ringway was typical of many such developments of the late 1930s. It had an extensive area of mown grass fields of 250 acres with room for expansion to 600 acres, and a set of grass runways of which the longest was 1,300 yards. At one corner of the airfield was the terminal building, a control tower and the aircraft hangars. Aeroplanes approached the terminal by taxiing off the grass field onto a small concrete apron.[62] The terminal was

FIGURE 8.3 *Opening of Manchester Airport terminal. Image Credit: Reproduced by permission of Historic England Archive.*

a modernist two-storey steel-framed building with white cement finish, and could have sat alongside the buildings of the Glasgow Empire Exhibition without a murmur. The interior of the terminal building was simplicity itself; there were four airline offices each with a low counter for passenger check-in. Customs and Excise staff had their own office, making it officially an airport rather than just a large aerodrome. There was a small seating area with a view of the airfield for passengers waiting for their flights and an adjacent restaurant that served both passengers and visitors.[63] On the floor above, there was a terraced viewing area with 'the little tables and covered umbrellas which are such a popular feature of all Continental airports' so that sightseers could get a clear view of the arrivals and departures.[64]

Ringway provided the latest in safety features. The most important was a clear site not encumbered by nearby houses. This was a particular problem at Croydon where suburban estates had surrounded the airfield, increasing the likelihood of accidents. For example, a KLM plane crashed into a thankfully unoccupied nearby house killing all on board in 1936.[65] Besides the large landing area, Ringway deployed traditional floodlighting (which pilots were beginning to consider a menace in very bad weather), an ultra-short-wave blind-approach radio beacon and, in a first for Britain, a set of runway marker lights, 'which showed an intense light to pilots at the correct 8-degree angle of approach'. The last quarter of the runway lights was red to show that it was time to stop or go around the airfield again, whichever seemed the best idea.[66]

Ringway, as was usual with new airport terminals in 1938, held a large public event to advertise the new services available, swell civic pride and justify the expenditure incurred on behalf of the weary ratepayers (see Figure 8.3).[67] The Lord Mayor of Manchester prophesized that 'there can be little doubt that the rising generation will accept air travel as a purely normal activity of daily life'.[68] It took, because of the coming war, two decades before this came to pass, but he was, in the end, correct. The Corporation of Manchester made sure that the event was well attended by making it free of charge if you were happy to stand. The wealthier middle-class attendee could sit and park the car for two shillings (10p).[69] As was also common at these events, there was a display of airport facilities, civilian planes such as the ultra-modern KLM DC2, an autogiro demonstration, gliders and a parachute descent. A display of military strength from the RAF added to the spectacle, reflecting the troubled times.[70] Two months later, the airport had become an established visitor attraction:

> The setting is pleasant, food and drink are to be had, and something is always happening. Many had their short 'flip' and the more serious business of service transport enjoyed a record day. The Isle of Man planes were duplicated to cope with demand … and the longer routes to Glasgow, London and Jersey had their day excursionists.[71]

Smaller, simpler aeroplanes than the brand new DC2 serviced Britain's domestic routes. One journey from London to Glasgow provides insights into the realities of passenger flight in 1938. Journalist F. D. Bradbrooke flew from Hatfield to Glasgow in June of that year and recorded his impressions.

> At 0500 hours there was a fog at Hatfield ... about 8 feet deep. By using the famous furrow as a fog line and unsticking to a height of two feet one could see all the rest of the landscape. The comfort of the Hornet cabin and the grand drone of the Gypsy Major [engine] were slightly soporific. Our speed averaged a steady 100 mph. The rain and the bumps had a whack at us but this is an aerial all-weather motor-car. Over the Solway the wind was getting up and we were behind schedule. Things were not bad to Dumfries, but there was obviously much up ahead and the question arose whether to circumnavigate Galloway or try the Sanquhar valley. This is narrow for about 10 miles and the nice behaviour of the vehicle so far made it worth trying. A suspicion that Glasgow was approaching was confirmed by seeing the Exhibition suddenly on the right. We landed at 0830 hours precisely to schedule.[72]

Negotiating eight feet of fog on a blind take-off and deciding on flying through a valley or round a mountain in bad weather demonstrates a contingency in domestic flying that is not apparent today. Our correspondent's suggestion that flying in this type of plane was similar to driving a closed-roofed car was not something nervous passengers would have agreed with.

KLM's DC2 plane serviced Ringway's connection to its Amsterdam hub. In contrast to the Hatfield to Glasgow service, its twin engines, pressurized cabin and much higher flight ceiling proposed a quieter, faster future for air travel that came about in the 1950s and beyond. As the *Manchester Guardian*'s blasé special correspondent recorded:

> The Ringway Aerodrome meets the requirements of their [KLM] big 14-seater passenger liners admirably ... to reach Amsterdam in less than three hours should be rapid enough for any Manchester businessman to say nothing of the thrill of air travel, which does not yet fail the Englishman, even though it is not exactly a novelty in these days.[73]

Networks

Network formation is both a symptom and promoter of modernity, and was evident in 1938's transport systems.[74] Lord Derby, in setting out his aspirations for Liverpool to be the nerve centre of the world, understood the modern possibilities of airports and airlines. He foresaw that airports would become nodal points in a new network that would transform travel and compress time and space in the same dramatic way as the railways had

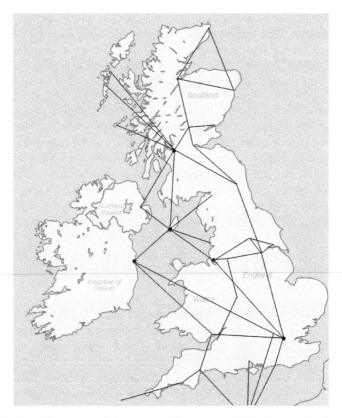

MAP 8.1 *Simplified map of domestic airline routes 1938. Image Credit: Creative Commons Attribution-Share Alike 3.0 Unported licence.*

achieved a century before. The problem was that this was the same role as Manchester wished to play. The consequences of a failure to implement a coordinated national policy on aerodrome development in the 1920s and 1930s met a laissez-faire attitude to who could fly from them. It was not until June 1938 that it was necessary to have a licence to run a domestic airline.[75] The result was an incoherent, inefficient set of airport and airline services that could not pay their own way.[76] A simplified version of this network in 1938 is shown in Map 8.1.[77]

The government thought that loss-making aerodromes and airlines would not build, of their own volition, a sensible self-supporting domestic flight network. Left to its own devices, a laissez-faire system presumably would have seen airlines bankrupted and aerodromes closed until a rationalized network emerged. This was not the mood of the late 1930s, which saw increased state intervention to accelerate rearmament connecting with a militarized version of airmindedness. In response, the Air Ministry set up the Maybury

Committee to investigate how it might improve the state of civil aviation in the United Kingdom. The committee presented its report in January 1937.[78]

It recommended, inter alia, that municipal authorities rather than private enterprise should continue to control airports and that competition should be restricted on key routes, for example, Manchester/Liverpool to London and to Belfast. The committee thought that by imposing a 'hub and spoke' system it could eliminate incoherent routings (we are familiar with hub and spoke systems today and they are particularly well developed in the United States). The committee's proposal for a simplified network is shown in Map 8.2, and its locus is a central junction in Lancashire. By using the term 'Manchester or Liverpool' in their report, the committee was negotiating the noted rivalry between these two cities and their airports. As discussed earlier, Manchester's location was a better hub as it was closer to Yorkshire's population centres. It is indicative that the maps published with the report showed the hub in Manchester. The committee believed that 'this

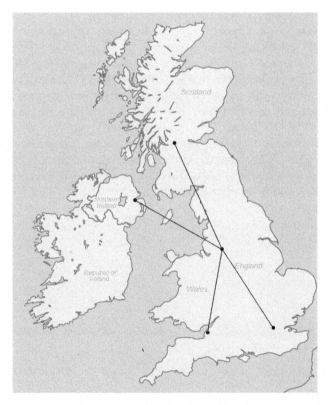

MAP 8.2 *Maybury Committee proposed hub and spoke network 1937. Image Credit: Creative Commons Attribution-Share Alike 3.0 Unported licence.*

Junction Aerodrome System is the scheme ... best calculated to secure the greatest measure of advantage both in facilities to the travelling public and in economical operation'.[79]

Conclusion

Domestic passenger flight was in an intriguing position in Britain in 1938. Some aspects of it were inefficient and, for such a young industry, a little archaic. The main international hub at Croydon was already out of date and no longer fit for purpose. There were too many airlines and insufficient regulation of their activities. There were too many municipal aerodromes, which caused route duplication, although, at the time, many people thought that private flying would follow the rapid pattern of acquisition seen with the motor car. However, some important aspects were changing. Aviation was shifting from its 1920s origins when it was individual, heroic and observed from a distance to, in the late 1930s, becoming one where the passenger, not the pilot, was the centre of attention.

New larger-scale airport terminal buildings in Gatwick, Liverpool, Manchester and Birmingham, together with elegant and efficient smaller buildings at Ramsgate and elsewhere, provided passengers with something akin to an airport experience that lasted up to the 1970s. Gatwick, the most innovative, but in the short-term least successful new airport, introduced airside gates and powered movable covered walkways to planes. KLM's deployment of American DC2 planes showed the way forward, they travelled at twice the speed of British-made planes, had pressurized cabins and flew higher, well above the clouds. The proposal for a hub and spoke system was clever and sensible and would, if implemented, have accelerated the progress of domestic flying in Britain.

CHAPTER NINE

Conclusion

This book reveals an unusual state of modernity in Britain in 1938, obscured by decades of historiography that has concentrated on the great events of that year. I am not suggesting that the historians involved were wrong-headed; evacuation and Air Raid Precautions were very important aspects of social history, just as Chamberlain's visit to Munich was a pivotal event in Britain's political history. However, when you ignore these big events, a different picture emerges of life in 1938.

This view of 1938 was not always recognized at the time. For example, contemporary commentators did not give it much space in their accounts. Malcolm Muggeridge, Robert Graves and Alan Hodge, authors who quickly produced social histories of the thirties, noticed little about the modern world around them.[1] Cicely Hamilton, in her report on the state of the nation, published in 1938, was clear that 'modern' meant urban. She was not especially interested in technology, but she did extol the virtues of the Mersey Tunnel, which was both an enormous construction project and an instrument of network formation.[2] However, the newsreel companies noticed. Movietone and Pathé gave Britain's innovative projects a good airing in their reviews of the year. What the newsreels thought was interesting was speed and size, the key ingredients of the modern wonder popular discourse that was at something of a peak in 1938. This idea was also evident in magazines aimed at boys and young men, books that covered the same themes, and popular cigarette card sets. The audience for this material was usually male, but there were signs, tellingly from Kodak, an American company publishing in Britain, of a recognition that some women enjoyed using new technologies.

The case studies that form the main part of this book document a modern life in Britain in 1938. Although some examine components of the modern wonders idea (aeroplanes, huge office blocks), what they tell us about social change is far more important than speed and size. A synthesis of these case studies provides an assessment of the condition of modernity in Britain in the last full year before the war and offers possible connections to future developments. Each of the elements of social change proposed in the introduction: Class and Wealth, Americanization, Consumption, Network Development and Urban Formation are now examined in turn.

Class and wealth

In interwar Britain, class infected everything, and it features in the case studies as the key means by which modernity distributed its benefits in 1938. For example, only a relatively few people could enjoy the time/space compression provided by Britain's budding airlines flying from their glamorous new airport buildings. The rich and leisured classes had always been the first to enjoy new, speedier forms of transport, whether in motor cars, luxurious transatlantic liners or aeroplanes. The price of this type of leisure was beyond the reach of all but the wealthiest private individuals, most explicitly shown by the Blue Riband service from London to Paris. Intriguingly, in the last years before the Second World War, another emerging class of airline traveller, the businessman, came to the fore. Manchester's Council built its smart new terminal to provide a means of rapid travel for northern businessmen and their foreign counterparts to move between European destinations. Head offices like the Adelphi Building also accommodated male executives, where they occupied a well-appointed top floor. The lower-middle-class typists, bookkeepers and clerks had to put up with the modern rows of simple desks on lower floors.

Two of the case studies, *Picture Post* and the Prospect Inn, suggest an attempt to break down the strict class barriers of the time. *Picture Post* was the product of an eastern European artistic sensibility meeting with British leftist journalism, all under the financial sponsorship of a well-meaning Conservative. This special mix produced a unique response to questions of class. For the first time, a national journal portrayed ordinary people (i.e. the working and lower middle classes) in a way that valued them rather than showing them as despicable or the source of unintentional humour. Most of *Picture Post*'s readers also came from an ordinary background. These characteristics, already evident in *Picture Post* in 1938, were amplified by the experience of the Second World War to form part of a radical change in British politics. The breaking down of class barriers at the Prospect Inn was more ambiguous. This small pub was unusual at the time in granting almost identical facilities to working-class patrons in its public bars as it did to the middle-class customers in its lounges. By being prepared to accept charabanc customers, this pub also recognized that not all 'charra' parties were vulgar or violent. This was progressive for the time, but in 1938 the Prospect Inn was not prepared to be fully democratic. Municipal and seaside lidos provided a single democratic space, but, consequently, members of the upper echelons of the middle classes would not dream of joining in. The Prospect's design, recognizing this, was equal but separate, maintaining a cultural apartheid that was to last for many years after the war.

Impoverished gentlefolk and temporary gentlemen may feature in accounts of interwar life, but, generally in 1938, class and wealth were quite closely aligned.[3] Clerks and factory workers had an engagement with modernity imposed on them by their use of new machines to simplify and expedite work practices, placing their traditional skills under threat. Wealth provided access to modernity, but structures in society ensured that those from the lower classes who had the money could not always take full advantage of it. Class, not wealth, often determined choices of leisure, transport and place of residence. Class, not wealth, was the key means of distorting modernity's benefits and promise in 1938. Forces were in play to bring about slow change, but much conservatism remained.

Americanization

Such were America's technological and commercial advantages in the 1930s that it was easy for commentators to conflate Americanization and modernity. Much that was new was American, but this was not always the case. As far as the case studies were concerned, there was little or no American influence in the ideas behind *Picture Post*, the Prospect Inn, the BBC radio and television service, the Emitron camera, or in the architecture at the Empire Exhibition. It was apparent at the Adelphi Building and in the use of American planes at Manchester airport.

Americanization came in many forms in the 1930s. One direct version was the arrival of American individuals and companies in Britain. Charles Lindbergh's exploits and subsequent fame in Britain was an example of this phenomenon. Companies such as Hoover and Firestone brought American consumer products to the British market. Philco, an American radio manufacturer, sold cheap mass-produced radios from a London base allowing them to evade British tariff barriers. However, the most prominent instance of consumer Americanization in the case studies was the impact Kodak had on British photography. Kodak's cheap and simple cameras, manufactured in Harrow from as early as 1890, had revolutionized photography for the ordinary consumer by 1938.[4] Its much-advertised cine-cameras were a good example of American technology finding its way into the lives of Britain's wealthy early adopters.

American companies brought their forward-thinking business methods with them. For example, Kodak's marketing and advertising was much more sophisticated than its British competitors. Its consumer magazine was educative but also designed to increase brand loyalty. It was unusual in the way that it recognized the importance of female photographers, featured women role models in its advertising and encouraged women to write technical articles on equal terms. The new Adelphi Building provided another example of the importation of American technology. British companies were regular buyers of American office automation equipment. The organization of the headquarters of the companies that occupied London's new offices also reflected American scientific management methods.

The case studies demonstrate that American sources were not always dominant in 1938. For example, local companies built most of the radios and televisions sold in Britain; there were many excellent British camera companies competing with Kodak. Workers in the Adelphi Building were just as likely to use British equipment as American. Despite the competing attractions of the highly Americanized Radio Luxembourg, the BBC broadcast much of its content in a defiantly British style. Although Hollywood films were a major influence on cinema audiences, Britain also produced its own major stars. For example, *Picture Post* lauded the careers and personalities of the glamorous Jessie Matthews and the more superficially ordinary stars such as Gracie Fields and George Formby. However, American ideas strongly influenced the books and magazines that examined Britain's modernity. The modern wonder trope was particularly sensitive to the question of America's technological leadership. The writers of this material consciously or unconsciously doffed their hat to America's growing technical dominance while remaining proud of British and imperial prowess in these fields. Britain's impoverishment from the Second World War altered this dialectic but it took decades to be resolved. It was, for instance, an important influence of the aerospace industry in the 1950s and 1960s resulting in abandoned projects such as the Comet passenger jet, the Blue Streak rocket and the TSR2 fighter.[5]

It is easy to overstate the influence of Americanization on Britain. The case studies reveal a very mixed picture with American influence clear in some areas, but excluded entirely from others. This reflects the wider state of play in Britain in 1938. Some areas as diverse as mass-production methods, jazz and swing music and Hollywood films had a profound influence on British life, but in other fields, such as sport and respect for the royal family, it was largely absent.

Consumption

Changing patterns of consumption fuelled much of Britain's experience of modernity in the interwar years. Consumption increased in both value and variety; by 1938, real incomes were 32 per cent higher than in 1920 and families with a wage earner spent their extra money on consumer durables and leisure.[6] These benefits occurred in a heterogeneous manner, with the middle classes and those working in administrative jobs and in light-industrial factories gaining the most. Spending on consumer durables was encouraged by wider access and changing attitudes to instalment credit.

People spent their money on holidays, cars, motorcycles, bicycles, electrical and gas appliances and (most people) on radios and (a very few people) on televisions.

Going to the cinema was very popular in 1938, and offered ordinary people luxurious surroundings and Americanized glamour on the screen. However, entertainment in Britain was in the middle of profound social change. Radio had almost reached a saturation point, where most people who wanted to had access to it, although there were some regional variations. Radio promoted much social change; its impact was similar to the internet's ability to provide unconstrained access to information and entertainment in the home. Families gathered around the radio to listen to their favourite shows, ensuring that they spent less time on communal entertainment. By 1938, television, even though at an early stage and with low levels of adoption, had begun to disrupt patterns of consumption established over the previous twenty years. It is telling, in a newsreel review of the year, that Pathé needed to defend its coverage by proposing that only its powerful cameras could show the Derby properly. The development of a sophisticated market in television sets showed the way for a more nuclear family life centred around a screen in the corner of the living room.

One aspect of how Britons spent their increased leisure time worked in the opposite direction to radio and television's encouragement of domestication. Compulsory paid holidays for most workers began in 1938, but even before this, many leisure activities were moving outdoors. By the end of the 1930s, increasing numbers of lower-middle-class and some working-class families had access to a car; those that did not could take advantage of improved motor coaches and charabancs. Wider access to transport encouraged city dwellers to visit the countryside or to stop at country pubs on the way to the seaside. The Prospect Inn and other new pubs were one response to this trend. This suggested a recognition that working-class consumers, used to luxurious cinemas and motor coaches, were beginning to demand equivalent levels of sophistication in their other leisure activities. It would be late into the 1950s before this would become more widely realized in Britain.

Network development

Manchester's new airport became part of an emerging transport network in 1938. Its sophisticated terminal, together with those at Gatwick, Liverpool and Birmingham, pointed to the future by organizing itself around the customer for the first time. In contrast, Britain's rail network was at a low ebb by the end of the 1930s. Years of poor investment and over-development of stations and lines had resulted in an inefficient and scruffy system. Much goods and some passenger traffic had moved from rail to road, encouraged by the interwar arterial road programme. This project, which mostly benefitted the south of England, provided the impetus for

independent haulage contractors and private coach companies to offer a
viable alternative to the train.

Change to Britain's physical transport networks was slow. However, in
the world of electric and electronic networks, rapid progress was underway,
controlled by the government's monopoly over Britain's broadcast and
communications network, executed directly or through the BBC. Although
telegram and telephone systems were old technologies by 1938, developments
in user control were improving access to a rapidly expanding network.
For example, in London automated exchanges permitted direct dialling of
local telephone numbers. Large businesses had their own exchanges that
offered multiple telephone lines to callers so they would not have to wait.
Teleprinters gave direct access to telegram messages, avoiding the need to
wait for a messenger to arrive from the telegraph office. Improved networks
lay at the heart of modern business providing rapid communication
to branches, factories, customers and suppliers. New communication
technologies provided flexible and quick responses, enabling a more fluid
style of management to develop. Broadcasting networks in Britain were
limited; the BBC providing one national radio channel with regional variants
and one television channel that only reached the innermost Home Counties.
Listeners could pick up commercial transmissions from Europe on medium
and long wave and from all over the world if their radios had access to
short-wave transmissions.

Physical network planning was rudimentary in 1938. The domestic airport
network was a good example of the incoherent interventions of public and
private bodies that typified government policy in the 1930s. There were
private airports, such as Croydon and Gatwick, but local councils owned
the most, such as at Manchester and Liverpool. Airline companies, in
contrast, were unregulated and were privately owned, but on occasion, such
as with Imperial Airways, were subsidized by the government. The confused
actions of the market and government generated an inefficient transport
network where few parties involved could make any money. Things were
about to change. The Mayhew Committee recommended a rationalization
and simplification of the domestic route network, proposing that airports
like Manchester could act as a hub with spokes to many other British cities.
This was a sensible approach aimed at providing Britain with an efficient
domestic airline system providing genuine competition for a struggling
privately owned railway network. Central and local government controlled
road building and vehicle and driver licencing.

Because of these developments, Britain in 1938 was experiencing
various shockwaves of time/space compression, comparable with the social
earthquake resulting from the introduction of railways a century earlier. The
rapid adoption of radios in the late 1930s meant that their transformative
powers were available to almost everybody who wanted them. In consequence,
London's latest news and fashion trends could be heard instantaneously in
Britain's remote outposts. Television offered viewing in an immediate form

allowing, for example, remote access to major sports events. Wider adoption of telephones and telegram systems did the same for written material. Cars and coaches provided rapid transport to wider and wider social groups. Scheduled airlines, particularly when across water, dramatically reduced journey times, allowing the social elite and businessmen to save days of travelling.

Urban formation

The buildings described in the case studies came in a variety of architectural styles, which shows that modernity was not always associated with modernism. Atypically, Manchester Airport was a functional modernist box. Liverpool's Speke Airport was brick built and looked more like a railway station or a hotel than an airport of today. Gatwick, Birmingham and Ramsgate airports deployed streamlined *moderne* designs to capture the glamour of air travel. The Glasgow Exhibition Pavilions showed a lightness of touch that looked to the future of British architecture. Specifically, Basil Spence's excellent designs for the Scottish Pavilions and the ICI Pavilion had much in common with the supposedly groundbreaking Festival of Britain of 1951. Tait's insistence on standardization of materials and prefabrication looked forward to post-war approaches.

The design of the Adelphi Building was influenced by Art Deco, which was an idea going out of style in 1938. The Prospect Inn, with its porthole windows and curves, was far from the Bauhaus ideal. However, both these buildings were modern, with the Adelphi Building generating the most social change. This office block created various new levels of order. First, it cleared the building's notorious undercroft, which had become a hiding place for vagrants, petty criminals, prostitutes and, more worryingly at the time, a famous 'cottage' for queer encounter. Second, it swept away a crumbling set of small tenancies that housed an eccentric selection of occupants, and generated a great increase in rental yields. A garage for well-ordered suburban young executives to park their cars replaced the chaos previously found below ground level. Although it was a failure, the conservationist campaign to retain the Adelphi's Georgian terraces was a relatively new idea. It presaged a way of thinking that came into full bloom in London in the 1970s, saving Covent Garden (a few hundred yards from the Adelphi) from the developers.

In summary

The case studies presented in this book complement the usual narrative of late 1930s historiography, which, through omission, proposes that modern life was in stasis in the years from the end of the slump to declaration of war. In contrast, they show that Britain was a dynamic country that in 1938 was undertaking many projects that brought change to its way of life. The British economy, that seven years earlier seemed to have come to a shuddering halt, was booming again. In conjunction with state control over some specific areas, it provided the impetus to develop new forms of transport, new ways of organizing leisure, new networks of business administration and control, and new types of print and broadcast media. In the background throughout was the slow movement of historical tectonic plates, which signalled the decline of British leadership in science and technology and the rise of the United States.

The idea that Britain in 1938 was the same as it was in 1931 can be refuted by considering the changes that these case studies have directly or indirectly identified. First, Britain was far more suburban than in 1931. For example, London's suburban ring saw a growth of 1.2 million people between the 1931 census and 1938, an increase of 27 per cent.[7] It was these suburban residents who fuelled the consumption of consumer durables. As Orwell observed, they were likely to own a radio. The BBC's adoption of an electronic system had promoted the launch of a comprehensive studio and outside broadcast high-definition television service. Here Britain led the world in what would become the most transformative technology of the second half of the twentieth century.

Across the country, people became more mobile. Working-class Britons took advantage of luxurious motor coaches to reach parts of the country not served by trains or took charabanc trips to the seaside. The middle classes were likely to buy cars as soon as they could afford to, fuelling an 80 per cent increase in the number of cars from 1931 to 1938.[8] Very wealthy individuals and senior businessmen had become regular users of airlines that now reached across Britain, Europe and the distant Empire. New air terminals reflected this change in habit. Class still had a stultifying effect on Britain in 1938, but there were some signs of change in the approach taken by Stefan Lorant and in a more democratic approach to leisure in lidos and pubs. New technologies had transformed office work in large companies, where clerks had lost their status and commercial skills to become specialist machine operatives in the same way that had previously been seen in factories. Instant communication fuelled a rise in Britain's major cities of large head offices to control newly formed conglomerates such as ICI. In 1931, British architecture was prone to an excessive use of mock-Tudor or a restrained form of classicism. By 1938, modern buildings were becoming more familiar to the public and were seen to great effect in Glasgow at the exhibition. The fashion for Art Deco had come and gone and Britain could now produce buildings to please both strict architectural critics and the public.

Throughout the period, Britons had an increasing sense of their own modernity, promoted and mediated by books and magazines specializing in modern wonder material and supplying technical information to hobbyists. This sense of the modern world was not confined to those building prototype television receivers from the instructions in *Television and Short-Wave*

World. Increasing use of the word modern occurred in many books of the period and items on modern technology informed collectors of cigarette cards and the very many people who watched the newsreel reviews of 1938.

As mentioned at the start of this book, historians discovering that developments happened earlier than we all thought can seem rather 'dreary'. It would be wrong to think that the histories portrayed in this book form an inevitable continuity to the 1950s, defying the impact of a world war, although some intriguing potential connections are revealed by the case studies. Historians are also tempted to explore presumptuous counterfactual histories of what might have occurred without a war. If this book has avoided dreariness and presumption, what remains is a set of cases that show that Britain was, in 1938, for some, a surprisingly modern country. Social changes evidenced this modernity, and in them are keys to understanding the future of Britain when similar circumstances reappeared after the war.

NOTES

Chapter 1

1   Maroula Joannou, 'Hamilton (Mary) Cicely (1872–1952)', *Oxford Dictionary of National Biography* (Oxford: Oxford University Press, 2004).

2   Stanley Baldwin, 'What England Means to Me', speech to the Royal Society of St George, 6 May 1924. At this time the terms 'England' and 'Britain' were often used interchangeably.

3   Stephan Kohl, 'Rural England: An Invention of the Motor Industries?', in Robert Burden and Stephan Kohl (eds), *Landscape and Englishness* (New York: Editions Rodopi, 2006), 185–206.

4   Cicely Hamilton, *Modern England* (London: Dent, 1938), x.

5   Ibid., xi.

6   George Orwell, *The Lion and the Unicorn: Socialism and the English Genius* (London: Secker and Warburg, 1941).

7   Kate Caffrey, '37-'39: Last Look Round* (London: Gordon & Cremonesi Publishers, 1978), 14.

8   Richard Overy, *The Morbid Age: Britain Between the Wars* (London: Allen Lane, 2009).

9   I have discussed the destructive aspects of modernity in Michael John Law, *The Experience of Suburban Modernity* (Manchester: Manchester University Press, 2014).

10 Martin Pugh, *'We Danced all Night': A Social History of Britain Between the Wars* (London: Bodley Head, 2008).

11 Juliet Gardiner, *The Thirties: An Intimate History* (London: Harper Press, 2010).

12 Dietrich Gerhard, 'Periodization in History', in Philip P. Wiener (ed.), *Dictionary of the History of Ideas* (New York: Scribner's, 1973), 476–8.

13 Marc Bloch, quoted in Dietrich Gerhard, 'Periodization in History'.

14 Jason Scott Smith, 'The Strange History of the Decade: Modernity, Nostalgia and the Perils of Periodization', *Journal of Social History* 32, no. 2 (Winter 1998): 263–85.

15 Frank Mort, *Capital Affairs: London and the Making of the Permissive Society* (New Haven, CT: Yale University Press, 2010); Jon Savage, *Teenage: The Creation of Youth Culture* (London: Chatto & Windus, 2007); Melanie Tebbutt, *Being Boys: Youth, Leisure and Identity in the Inter-War Years* (Manchester: Manchester University Press, 2012); Kate Fisher, *Birth Control, Sex, and Marriage in Britain 1918-1960* (Oxford: Oxford University Press,

2006); Judy Giles, '"Playing Hard to Get": Working-class Women, Sexuality and Respectability in Britain, 1918-40', *Women's History Review* 1 (1992): 239–55.

16 David Taylor, *Bright Young People: The Rise and Fall of a Generation, 1918-1940* (London: Chatto & Windus, 2007).

17 Noreen Branson, *Britain in the Nineteen Thirties* (London: Weidenfeld and Nicolson, 1971); John Stevenson, *The Slump* (London: Quartet, 1979); Pugh, *'We Danced all Night'*.

18 Caffrey, *'37-'39: Last Look Round*, Brian Cleeve, *1938, A World Vanishing* (London: Buchan & Enright, 1982).

19 Charles S. Maier, 'Consigning the Twentieth Century to History: Alternative Narratives for the Modern Era', *American Historical Review* 105, no. 3 (2000): 807–31.

20 Marshall Berman, *All That is Solid Melts into Air: The Experience of Modernity* (London: Penguin, [1982] 1988), 290.

21 Bernhard Rieger, *Technology and the Culture of Modernity in Britain and Germany, 1890-1945* (Cambridge: Cambridge University Press, 2005); M. J. Daunton and Bernhard Rieger, *Meanings of Modernity: Britain from the Late-Victorian Era to World War II* (Oxford: Berg, 2001).

22 Miles Ogborn, *Spaces of Modernity: London's Geographies, 1680–1780* (London: The Guilford Press, 1998), 2.

23 Berman, *All That is Solid Melts into Air: The Experience of Modernity*; Daunton and Rieger, *Meanings of Modernity: Britain from the Late-Victorian Era to World War II*; David Gilbert, David Matless and Brian Short (eds), *Geographies of British Modernity: Space and Society in the Twentieth Century* (Oxford: Blackwell, 2003); Mica Nava and Alan O'Shea (eds), *Modern Times: Reflections on a Century of English Modernity* (London: Routledge, 1996); Rieger, *Technology and the Culture of Modernity in Britain and Germany, 1890-1945*; Andrew Thacker, *Moving through Modernity: Space and Geography in Modernism* (Manchester: Manchester University Press, 2003).

24 For rural modernity, see David Matless, *Landscape and Englishness* (London: Reaktion, 1998).

25 Brad Beaven, *Leisure, Citizenship and Working-Class Men in Britain, 1850-1945* (Manchester: Manchester University Press, 2005); Richard Hoggart, *The Uses of Literacy: Aspects of Working-Class Life, with Special Reference to Publications and Entertainments* (London: Chatto and Windus, 1957); Robert James, *Popular Culture and Working-Class Taste in Britain, 1930-1939* (Manchester: Manchester University Press, 2010); Jonathan Rose, *The Intellectual Life of the British Working Classes* (New Haven, CT: Yale University Press, 2001); E. P. Thompson, *The Making of the English Working Class* (London: Gollancz, 1963); Ken Worpole, *Dockers and Detectives: Popular Reading, Popular Writing* (London: Verso, 1983).

26 One exception is Alan A. Jackson, *The Middle Classes 1900-1950* (Nairn: David St. John Thomas, 1991). For suburbanization, see Paul Barker, *The Freedoms of Suburbia* (London: Frances Lincoln, 2009); Mark Clapson, *Suburban Century: Social Change and Urban Growth in England and the United States* (Oxford: Berg, 2003); Alan A. Jackson, *Semi-Detached London:*

Suburban Development, Life and Transport, 1900-39 (London: Allen & Unwin, 1973); Paul Oliver, Ian Davis and Ian Bentley, *Dunroamin: The Suburban Semi and its Enemies* (London: Barrie & Jenkins, 1981); Peter Scott, *The Making of the Modern British Home: The Suburban Semi and Family Life between the Wars* (Oxford: Oxford University Press, 2013).

27 Robert W. Rydell, *Buffalo Bill in Bologna: The Americanization of the World, 1869-1922* (Chicago, IL: University of Chicago Press, 2005); Neil Campbell, Jude Davies and George McKay, *Issues in Americanisation and Culture* (Edinburgh: Edinburgh University Press, 2004); Frank Costigliola, *Awkward Dominion: American Political, Economic, and Cultural Relations with Europe, 1919-1933* (Ithaca, NY: Cornell University Press, 1984); Victoria De Grazia, *Irresistible Empire: America's Advance through Twentieth-Century Europe* (Cambridge, MA: Belknap, 2005); Chris Waters, 'Beyond "Americanization" Rethinking Anglo-American Cultural Exchange between the War', *Cultural and Social History* 4 (2007): 451–9.

28 Law, *The Experience of Suburban Modernity.*

29 James Nott, *Music for the People: Popular Music in Britain between the Wars* (Oxford: Oxford University Press, 2002).

30 Mark Glancy, '"Temporary American Citizens"? British Audiences, Hollywood Films and the Threat of Americanisation in the 1920s', *Historical Journal of Film, Radio and Television* 26, no. 4 (2006): 461–84, Lawrence Napper, *British Cinema and Middlebrow Culture in the Interwar Years* (Exeter: University of Exeter Press, 2009); Kelly Boyd, *Manliness and the Boys' Story Paper in Britain: A Cultural History, 1855-1940* (Basingstoke: Palgrave Macmillan, 2003); Worpole, *Dockers and Detectives: Popular Reading, Popular Writing.*

31 Sue Bowden, 'The New Consumerism', in Paul Johnson (ed.), *Twentieth-Century Britain, Economic, Cultural and Social Change* (London: Longman, 1994), 242–60.

32 Stephen G. Jones, *Workers at Play: A Social and Economic History of Leisure, 1918-1939* (London: Routledge & Kegan Paul, 1986); Josephine Kane, *The Architecture of Pleasure: British Amusement Parks 1900-1939* (Farnham: Ashgate, 2013); John K. Walton, *The British Seaside: Holidays and Resorts in the Twentieth Century* (Manchester: Manchester University Press, 2000).

33 Rex Walford, *The Growth of 'New London' in Suburban Middlesex (1918-1945) and the Response of the Church of England* (Lampeter: Edwin Mellen Press, 2007); George Orwell, *The Lion and the Unicorn: Socialism and the English Genius* (London: Secker & Warburg, 1941).

34 Law, *The Experience of Suburban Modernity.*

35 Maria Kaika, *City of Flows: Modernity, Nature, and the City* (Abingdon: Routledge, 2005).

36 Christopher Savage and T. C. Barker, *Economic History of Transport in Britain* (Abingdon: Routledge, 1959).

37 Richard Dennis, *Cities in Modernity: Representations and Productions of Metropolitan Space, 1840-1930* (Cambridge: Cambridge University Press, 2008).

38 John Burnett, *A Social History of Housing, 1815-1985* (London: Methuen, 1986).

39 Edward Jones and Christopher Woodward, *A Guide to the Architecture of London* (London: Seven Dials, 2000) records the new offices and blocks of flats of the 1930s.

Chapter 2

1 *Modern Wonder*, 22 May 1937.

2 David Kynaston, *Modernity Britain: 1957-1962* (London: Bloomsbury, 2013).

3 See https://books.google.com/ngrams.

4 For example, I was intrigued to see, in researching for this chapter, an advert in a 1938 *Kodak* magazine that offered an expensive 'sub-standard' cine-camera, by which the advertiser meant small rather than inferior.

5 Searching Ngram for 'modern war' demonstrates peaks in the late 1930s, but this phrase accounts for only 1 per cent of the rise in the use of the word 'modern'.

6 See also Nava and O'Shea, *Modern Times: Reflections on a Century of English Modernity*; Thacker, *Moving Through Modernity: Space and Geography in Modernism*; Gilbert, Matless and Short (eds), *Geographies of British Modernity: Space and Society in the Twentieth Century*.

7 Rieger, *Technology and the Culture of Modernity in Britain and Germany, 1890-1945*; Daunton and Rieger, *Meanings of Modernity: Britain from the Late-Victorian era to World War II*.

8 'Airmindedness' can be thought of as marketing campaigns by governments and others to increase awareness of aviation matters.

9 Penny Tinkler and Cheryl Krasnick Warsh, 'Feminine Modernity in Interwar Britain and North America: Corsets, Cars, and Cigarettes', *Journal of Women's History* 20, no. 3 (2008): 133–43; Adrian Bingham, '"An Era of Domesticity"? Histories of Women and Gender in Interwar Britain', *Cultural and Social History* 1 (2004): 225–33; Alison Light, *Forever England: Femininity, Literature and Conservatism Between the Wars* (London: Routledge, 1991).

10 Philipp Blom, *The Vertigo Years: Change and Culture in the West, 1900-1914* (London: Weidenfeld & Nicolson, 2008).

11 Paul Virilio, *The Original Accident* (Cambridge: Polity, 2007).

12 Law, *The Experience of Suburban Modernity*.

13 Charles Joseph Thomas Gardner, *Fifty Years of Brooklands* (London: Heinemann, 1956).

14 Charles Jennings, *The Fast Set: Three Extraordinary Men and Their Race for the Land Speed Record* (London: Little, Brown, 2004).

15 See Chapter 8 for more on Amy Johnson.

16 E. F. Spanner, 'Companion Vessels', *Times*, 27 September 1938.

17 Rieger, *Technology and the Culture of Modernity in Britain and Germany, 1890-1945*, 33.

18 Geoffrey Cantor, 'Emotional Reactions to the Great Exhibition of 1851', *Journal of Victorian Culture* 20, no. 2 (2015): 230–45.

19 David E. Nye, *American Technological Sublime* (Cambridge, MA: MIT Press, 1994).

20 *Review of the Year* [film], UK, British Pathé, 1938.

21 *Movietone Reviews 1938* [film], UK, British Movietone, 1938.

22 Tinkler and Krasnick Warsh, 'Feminine Modernity in Interwar Britain and North America: Corsets, Cars, and Cigarettes', 116.

23 The London Cigarette Card Company, *The Complete Catalogue of British Cigarette Cards* (Exeter: Webb & Bower, 1981).

24 Matthew Hilton, *Smoking in British Popular Culture 1800-2000: Perfect Pleasures* (Manchester: Manchester University Press, 2000), 96.

25 Ibid., 12.

26 Martin Murray, *The Story of Cigarette Cards* (London: Murray Cards (International) Ltd, 1987), 40.

27 I remember as a child in the 1960s pestering my father for the vouchers for cheap gifts that were included in packets of 'Guards' cigarettes. We collected two vouchers a day.

28 Records taken from 1934 and 1938 issues shown in Tessa Bennett, *Antiques and Their Values – Cigarette Cards* (Galashiels: Lyle Publications, 1982).

29 Both from author's collection.

30 *Popular Flying*, May 1938, 2.

31 Hilton, *Smoking in British Popular Culture 1800-2000: Perfect Pleasures*, 96.

32 W. D. and H. O. Wills, 'Speed' Cigarette Card Set, 1938.

33 W. D. and H. O. Wills, 'Speed' Cigarette Card Set, #13, 'Heinkel He. 111 Bomber', 1938.

34 W. A. and A. C. Churchman, 'Modern Wonders' Cigarette Card Set, #27, 'Magnet that Lifts 46 Tons', 1938.

35 W. A. and A. C. Churchman, 'Modern Wonders' Cigarette Card Set, #22, 'High-Power Grid-Glow Tube', 1938.

36 Harry Golding, *The Wonder Book of Empire for Boys and Girls* (London: Ward, Lock & Co., 1915).

37 Harry Golding, *The Wonder Book of Why & What? Answers to Children's Questions* (London: Ward, Lock & Co., 1921); Harry Golding (ed.), *The Wonder Book of Inventions* (London: Ward, Lock & Co., 1930); Harry Golding (ed.), *The Wonder Book of Do You Know?* (London: Ward, Lock & Co., 1934).

38 Boyd, *Manliness and the Boys' Story Paper, 1855-1940*.

39 *Modern Boy*, British Library Catalogue PP.5993.NDW.

40 This idea can also be seen in, and is most associated with, *Boy's Own Paper*. See, for example, 'Comrades Three', *Boy's Own Paper*, June 1938.

41 *Modern Boy*, 16 July 1938.

42 *Modern Wonder*, 22 May 1937.

43 Ibid.

44 *Modern Wonder*, 20 January 1938.

45 Ibid., 'Newsreel', 2.

46 Ibid., 'Learning how to Land', 3.

47 Ibid., 'Giant American Air Liner', 8–9.

48 Ibid., 'One-day Wonder Cruise', 12.

49 *Modern Wonder*, 26 February 1938, cover.

50 Ibid., 3.

51 Guy Arnold, *Held Fast for England: G. A. Henty, Imperialist Boy's Writer* (London: Hamish Hamilton, 1980), 75.

52 Ibid.

53 'Miracles in Ferro-Concrete', in Harold Wheeler (ed.), *Marvels of the Modern World* (London: Odhams Press Limited, 1938).

54 'Speeding up the Railways', in Wheeler (ed.), *Marvels of the Modern World*.

55 *Times*, 4 July 1938.

56 Michael John Law, *1930s London – The Modern City* (Canterbury: Yellowback, 2015), 80.

57 'Speeding up the Railways', in Wheeler (ed.), *Marvels of the Modern World*, 126.

58 John R. Crossland, *The Modern Marvels Encyclopedia* (London: Collins, 1938).

59 Peter J. Bowler, 'Discovering Science from an Armchair: Popular Science in British Magazines of the Interwar Years', *Annals of Science* 73, no. 1 (2016): 89–107.

60 Ursula Bloom, *He Lit the Lamp* (London: Burke, 1958), 11.

61 Archibald M. Low, *Our Wonderful World of To-Morrow. A Scientific Forecast of the Men, Women, and the World of the Future* (London: Ward, Lock & Co., 1934); *Conquering Space and Time* (London: T. Nelson & Sons, 1937); *What New Wonders! The Story of the Pasadena Telescope* (London: Herbert Joseph, 1938).

62 Low, *What New Wonders! The Story of the Pasadena Telescope*, 19.

63 *Armchair Science*, British Library Catalogue, PP.1447.BAC.

64 *Armchair Science*, June 1938.

65 Ibid., 36 and 45.

66 *Reader's Digest*, British Library Catalogue, PP.6365.be.

67 John Langdon-Davies, 'Science To-Day', *Picture Post*, 22 October 1938.

68 Ibid.

69 Bowler, 'Discovering Science from an Armchair: Popular Science in British Magazines of the Interwar Years', 92.

70 Stanley Weintraub, 'Snow, Charles Percy, Baron Snow (1905–1980)', *Oxford Dictionary of National Biography* (Oxford: Oxford University Press, 2004).

71 *Discovery*, August 1938, iii.

72 Ros Ballaster, *Women's Worlds: Ideology, Femininity and the Woman's Magazine* (London: Macmillan, 1991).

73 *Modern Woman* Booklets: 'Good Looks'; 'Good Manners'; 'Home Laundry Work'; 'Interior Decoration'; 'Party Games'; 'The Domestic Worker'.

74 David Taylor, *Bright Young People: The Rise and Fall of a Generation, 1918-1940* (London: Chatto & Windus, 2007), 225.

75 Sunday Wilshin, 'The Rolling Road', *Modern Woman*, May 1938.

76 *Modern Woman*, May 1938.

77 They were introduced in the United States in 1936/7, http://tampax.com/en-us/about-us/tampax-history [accessed 21 September 2016].

78 For example, *Television and Short-Wave World, Wireless World, Amateur Photographer and Cinematographer.*

79 www.brownie.camera shows a comprehensive collection of 1930s British Kodak Brownie cameras, www.brownie.camera [accessed 26 August 2016].

80 *Kodak*, June 1938.

81 John Taylor, 'Kodak and the "English" Market between the Wars', *Journal of Design History* 7, no. 1 (1994): 29–42.

82 *Kodak*, June 1938.

83 M. Taylor, '- and your Gum-boots', *Kodak*, April 1938.

84 *Amateur Photographer and Cinematographer*, various issues from 1938.

85 For this idea in another context, see Mark Glancy, '"Temporary American citizens"? British Audiences, Hollywood films and the Threat of Americanisation in the 1920s', *Historical Journal of Film, Radio and Television* 26, no. 4 (2006): 461–84.

86 For example, 'China Hunts for Scientific Glory, and Aliens, With New Telescope', *New York Times*, 25 September 2016.

Chapter 3

1 Lord Kelmsley, 'Youth and the Exhibition', *A Souvenir of the Empire Exhibition 1938* (Glasgow: The Daily Record and Evening News, 1938), unpaginated.

2 *Daily Mail*, 2 May 1938.

3 Per Kinchin, *Glasgow's Great Exhibitions: 1888, 1901, 1911, 1938, 1988* (Wendlebury: White Cockade, 1988), 128.

4 Robert A. Crampsey, *The Empire Exhibition of 1938: The Last Durbar* (Edinburgh: Mainstream, 1988), 40.

5 Kinchin, *Glasgow's Great Exhibitions.*

6 John M. MacKenzie, 'The Second City of Empire', in Felix Driver and David Gilbert (eds), *Imperial Cities: Landscape, Display and Identity* (Manchester: Manchester University Press, 1999), 215–37; Colin McArthur, 'The Glasgow Empire Exhibition', in Tony Bennett, Colin Mercer and Janet Woollacott, *Popular Culture and Social Relations* (Milton Keynes: Open University Press, 1986), 117–34. Sarah Britton, '"Come and See the Empire by the All Red Route!": Anti-imperialism and Exhibitions in Interwar Britain', *History Workshop Journal* 69, no. 1 (2010): 68–89; Sarah Britton, 'Urban Futures/Rural Pasts', *Cultural and Social History* 8, no. 2 (2011): 213–32; J. Neil

Baxter, 'Thomas S. Tait and the Glasgow Empire Exhibition 1938', *Thirties Society Journal* 4 (1984): 26–30.

7   Anon, *Empire Exhibition, Scotland-1938, Official Guide,* Glasgow: Corporation of Glasgow, 1938.

8   *Scotland Calling,* Marketing Brochure, c. 1937.

9   Kinchin, *Glasgow's Great Exhibitions,* 134.

10 David. M. Walker, 'Tait, Thomas Smith (1882–1954)', *Oxford Dictionary of National Biography* (Oxford: Oxford University Press, 2004); John Robert Gold, *The Experience of Modernism: Modern Architects and the Future City, 1928-53* (London: E & FN Spon, 1997).

11 Harriet Atkinson, *The Festival of Britain: A Land and its People* (London: I. B. Tauris, 2012), 49.

12 Alastair Borthwick, 'Building Scotland's Exhibition', *Listener,* 2 March 1938.

13 Only a small monument remains from the exhibition, save for the repurposed Palace of Arts, which is now a sports club. Author's site visit, July 2016.

14 *King George VI Opens Scottish Exhibition* (film) British Movietone, 1938.

15 Glasgow City Archives, TD655/10/2/2.

16 *Architectural Review*, July 1938, 3.

17 Ibid., 4–5.

18 Baxter, 'Thomas S. Tait and the Glasgow Empire Exhibition 1938'.

19 Charles McKean, *The Scottish Thirties: An Architectural Introduction* (Edinburgh: Scottish Academic, 1987), 189.

20 *Observer*, 17 April 1938.

21 *Scottish Exhibition* (film) UK, British Pathé, 1938.

22 Anon., *Empire Exhibition, Scotland-1938. Official Guide,* Glasgow 1938, 107.

23 Anon., *Glasgow's Greatest Exhibition: Recreating the 1938 Empire Exhibition* (Edinburgh: RIAS, 2008).

24 *Country Life*, 7 May 1938, 487.

25 Alastair Borthwick and BBC Scotland, *The Empire Exhibition Fifty Years On: A Personal Reminiscence* (Edinburgh: Mainstream, 1988).

26 McArthur, 'The Glasgow Empire Exhibition', 130.

27 *Sunday Post*, 22 May 1938.

28 John Summerson, 'Architecture at the Empire Exhibition' *Listener,* 18 May 1938.

29 *Daily Mail*, 15 April 1938.

30 Gold, *The Experience of Modernism*, 87.

31 *Architectural Review*, July 1938, 18.

32 McKean, *The Scottish Thirties: An Architectural Introduction*, 187.

33 McArthur, 'The Glasgow Empire Exhibition', 130.

34 from www.ici.com/History via wayback machine at archive.org.

35 Edwards, *Basil Spence*, 52.

36 *Architectural Review*, July 1938, 35.

37 Kinchin, *Glasgow's Great Exhibitions*, 162.

38 Robert Hurd quoted in Charles McKean, *The Scottish Thirties*, 187.

39 http://www.basilspence.org.uk/work/buildings/empire-exhibition.

40 Lord Kelmsley, 'Youth and the Exhibition', *A Souvenir of the Empire Exhibition 1938*, unpaginated.

41 *Architectural Review*, July 1938.

42 Brian Edwards, 'Exhibition Design', in Philip Long and Jane Thomas, *Basil Spence: Architect* (Edinburgh: National Galleries of Scotland in Association with the Royal Commission on the Ancient and Historical Monuments of Scotland, 2007), 49–61.

43 An idea shown clearly, for example, in the title of Barry Turner, *Beacon for Change: How the 1951 Festival of Britain Helped to Shape a New Age* (London: Aurum, 2011).

44 Alan Powers, 'Casson, Sir Hugh Maxwell (1910–1999)', *Oxford Dictionary of National Biography* (Oxford: Oxford University Press, 2004).

45 Brian Edwards, *Basil Spence, 1907-1976* (Edinburgh: Rutland Press, 1995), 52.

46 Gold, *The Experience of Modernism*, 212.

47 Kinchin, *Glasgow's Great Exhibitions*, 167.

48 Kane, *The Architecture of Pleasure: British Amusement Parks 1900-1939*.

49 Anon, *Empire Exhibition, Scotland-1938, Official Guide*, Glasgow 1938, 206.

50 *Architectural Review*, July 1938, 29.

51 Graham Moss, The *Post Office and the Empire Exhibition, 1938* (Ross-shire: Scottish Postal History Society, 1988), 43.

52 Anon, *Empire Exhibition, Scotland-1938, Official Guide* (Glasgow: 1938), 205.

53 *Architectural Review*, July 1938, 29.

54 Ibid., 7.

55 *Sunday Post*, 29 May 1938.

56 www.ebay.co.uk, Historian Richard Hornsey brought to my attention the idea of eBay as an archival source.

57 *Dundee Courier*, 29 April 1938.

58 *Architectural Review*, July 1938, 19; Anon, *Empire Exhibition, Scotland-1938, Official Guide*, 163.

59 *Empire Exhibition, Scotland-1938, Official Guide*, 112–13.

60 Ibid., 104.

61 See 'Moderne', Jonathan M. Woodham, *A Dictionary of Modern Design* (Oxford: Oxford University Press, 2004), Oxford Reference Online. http://www.oxfordreference.com (accessed 28 August 2008).

62 *Architectural Review*, July 1938, plate viii. A reproduction of the design is featured in Anon., *Glasgow's Greatest Exhibition: Recreating the 1938 Empire Exhibition,* and can be seen online at http://www.empireexhibition.com/html/atlanticRestaurant.html (accessed 11 December 2015).

63 *Empire Exhibition, Scotland-1938, Official Guide*, 105 and 167–8.

64   This is the very rough equivalent of £10 and £5 in 2014, www.
     measuringworth.com (accessed 11 December 2015).

65   McKean, *The Scottish Thirties*, 188.

66   *Lancashire Evening Post*, 21 June 1938.

67   Harold Dickson, 'The Spirit and Splendour of Empire', *A Souvenir of the
     Empire Exhibition 1938* (Glasgow: The Daily Record and Evening News,
     1938), unpaginated.

68   *The Sunday Post*, 13 February 1938.

69   James Morrison, 'National Life Story Collection: Artists' Lives', www.sounds.
     bl.uk (accessed 2 August 2014).

70   Crampsey, *The Empire Exhibition of 1938*, 25.

71   'Memories of Bellahouston', *Empire Exhibition Souvenir Glasgow 1938*,
     presented with *Weekly News*, undated.

72   Kinchin, *Glasgow's Great Exhibitions,* 162.

73   Estimate based on Society of Motor Manufacturers and Traders, Ltd.
     Statistical Dept., *The Motor Industry of Great Britain 1937* (London: SMMT,
     1937).

74   Borthwick and BBC Scotland., *The Empire Exhibition Fifty Years On*,
     foreword.

75   *Dundee Courier*, 4 August 1938.

76   The films for this camera were processed without enlargement and measured
     2.25" x 4.25".

77   *Valentine's Snapshots: 12 Real Photographs, Empire Exhibition Scotland,
     1938*, bought on eBay for a few pounds.

78   George Bamber, 'Empire Exhibition Glasgow', *Kodak*, September 1938, 194–5.

79   Rieger, *Technology and the Culture of Modernity in Britain and Germany,
     1890-1945*, 201. Estimate of cars based on Society of Motor Manufacturers
     and Traders, *The Motor Industry of Great Britain 1937*.

80   Calculated using the 1931 census, visionofbritain.org.uk (accessed 25 January
     2010).

81   Rieger, *Technology and the Culture of Modernity in Britain and Germany*,
     196; Kodak advertisement, *Times*, 12 August 1938.

82   National Library of Scotland, Moving Image Archive, Glasgow Empire
     Exhibition 1938, films: 0065, 3035, 5653, 6710, 8686, 8782.

83   Stefan Szczelkun, 'Public History: The Value of Home Movies', *Oral History*,
     Autumn (2000): 94–8.

84   Rieger, *Technology and the Culture of Modernity in Britain and Germany*, 206.

85   National Library of Scotland, Moving Image Archive, 'Empire Exhibition'
     (film) dir. Don McLachlan, 1938 (Ref. 8686).

86   H. Norris Nicholson, 'In Amateur Hands: Framing Time and Space in Home-
     Movies', *History Workshop Journal* 43, Spring (1997): 198–212.

87   Alan Powers, *Modern – The Modern Movement in Britain* (London: Merrell,
     2007), 32.

Chapter 4

1 *Times*, 'Enlarged Screen Television', 17 August 1938.

2 Seán Street, *Historical Dictionary of British Radio* (Oxford: The Scarecrow Press, 2006), 231.

3 Shaun Moores, '"The Box on the Dresser": Memories of Early Radio and Everyday life', *Media, Culture and Society* 10 (1988): 23–40.

4 British Broadcasting Corporation, *BBC Handbook 1939* (London: The British Broadcasting Corporation, 1939), 156.

5 'This Year's Radiolympia', *Radio Pictorial*, 19 August 1938, 16.

6 This remained the standard for television in Britain until 1964 and was not supplanted until 1985.

7 Asa Briggs, *The History of Broadcasting in the United Kingdom, Volume 2* (London: Oxford University Press, 1965); Stephen Herbert, *A History of Early Television* (London: Routledge, 2004); Paddy Scannell, *A Social History of British Broadcasting, Volume 1, 1922-1939 – Serving the Nation* (Oxford: Basil Blackwell, 1991); Andrew Crisell, *An Introductory History of British Broadcasting* (London: Routledge, 1997); R. W. Burns, *British Television, the Formative Years* (London: Peter Peregrinus Ltd., 1986).

8 Bowden, 'The New Consumerism'.

9 Ibid., 242.

10 Philip Massey, 'The Expenditure of 1,360 British Middle-Class Households in 1938-9', *Journal of the Royal Statistical Society* 105, no. 3 (1942): 159–96.

11 Law, *The Experience of Suburban Modernity*.

12 Bowden, 'The New Consumerism', 245.

13 *BBC Handbook 1939*, 129, 156 et seq. Bowden misstated these numbers in her chapter, showing them as rates per thousand in both text and table, she also understated the 1938 adoption rate; the highest adoption rate was Dorset and Wiltshire at 86 per cent and the lowest was North of Scotland with 37 per cent.

14 Bowden, 'The New Consumerism', 245.

15 *Radio Pictorial*, 19 August 1938; Bowden; 'The New Consumerism', Table 14.5.

16 Briggs, *The History of Broadcasting in the United Kingdom, Volume 2*, 597.

17 *Observer*, 'Television in the Home', 4 September 1938.

18 British Broadcasting Corporation, *The London Television Station, Alexandra Palace* (London: British Broadcasting Corporation, 1937), 34; 'Map of service area of London Television Station', *Television and Short-Wave World*, December 1938, 737.

19 Crisell, *An Introductory History of British Broadcasting*, 72; Ernest Thomson, 'This is Where We Left Off' in British Broadcasting Corporation, *Television Again* (London: British Broadcasting Corporation, 1946), 25; 'Map of Service Area of London Television Station', *Television and Short-Wave World*, December 1938, 737. Television and short-wave radio were associated together because television was broadcast on the short-wave band.

20   Everett M. Rogers, *Diffusion of Innovations* (New York: The Free Press, 1995), 35, discussing Bryce Ryan and Neal C. Gross, 'The Diffusion of Hybrid Seed Corn in Two Iowa Communities', *Rural Sociology* 8, no. 15 (1943): 15–24.

21   Thomson, 'This is Where We Left Off', 24.

22   The attribution for this quote is somewhat uncertain.

23   'Editorial Comment', *Wireless World*, 25 August 1938.

24   *Radio Pictorial*, 19 August 1938.

25   'Olympia Show Report', *Wireless World*, 25 August 1938.

26   'fine-tuning', OED *Online*. Oxford University Press, March 2016, www.oed. com [accessed 25 May 2016]; *Wireless World & Radio Review,* 3 September 1924, 659.

27   Advertisement in Southend Flying Club, *At Home*, 27 August 1938.

28   See, for example, the online RGD museum at www.rgd.org.uk for a comprehensive catalogue of this company's console sets from the period.

29   'Olympia Show Report', *Wireless World*, 25 August 1938.

30   www.measuringworth.com/ukcompare (accessed 25 May 2015).

31   Roy Armes, *On Video* (London: Routledge, (1988) 1995), provides a succinct introduction to recording and broadcast technologies.

32   *Gramophone*, September 1938.

33   Kenneth Jowers, 'What's New in Radio', *Radio Pictorial*, 19 August 1938, 19.

34   See Scannell, *A Social History of British Broadcasting, Volume 1*, Chapter 13 and Crisell, *An Introductory History of British Broadcasting,* 38 et seq.

35   Scannell, *A Social History of British Broadcasting, Volume 1*, 264 et seq.

36   BBC programme for 21 August 1938, *Radio Times*, 19 August 1938.

37   Radio Luxembourg, programme for 21 August 1938, *Radio Pictorial*, 19 August 1938.

38   Scannell, *A Social History of British Broadcasting, Volume 1*, 296.

39   *Radio Pictorial*, 19 August 1938.

40   Scannell, *A Social History of British Broadcasting, Volume 1*, 297.

41   Ibid., 271.

42   Seán Street, 'Pre-War UK Commercial Radio and the BBC', Radio Studies Conference, York University, Toronto, July 2009.

43   'Olympia Show Report', *Wireless World*, 25 August 1938.

44   www.freemaptools.com (accessed 6 January 2016).

45   Briggs, *The History of Broadcasting in the United Kingdom, Volume 2*, 593.

46   Armes, *On Video,* 57.

47   This was known as the Marconi-EMI system.

48   John Trenouth, 'Behind the Cameras: No. 2 – The Emitron Camera', *405 Alive*, 25, First Quarter (1995).

49   'The Marconi EMI Emitron Camera', http://www.earlytelevision.org/pdf/ emitron_brochure.pdf (accessed 29 May 2016).

50 Thomson, 'This is Where We Left Off', 24.

51 *Radio Pictorial*, 19 August 1938.

52 *Television and Short-Wave World*, October 1938, 598.

53 Ibid., September 1938, 521.

54 'Progress of Television', *Spectator*, 26 August 1938.

55 *Wireless World*, 1 September 1938, 210.

56 *Television and Short-Wave World*, October 1938, 598.

57 'Sensation at the London Broadcast Exhibition 1938', Getty Images, # 56460902, Hulton Archive, Imagno.

58 G. E. C., *G. E. C. Television*, Brochure, 1938; Murphy, *Murphy Television*, Brochure, 1938, Ferranti, *Ferranti Television – 'Masters of Power'*, Brochure, 1938, Ultra, *Ultra Television – The Gift of Sight*, Brochure, 1938, PYE, *PYE Television*, Brochure, 1938.

59 *Wireless World*, 1 September 1938, 210.

60 *Television and Short-Wave World*, October 1938, 598; E. H. Traub, 'English and Continental Television', *Journal of the Television Society*, December, (1938).

61 'World's Largest Cathode-Ray Tube', *Television and Short-Wave World*, April 1938, 203.

62 Traub, 'English and Continental Television'.

63 *Television in Your Home – The Receivers You Can Buy – A Complete Guide*, Brochure, 1938, http://www.earlytelevision.org/pdf/television_in_your_home. pdf (accessed 4 June 2016).

64 'Enlarged Screen Television', *Times*, 17 August 1938.

65 It is beyond the scope of this book and its author to explain the Scophony or indeed any other system in detail. For those who wish to know more, please consult *Television and Short-Wave World*, January 1938, 23; Thomas Singleton, *The Story of Scophony* (London: Royal Television Society, 1988).

66 Singleton, *The Story of Scophony*, 87.

67 *Television and Short-Wave World*, October 1938, 598.

68 Singleton, *The Story of Scophony*, 86.

69 Gerald Cock. 'Television Today', *Listener*, 2 February 1938.

70 H. M. V., 'His Master's Voice' Television: The Birth of Television for Home Entertainment, Brochure, 1937; 'On Television – You See It Better Than If You Were There!', Radiolympia brochure, August 1938, http://www.tvhistory.tv/ magazines1.htm (accessed 1 May 2015).

71 'London Television, Alexandra Palace' *Times*, 6 August 1938.

72 http://bufvc.ac.uk/screenplays/index.php/prog/818 (accessed 15 August 2015).

73 'The Development of Television', *Times*, 24 August 1938.

74 'On Television'.

75 'On Television', inside front cover.

76 'On Television', 1.

77 'The Derby Television Broadcast', *Television and Short-Wave World*, July 1938, 409–10.

78 'The Race Televised – Vivid Last Quarter Mile', *Times*, 2 June 1938.

Chapter 5

1 John A. Milne, letter to *Times*, 13 February 1933.

2 See Chapter 3, note 41.

3 Hugh Casson, *New Sights of London* (Westminster: London Transport, 1938), cover.

4 I refer to the original buildings as 'the Adelphi' and the new offices as 'the Adelphi Building'.

5 John Newenham Summerson, *Georgian London* (London: Pleiades Books, 1945).

6 David G. C. Allan, *The Adelphi Past and Present: A History and a Guide* (London: Calder Walker, 2001); Charles Pendrill, *The Adelphi; or, old Durham House in the Strand* (London: Sheldon Press, 1934).

7 Steen Eiler Rasmussen, *London: The Unique City* (London: Jonathan Cape, 1948), 183.

8 David Pike, '"Down by the Dark Arches": A Cultural History of the Adelphi', *London Journal* 27, no. 1 (2002): 19–41.

9 Matt Houlbrook, *Queer London: Perils and Pleasures in the Sexual Metropolis, 1918-1957* (Chicago, IL: University of Chicago Press, 2005), 63.

10 Allan, *The Adelphi Past and Present*, 148, provides a canonical record of the occupants of all of the Adelphi's buildings from inception to demolition.

11 Wine merchants were quite common tenants of the Adelphi because of the cellaring it provided.

12 Richard Davenport-Hines, 'Weir, William Douglas, first Viscount Weir (1877–1959)', *Oxford Dictionary of National Biography* (Oxford: Oxford University Press, 2004).

13 *Daily Telegraph*, 29 June 1935.

14 Allan, The *Adelphi Past and Present*, 82.

15 Parliamentary exchange between Ormsby-Gore and Lovat-Fraser, reported *Times*, 8 February 1933.

16 John A. Milne, letter to the editor, *Times*, 13 February 1933.

17 A. R. Powys, letter to the editor, *Times*, 20 February 1933.

18 Editorial, *Times*, 21 February 1933.

19 Allan, The *Adelphi Past and Present*, 68; Clough Williams-Ellis and John Newenham. Summerson, *Architecture Here and Now* (London: T. Nelson and Sons, Ltd, 1934).

20 G. H. Drummond, letter to the editor, *Times*, 12 July 1933.

21 Gavin Stamp, 'Origins of the Group', *Architectural Review*, 31 March 1982, 35.

22   Robert Byron, 'The Destruction of Georgian London', *New Statesman and Nation*, 11 December 1937.

23   Terry Gourvish, *Dolphin Square: The History of a Unique Building* (London: Bloomsbury, 2014).

24   Charlotte Benton, Tim Benton and Ghislaine Wood, *Art Deco 1910-1939* (London: V&A, 2003), 217.

25   Miles Ogborn, *Indian Ink: Script and Print in the Making of the English East India Company* (Chicago, IL: University of Chicago Press, 2007).

26   The railways had the greatest impact on the largest number of people in Britain.

27   Roderick Floud and Paul Johnson (eds), *The Cambridge Economic History of Modern Britain (Volume 1)* (Cambridge: Cambridge University Press, 2004).

28   This persisted well into the twentieth century, for example, my father, when he worked in a provincial bank in the 1960s, had to stay at the office every day until the branch's books were balanced to the penny.

29   Adrian Forty, *Objects of Desire: Design and Society, 1750-1980* (London: Thames and Hudson, 1986), 123.

30   Ibid., 121.

31   Stephen Broadberry and Sayantan Ghosal, 'From the Counting House to the Modern Office: Explaining Anglo-American Productivity Differences in Services, 1870-1990', *Journal of Economic History* 62, no. 4 (2002): 967–8.

32   Gregory Anderson, 'The White-Blouse Revolution', in Gregory Anderson (ed.), *The White-Blouse Revolution: Female Office Workers Since 1870* (Manchester: Manchester University Press, 1988), 5.

33   Martin Campbell-Kelly, 'Large-scale Data Processing in the Prudential, 1850–1930', *Accounting, Business & Financial History* 2, no. 2 (1992): 117–40.

34   The first six buildings in this list from Edward Jones and Christopher Woodward, *A Guide to the Architecture of London* (London: Seven Dials, 2000).

35   https://www.historicengland.org.uk/listing/the-list/list-entry/1222795 (accessed 19 April 2014).

36   Anon., *Shell-Mex House* (London: Shell-Mex Ltd, 1935).

37   Ibid., 19.

38   Allan, *The Adelphi Past and Present*, 90.

39   Stanley E. Bragg, *Down Memory Lane: Thoughts of the Adelphi: Being Reminiscences of his Time in Collcutt & Hamp's Office During the Rebuilding of the Adelphi, Westminster, in 1934*, unpublished memoir (London, 1984), RIBA archive, BrS/1.

40   'Stanley Hamp', RIBA archive, Biographical File: Microfiche 67/G7.

41   See Chapter 3, note 16.

42   Stanley Hamp, Obituary, *Times*, 18 April 1968.

43   See illustrations in Allan, *The Adelphi Past and Present*.

44   Farebrother, Ellis & Co.'s advertisement 'The Adelphi London', *Times*, 26 July 1938.

45   'The Adelphi (London) Limited', *Times*, 5 January 1949.

46 'The New Adelphi', *Builder*, 4 November 1938, 870.

47 See Law, *The Experience of Suburban Modernity*.

48 'The New Adelphi', *Builder*, 4 November 1938, 876.

49 'Office Building – Adelphi', *Architect's Journal*, 10 November 1938, 772.

50 http://www.hse.gov.uk/contact/faqs/toilets.htm (accessed 24 March 2016).

51 Anderson (ed.), *The White-blouse Revolution: Female Office Workers Since 1870*.

52 Anderson, 'The White-Blouse Revolution', 2.

53 Ibid., 7. This was the nearest full census to 1938. In that year, a partial census was taken to facilitate the issue of identity cards.

54 Author's personal knowledge.

55 Anderson, 'The White-Blouse Revolution', 18.

56 Jane. E. Lewis, 'Women Clerical Workers', in Anderson (ed.), *The White-Blouse Revolution: Female Office Workers Since 1870*, 37, quoting from Hilda Martindale, *Women Servants of the State, 1870–1938* (London: Allen and Unwin, 1938).

57 Hilda Martindale, *Women Servants of the State, 1870-1938. A History of Women in the Civil Service* (London: Allen and Unwin, 1938), 156.

58 Anderson, 'The White-Blouse Revolution', 11.

59 Ibid., 9.

60 1931 Census, visionofbritain.org.uk and L. P. Abercrombie, *Greater London Plan 1944*, London 1945, 188.

61 Lewis, 'Women Clerical Workers', 34.

62 Forty, *Objects of Desire: Design and Society, 1750-1980*, 132.

63 www.lightstraw.co.uk/ate/tass/telex1.html (accessed 26 April 2014).

64 Broadberry and Ghosal, 'From the Counting House to the Modern Office: Explaining Anglo-American Productivity Differences in Services, 1870-1990', Table 5.

65 *Shell-Mex House*, 23.

66 See British Pathé newsreel 'Towards 100%', 1937.

67 International Office Machines Research Limited, *Office Machine Manual. A Loose Leaf Reference on Office Machines and Appliances* (London: IOMRL, 1938).

68 Anon., *Office Machine Manual*, Index.

69 Broadberry and Ghosal, 'From the Counting House to the Modern Office: Explaining Anglo-American Productivity Differences in Services, 1870-1990', Table 6; Forty, *Objects of Desire: Design and Society, 1750-1980*, 133.

70 Author's personal knowledge.

71 Campbell-Kelly, 'Large-scale Data Processing in the Prudential, 1850–1930', 123.

72 James W. Cortada, *Before the Computer* (Princeton, NJ: Princeton University Press, 1993).

73 International Office Machines Research Limited, *Office Machine Manual. A Loose Leaf Reference on Office Machines and Appliances*, 'Punched Card Machines', 1–2.

74 H. W. Simpson, *Modern Office Management* (London: Pitman, 1937), 42.

75 'Offices of the New Adelphi Building, London; Designed by Michael Rachlis', *Architectural Review*, November 1939, 207.

Chapter 6

1 Editorial (abridged) in response to a letter from William Freeman, *Picture Post*, 19 November 1938, 4.

2 Stuart Hall, 'The Social Eye of Picture Post' in Centre for Contemporary Cultural Studies, *Working Papers in Cultural Studies* (Birmingham: University of Birmingham, 1971), 71–120.

3 The term 'ordinary' has a variety of constructed meanings, see Raymond Williams, *Keywords: A Vocabulary of Culture and Society* (London: Fontana, 1976), 226.

4 Tom Hopkinson, *Picture Post 1938-50* (London: Allen Lane, The Penguin Press, 1970); Robert Kee, *The Picture Post Album* (London: Barrie & Jenkins, 1989); Gavin Weightman, *'Picture Post' Britain* (London: Collins & Brown, 1991); Michael Hallett, *The Real Story of Picture Post* (Birmingham: ARTicle Press, 1994); David J. Marcou, *All the Best: Britain's Picture Post Magazine, Best Mirror and Old Friend to Many, 1938-57* (La Crosse: Digicopy, 2013).

5 Robert McG. Thomas Jr., 'Stefan Lorant', *New York Times*, 18 November 1997.

6 Christopher H. Sterling (ed.), *Encyclopedia of Journalism* (London: Sage, 2009), 1071.

7 Michael Hallett, *Stefan Lorant: Godfather of Photojournalism* (Lanham, MD: Scarecrow, 2006).

8 Michael Hallett, 'Lorant, Stefan (1901–1997)', *Oxford Dictionary of National Biography* (Oxford: Oxford University Press, 2004).

9 Hopkinson, *Picture Post 1938-50*, 9.

10 Colin Seymour-Ure, 'Hulton, Sir Edward George Warris (1906–1988)', rev. *Oxford Dictionary of National Biography* (Oxford: Oxford University Press, 2004).

11 Kee, *The Picture Post Album*, introduction.

12 Charles Wintour, 'Hopkinson, Sir (Henry) Thomas (1905–1990)', rev. *Oxford Dictionary of National Biography* (Oxford: Oxford University Press, 2004).

13 Hallett, 'Lorant, Stefan (1901–1997)'.

14 *John Bull*, 1 October 1938.

15 Hopkinson, *Picture Post 1938-50*, 10.

16 David Reed, *The Popular Magazine in Britain and the United States 1880-1960* (London: The British Library, 1997), 185.

17 See advertisement in *Picture Post*, 19 November 1938, 4.

18 *Picture Post*, 29 October 1938, 6.

19 Ibid., 24 December 1938, 1.

20 The full run of *Picture Post* is available online at Gale Cengage Picture Post Historical Archive by subscription. Individual copies are still readily available for a few pounds on auction sites.

21 *Picture Post*, 22 October 1938, 7.

22 Ibid., 22 October 1938, 55.

23 David Matless, *Landscape and Englishness* (London: Reaktion, 1998).

24 *Picture Post*, 22 October 1938, 63.

25 The class and location of *Picture Post*'s readership can be seen in contributions to the readers' letters and photographs sections, which give a full address. Tracing them on Google Maps 'street view' is useful in establishing a rough idea of a reader's class origins based on the size of their house. For cars, see Law, *The Experience of Suburban Modernity*.

26 Mike Huggins and Jack Williams, *Sport and the English 1918-1939* (London: Routledge, 2006).

27 *Picture Post*, 22 October 1938, 44.

28 Stuart Hall, 'The Social Eye of Picture Post', 72.

29 *Picture Post*, 22 October 1938, 35.

30 Ibid., 22 October 1938, 12.

31 Ibid.

32 'Women's Enthusiasm for Flying', *Times*, 2 August 1938.

33 *Picture Post*, 22 October 1938, 47.

34 See note 25.

35 Letter from William Freeman and editorial response, *Picture Post*, 19 November 1938, 4.

36 D. L. LeMahieu, *A Culture for Democracy: Mass Communication and the Cultivated Mind in Britain Between the Wars* (Oxford: Clarendon, 1988), 47.

37 Jeffrey Richards, *The Age of the Dream Palace: Cinema and Society in Britain, 1930-1939* (London: Routledge, 1989).

38 Robert James, *Popular Culture and Working-class Taste in Britain, 1930-1939* (Manchester: Manchester University Press, 2010), Appendices.

39 M. Glancy, '"Temporary American citizens"? British Audiences, Hollywood films and the Threat of Americanisation in the 1920s', *Historical Journal of Film, Radio and Television* 26, no. 4 (2006): 461–84.

40 LeMahieu, *A Culture for Democracy: Mass Communication and the Cultivated Mind in Britain Between the Wars*, 48.

41 James, *Popular Culture and Working-class Taste in Britain, 1930-1939*, Appendices.

42 David Bret, *George Formby: A Troubled Genius* (London: Robson, 1999).

43 *I See Ice* [film] and *It's in the Air* [film], both Dir. Anthony Kimmins, Associated Talking Pictures, 1938.

44 Richards, *The Age of the Dream Palace: Cinema and Society in Britain, 1930-1939*, 169.

45 *Picture Post*, 29 October 1938. This photograph showed black Londoners waving the union flag with the caption 'white faces, coloured faces, bright eyes, dark eyes, straight hair, curly hair – but all loud voices'.

46 'A day with Gracie', *Picture Post*, 29 October 1938, 12.

47 See www.measuringworth.com for an explanation and alternative calculations.

48 'Fields, Dame Gracie (1898–1979),' Jeffrey Richards in *Oxford Dictionary of National Biography* (Oxford: Oxford University Press, 2004).

49 *Picture Post*, 5 November 1938, 69.

50 *The Lady Vanishes* [film] Dir. Alfred Hitchcock, UK, Gainsborough Pictures, 1938.

51 Su Holmes, '"You Don't Need Influence ... All You Need is Your First Opportunity!"': The Early Broadcast Talent Show and the BBC', *Critical Studies in Television: The International Journal of Television Studies* 9, no. 1 (2014): 23–42.

52 *The Gang Show* [film], Dir. Alfred J. Goulding, UK, Herbert Wilcox Productions, 1937.

53 Ross McKibbin, *Classes and Cultures: England, 1918-1951* (Oxford: Oxford University Press, 1998), 335.

54 Matthew Taylor, 'Beyond the Maximum Wage: The Earnings of Football Professionals in England, 1900-39', *Soccer & Society* 2, no. 3 (2001): 101–18.

55 Ian Aitken, 'The British Documentary Movement in the 1930s', *In Land of Promise – The British Documentary Movement 1930-1950*, Booklet accompanying DVD box set, undated (London, BFI), 8–11.

56 Richards, *The Age of the Dream Palace*, 248.

57 *Housing Problems* [film], Dir. Arthur Elton, UK, British Commercial Gas Association, 1935.

58 Anthony Aldgate and Jeffrey Richards, *Best of British: Cinema and Society from 1930 to Present* (London: I. B. Tauris, 1999), 5.

59 Ben Highmore, *Everyday Life and Cultural Theory: An Introduction* (New York: Routledge, 2001), 77.

60 Nick Hubble, *Mass-Observation and Everyday Life: An Introduction* (London: Palgrave Macmillan, 2010); Charles Madge and Tom Harrisson, *Britain by Mass-Observation* (Harmondsworth: Penguin, 1939).

61 Madge and Harrisson, *Britain by Mass-Observation*, 67.

62 Highmore, *Everyday Life and Cultural Theory: An Introduction*.

63 Clive Bloom, *Bestsellers: Popular Fiction Since 1900* (Basingstoke: Palgrave, 2002); Andy Croft, *Red Letter Days: British Fiction in the 1930s* (London: Lawrence & Wishart, 1990).

64 'Pickles, Wilfred (1904–1978)', John A. Hargreaves in *Oxford Dictionary of National Biography* (Oxford: Oxford University Press, 2004).

65 Su Holmes, 'The "Give-away" Shows – Who is Really Paying?: "Ordinary" People and the Development of the British Quiz Show', *Journal of British Cinema and Television* 3, no. 2 (2006): 266–83.

66 *Radio Times*, 29 December 1946.

67 http://whirligig-tv.co.uk/radio/downyourway.htm [accessed 28 May 2015].

68 Claire Langhamer, '"Who the Hell are Ordinary People?", Ordinariness as a Category of Historical Analysis', paper given to the Royal Historical Society, 10 February 2017. Claire Langhamer has shown that the idea of ordinary people became 'slippery and dynamic' in the 1950s and 1960s when it became increasingly deployed for political purposes.

69 Su Holmes, 'The "Give-away" Shows – Who is Really Paying?'.

Chapter 7

1 H. V. Morton, *In Search of England* (London: Methuen, 1927), vii.

2 Much of this chapter first appeared in: Michael John Law, 'Charabancs and Social Class in 1930s Britain', *Journal of Transport History* 36, no. 1 (2015): 41–57.

3 This idea, often associated with suburbanization, is seen in the writing of, for example, Evelyn Waugh, George Orwell and John Betjeman. See John Carey, *The Intellectuals and the Masses: Pride and Prejudice Among the Literary Intelligentsia, 1880-1939* (London: Faber, 1992).

4 For the proposition that increased leisure led to greater social cohesion and cultural convergence, see LeMahieu, *A Culture for Democracy: Mass Communication and the Cultivated Mind in Britain Between the Wars*, 227; McKibbin, *Classes and Cultures: England, 1918-1951*, 527; John Stevenson, *British Society, 1914-45* (Harmondsworth: Penguin, 1984), 381. For working-class agency and leisure, see Jones, *Workers at Play: A Social and Economic History of Leisure, 1918-1939*.

5 The history of the charabanc and motor coach has not received much attention from leisure and transport historians who have emphasized the impact of the railway on how seaside holidays became open to wider social groups; see Walton, *The British Seaside: Holidays and Resorts in the Twentieth Century*; John K. Walton, 'The Origins of the Modern Package Tour?: British Motor-coach Tours in Europe, 1930-70', *Journal of Transport History* 32, no. 2 (2011): 145–63; Bob Gibson, 'From the Charabanc to the Gay Hostess', in Leisure Studies Association (Great Britain), *Recording Leisure Lives: Holidays and Tourism in 20th Century Britain* (Eastbourne: Leisure Studies Association, 2011), 99–118. This chapter draws on work on the history of working-class leisure that has revealed it to be far more heterogeneous than contemporary critics of interwar 'mass' culture had imagined: Brad Beaven, *Leisure, Citizenship and Working-Class Men in Britain, 1850-1945* (Manchester: Manchester University Press, 2005); Kane, *The Architecture of Pleasure: British Amusement Parks 1900-1939*.

6   Christian Wolmar, *Fire & Steam: A New History of the Railways in Britain* (London: Atlantic Books, 2007).

7   J. B. Priestley, *English Journey* (London: Heinemann, 1934), 3.

8   William Plowden, *The Motor Car and Politics 1896-1970* (London: The Bodley Head, 1971), 456.

9   Law, '"The Car Indispensable" The Hidden Influence of the Car in Inter-War Suburban London'.

10 Stan Lockwood, *Kaleidoscope of Char-a-bancs and Coaches* (London: Marshall Harris & Baldwin, 1980).

11 Miles Burton, *The Charabanc Mystery* (London: Collins, 1934), 9.

12 Advertisement for English Electric Company in Stan Lockwood, *Kaleidoscope of Char-a-bancs and Coaches*, figure 110.

13 *Daily Mirror*, 16 May 1931. In this chapter, I use the term 'charabanc' for special journeys made for outings and 'motor coach' for scheduled journeys that competed with the railways.

14 The total number of passenger journeys, excluding those originating in London, was 37.2 million in 1937; the additional London-based element was typically less than 10 per cent of the rest of the UK total. The 1951 figure is for the whole of the UK. These figures probably exclude the smallest charabanc operators. D. L. Munby, *Inland Transport Statistics, Great Britain, 1900-1970* (Oxford: Oxford University Press, 1978), Table B 6.5.

15 *Motor Coach A. B. C.*, London 1929.

16 *A. B. C. Railway Guide*, July 1932.

17 Hoggart, *The Uses of Literacy*, 146.

18 *Roadways*, (film) director, A. Cavalcanti, S. Legg and W. Coldstream, UK, GPO Film Unit, 1937. For a theoretical analysis of circulation and regulation, see C. Lopez Galviz, 'Mobilities at a Standstill: Regulating Circulation in London c. 1863-1870', *Journal of Historical Geography* 42 (2013): 62–76.

19 This is the rail fare from Charing Cross. If you lived in Croydon you would have to go in and out of London to get to Ramsgate by train making the coach even cheaper and more convenient, if a little slower.

20 Bennett's Coaches leaflet, http://thecroydoncitizen.com/history/23-london-road-prestige-barber (accessed 4 March 2012).

21 Christopher T. Brunner, *The Problem of Motor Transport. An Economic Analysis* (London: Ernest Benn Ltd, 1928), 60.

22 Ibid., 61.

23 *Skinners' Motor Coach Tours from Hastings and St. Leonards* (Gloucester: British Publishing Co., 1937), 9.

24 Hoggart, *The Uses of Literacy*.

25 Eric Newby, *A Traveller's Life* (London: Pan, 1982), 82, abridged quotation.

26 'A Devil's Dictionary', in Clough Williams-Ellis, *England and the Octopus* (London: Geoffrey Bles, 1928).

27 Norah Richardson, review of S. P. B. Mais, *The Home Counties* (London: Batsford, 1942), *Journal of the Royal Society of the Arts*, 27 October 1944.

28 D. N. Jeans, 'Planning and the Myth of the English Countryside in the Interwar Period', *Rural History* 1, no. 2 (1990): 249–64.

29 Morton, *In Search of England*, vii.

30 Matless, *Landscape and Englishness*.

31 E. Varah, account of a 1947 trip, in Clare Jenkins (ed.), *The Bumper Book of Beanos: South Yorkshire People Reminisce About Works Outings, Trips to the Seaside and Other Merry Sprees* (Castleford: Yorkshire Art Circus in Association with Sheffield City Libraries and Ventura Holidays, 1988), 7.

32 Charles Graves, *– And the Greeks* (London: Geoffrey Bles, 1930), 193.

33 Varah, *The Bumper Book of Beanos*, 1.

34 George Bernard Shaw, *The Intelligent Woman's Guide to Socialism and Capitalism* (New Brunswick, NJ: Transaction Publishers, (1928) 1984), 165.

35 C. Delisle Burns, *Leisure in the Modern World* (London: The Century Co., 1932), 228.

36 Mass-Observation, *The Pub and the People: A Worktown Study* (London: Victor Gollancz Ltd., 1943), 273.

37 Holidays With Pay Act, November 1938, House of Commons Parliamentary Papers.

38 Walton, *The Seaside*.

39 Priestley, *English Journey*, 264. A discussion on Priestley's status as an intellectual can be found in John Baxendale, 'Priestley and the Highbrows', in Erica Brown and Mary Grover (eds), *Middlebrow Literary Cultures* (Basingstoke: Palgrave Macmillan UK, 2012), 69–81; For Blackpool, see Rebecca Conway, 'Making the Mill Girl Modern?: Beauty, Industry and the Popular Newspaper in 1930s England', *Twentieth Century British History* 24, no. 4 (2013): 518–41.

40 C. E. M. Joad, 'The Horrors of the Countryside', *The Book of Joad* (London: Faber and Faber, 1935), 136.

41 Yvonne Cloud, 'Margate', in Yvonne Cloud (ed.), *Beside the Seaside, Six Variations* (London: John Lane, The Bodley Head, 1934), 258.

42 For the Fylde Coast, see Gary S. Cross and John K. Walton, *The Playful Crowd: Pleasure Places in the Twentieth Century* (New York: Columbia University Press, 2005).

43 Cloud, 'Margate', 258.

44 Kane, *The Architecture of Pleasure: British Amusement Parks 1900-1939*.

45 John Armstrong and David M. Williams, 'The Steamboat and Popular Tourism', *Journal of Transport History* 26, no. 1 (2005): 61–77.

46 Editorial in *The Preston Pilot*, quoted in John Walvin, *Beside the Seaside: A Social History of the Popular Seaside Holiday* (London: Viking, 1978), 38.

47 Anthony Hern, *The Seaside Holiday. The History of the English Seaside Resort* (London: Cresset Press, 1967), 98; Jack Simmons, *The Victorian Railway* (London: Thames and Hudson, 1991), 286.

48 Caste was a frequently used term in the interwar period to describe social class.

49 Beaven, *Leisure, Citizenship and Working-Class Men in Britain, 1850-1945*.

50 Bruce Peter, *Form Follows Fun: Modernism and Modernity in British Pleasure Architecture 1925-1940* (London: Routledge, 2007),

51 Jenkins (ed.), *The Bumper Book of Beanos*.

52 Alan Delgado, *The Annual Outing and Other Excursions* (London: Allen and Unwin, 1977), 146.

53 David W. Gutzke, *Pubs and Progressives: Reinventing the Public House in England, 1896-1960* (DeKalb, IL: Northern Illinois University, 2006), 176–7. This pub has been demolished and is now a McDonald's restaurant.

54 P. D. Hopkins, *Minster-in-Thanet: An Outline History for the Visitor* (Minster: Minster Parish Council, 1985).

55 *Times*, 11 April 1933.

56 Basil Oliver, *The Renaissance of the English Public House* (London: Faber, 1947), 22.

57 Gutzke, *Pubs and Progressives*.

58 Law, '"The Car Indispensable" The Hidden Influence of the Car in Inter-War Suburban London'.

59 Harold P. Clunn, *The Face of the Home Counties* (London: Spring Books, (1936) 1959), 254 and 242.

60 Ministry of Transport, *Road Traffic Census 1938 Report* (London: HMSO, 1939).

61 Kent Drawings and Archives Collections and Local History Service, 'large photographs of Tomson and Wotton public houses', U3555/5/TW/1/Bp4/2.

62 Alan Powers, *Oliver Hill: Architect & Lover of Life 1887-1968* (London: Methuen, 1989), 3; Jessica Holland, 'An English Sensibility: The Architecture of Oliver Hill', Unpublished Thesis, University of Portsmouth, 2011; Michael Bracewell, 'Morecambe: The Sunset Coast', in Lara Feigel and Alexandra Harris (eds), *Modernism on Sea: Art and Culture at the British Seaside* (Witney: Peter Lang, 2009), 35–44.

63 Rex Pope, 'Railway Companies and Resort Hotels Between the Wars', *Journal of Transport History* 22, no. 1 (2001): 62–73.

64 Oliver Hill letter to Tomson and Wotton 8 May 1933, RIBA Drawings and Archives Collections at the V&A, HiO/56/2.

65 David W. Gutzke and Michael John Law, *The Roadhouse Comes to Britain: Drinking, Driving and Dancing 1925–1955* (London: Bloomsbury Academic, 2017).

66 Hoggart, *The Uses of Literacy*, 147.

67 RIBA Drawings and Archives Collections at the V&A, HiO/55/6.

68 Oliver Hill's notes, 29 November 1938, RIBA Drawings and Archives Collections at the V&A, HiO/79/1.

69 RIBA Drawings and Archives Collections at the V&A, HiO/55/6 letter from Claude-General Neon Lights Ltd., 9 November 1937.

70 Letter from Group Services Ltd. (the building subsidiary of Tomson and Wotton) to Oliver Hill, 29 December 1936, RIBA Drawings and Archives Collections at the V&A, HiO/56/1.

71 Historic England, Minster, A253 TR 36 NW 2/59 Prospect Inn – II Public House, 1939.

72 RIBA Drawings and Archives Collections at the V&A, HiO/55/6.

73 Oliver, *The Renaissance of the English Public House,* 33.

74 See the examples in Oliver, *The Renaissance of the English Public House.*

75 Clunn, *The Face of the Home Counties,* 36.

76 W. G. McMinnies, *Signpost to the Road Houses, Country Clubs and Better and Brighter Inns and Hotels of England* (London: Simpkin Marshall, 1935), 26.

77 Ibid.

78 This and other plan details from Oliver, *The Renaissance of the English Public House,* 37.

79 Sean O'Connell, *The Car and British Society: Class, Gender and Motoring 1896-1939* (Manchester: Manchester University Press, 1998).

80 In the late 1930s, the car began to be used extensively for more quotidian purposes such as going shopping, visiting the cinema and for commuting to work, see Law, '"The Car Indispensable" The Hidden Influence of the Car in Inter-War Suburban London'.

81 For example, Morton, *In Search of England.*

82 Peter Thorold, *The Motoring Age; The Automobile and Britain 1896-1939* (London: Profile, 2003).

83 *Autocar,* 23 January 1925.

84 T. Craven, quoted in O'Connell, *The Car and British Society,* 84.

85 Law, '"The Car Indispensable" The Hidden Influence of the Car in Inter-War Suburban London'.

86 The 'Tudor' saloon bar is well described in Patrick Hamilton's novel, *Mr. Stimpson and Mr. Gorse* (London: Constable, 1953).

87 Gutzke, *Pubs and Progressives,* 158.

88 Brewery officials discussing Norbury Tavern, David W. Gutzke, *Pubs and Progressives,* 171.

89 Gutzke, *Pubs and Progressives,* 175.

90 Correspondence with David Gutzke, 5 January 2014.

91 Powers, *Oliver Hill: Architect & Lover of Life 1887-1968,* 3. Only one of these was built due to the Second World War.

92 See plans in Oliver, *The Renaissance of the English Public House.*

93 *Architects' Journal,* 24 November 1938; *Architect and Building News,* 6 January 1939.

94 Oliver Hill's notes, 29 November 1938, RIBA Drawings and Archives Collections at the V&A, HiO/79/1.

95 Peter, *Form Follows Fun,* 46.

96 Architecture Club, *Recent English Architecture 1920-1940* (London: Country Life, 1947), Plate 17.

97 Peter, *Form Follows Fun,* 63.

98 Ibid., 41.

99 *Times,* 21 July 1934.

100 The Prospect Inn, in decline, can be seen on 'Lightening Coach Tours' (film), It's Marty, BBC broadcast 1968, http://youtu.be/Z7CpkzJU9kA.

Chapter 8

1 Joseph Crookes Grime, Lord Mayor of Manchester, 'Foreword', *Manchester (Ringway) Airport – Official Opening and Air Display,* 3.

2 Law, '"The Car Indispensable" The Hidden Influence of the Car in Inter-War Suburban London'.

3 *The People's Year Book 1939* (Stockport: Co-operative Wholesale Society, 1939), 162.

4 *Times,* 4 July 1938.

5 Peter Adey, 'Airports and Air-mindedness: Spacing, Timing and Using the Liverpool Airport, 1929-1939', *Social & Cultural Geography* 7, no. 3 (2006): 343–63.

6 *Aeroplane,* 3 July 1935.

7 Rieger, *Technology and the Culture of Modernity in Britain and Germany, 1890-1945,* 132.

8 *Times,* 16 June 1919.

9 H. J. Penrose, 'Cobham, Sir Alan John (1894–1973)', rev. *Oxford Dictionary of National Biography* (Oxford: Oxford University Press, 2004); Alan J. Cobham, Sir, *A Time to Fly* (London: Shepheard-Walwyn, 1978).

10 Janet R. Daly Bednarek, 'The Flying Machine in the Garden: Parks and Airports, 1919-1938', *Technology and Culture* 46, no. 2 (2005): 350–73.

11 *Flight,* 2 June 1927.

12 Law, *The Experience of Suburban Modernity.*

13 *Flight,* 2 June 1927.

14 Midge Gillies, *Amy Johnson* (London: Weidenfeld & Nicolson, 2003).

15 *Flight,* 8 August 1930.

16 David Oliver, *Hendon Aerodrome – A History* (Shrewsbury: Airlife Publishing, 1994).

17 A. C. Cruddas, *Those Fabulous Flying Years: Joy-Riding and Flying Circuses Between the Wars* (Tunbridge Wells: Air-Britain Historians, 2003); Cobham, *A Time to Fly.*

18 'Great Air Display', *Surrey Comet,* 23 September 1933.

19 Bob Learmonth, Joanna Nash and Douglas Cluett, *First Croydon Airport, 1915–1928* (Sutton: Sutton Libraries and Art Services, 1977); Douglas Cluett, Joanna Nash and Bob Learmonth, *Croydon Airport: The Great Days, 1928-1939* (Sutton: London Borough of Sutton Libraries and Art Services, 1980).

20 Air Ministry, Brochure, *Guide to Croydon Aerodrome: (the Air Port of London)*, London, 1929.

21 John Myerscough, 'Airport Provision in the Inter-War Years', *Journal of Contemporary History* 20 (1985): 41–70.

22 W. F. Nicholson (secretary, Air Ministry), Letter to Town Clerks, 25 October 1928, The National Archives, AVIA 2/526.

23 Cobham, *A Time to Fly*, 150.

24 *Flight*, 8 November 1929.

25 Alan J. Cobham, *Report on the Present Situation with regard to the Establishment of Aerodromes in Great Britain and Northern Ireland*, presented to the secretary of state for air, 9 January 1931, The National Archives, AVIA 2/526.

26 *Times*, 9 December 1933.

27 *Flight*, 16 November 1933.

28 Edward, Prince of Wales, 'Think in Terms of 250 m.p.h.', speech reported in *Flight*, 14 December 1933.

29 *Times*, 9 December 1933.

30 'Air Travel and Transport', *Aeroplane*, 15 December 1933.

31 Myerscough, 'Airport Provision in the Inter-War Years'.

32 R. Ashley Hall, 'Organisation of Air Transport in Great Britain', *Aerodrome Owners Association – Papers Read at Conferences*, 1937, National Aerospace Library.

33 Advertisement in *Aeroplane*, 6 July 1938.

34 Air Ministry, *Report of the Committee to Consider the Development of Civil Aviation in the United Kingdom* (London: HMSO, 1937), 32.

35 *Popular Flying*, February 1938.

36 Wolfgang Voigt, 'From the Hippodrome to the Aerodrome, from the Air Station to the Terminal: European Airports 1909-45', in John Zukowsky (ed.), *Building for Air Travel* (Chicago, IL: Art Institute of Chicago, 1996), 27–51.

37 Alastair Gordon, *Naked Airport: A Cultural History of the World's Most Revolutionary Structure* (New York: H. Holt, 2004), 83.

38 M. H. Volk, 'Some Practical Suggestions on Aerodrome Organization and Management', *Aerodrome Owners Association – Papers Read at Conferences*, 1938, National Aerospace Library.

39 This paragraph first appeared in Michael John Law, *1930s London – The Modern City* (Canterbury: Yellowback, 2015).

40 John King, 'Gatwick's Beehive: A Forgotten Development', *Thirties Society* 2 (1982): 25–8.

41 Sonja Dümpelmann, *Flights of Imagination: Aviation, Landscape, Design* (Charlottesville, VA: University of Virginia Press, 2014).

42 Voigt, 'From the Hippodrome to the Aerodrome, from the Air Station to the Terminal: European Airports 1909-45', 47.

43 Anon., *Airports and Airways 1937* (London: Royal Institute of British Architects, 1937).

44 Architecture Club, *Recent English Architecture 1920-1940* (London: Country Life, 1947).

45 'A Thanet Inauguration', *Flight*, 8 July 1937.

46 Peter G. Masefield, 'Straight, Whitney Willard (1912–1979)', *Oxford Dictionary of National Biography* (Oxford: Oxford University Press, 2004).

47 *Straightaway Review 1938* (London: Straight Corporation Limited, 1938), 52.

48 *Straightaway Review 1938*, 54.

49 'Suffolk Air Day' programme, Ipswich Airport, 9 July 1938, Suffolk Record Office, HD2272/153/9/12/1.

50 Speke was opened in sections between 1937 and 1939, Birmingham was opened in early 1939, Manchester in 1938.

51 'Manchester's New Airport', *Manchester Guardian*, 24 June 1938.

52 *Manchester Airport, Ringway* (Manchester: Municipal Information Bureau, undated c.1940s); Barry Abraham and Les Jones, *Manchester Airport – Ringway Remembered* (Stroud: Tempus, 2001).

53 Adey, 'Airports and Air-mindedness', 351.

54 'Manchester's New Airport', *Manchester Guardian*, 24 June 1938.

55 'Wants City to Sell Airport' note of interview in *Daily Dispatch*, 29 January 1938, The National Archives, AVIA 2/928.

56 'Ringway Air Services', *Manchester Guardian*, 25 May 1938.

57 Derek H. Aldcroft, *British Railways in Transition* (London: Macmillan, 1968), 80; London Midland & Scottish Railway – Timetable, June 1947, http://timetableworld.com (accessed 20 November 2015).

58 John Stroud, *Railway Air Services* (Shepperton: Ian Allan Ltd, 1987), 57.

59 Railway Air Services, *General Timetable 1938*, National Aerospace Library.

60 'Ringway Air Services', *Manchester Guardian*, 25 May 1938.

61 Manchester (Ringway) Airport, *Official Opening and Air Display*, programme, 25 June 1938, Trafford Local Studies Archives, Ref. 91390508, 57.

62 'Ringway is Ready', *Flight*, 23 June 1938.

63 'Airports – 1', *Architectural Review*, February 1939, 90.

64 'Ringway is Ready', *Flight*, 23 June 1938.

65 Law, *1930s London – The Modern City*, 84.

66 R. A. Scholefield, *Manchester Airport* (Stroud: Sutton Publishing Limited, 1998), 10.

67 Manchester (Ringway) Airport, *Official Opening and Air Display*; see also programmes for opening of Ipswich Airport at Suffolk Record Office, Ipswich and programmes for opening of Luton, Derby and Cambridge Airports, all 1938, at National Aerospace Library, Farnborough.

68 Joseph Crookes Grime, Lord Mayor of Manchester, 'Foreword', *Manchester (Ringway) Airport – Official Opening and Air Display*, 3.

69 *Manchester (Ringway) Airport – Official Opening and Air Display*, 12.

70 Ibid., 15; 'Ringway's Send-Off', *Flight*, 30 June 1938.

71 'Manchester Discovers its Airport', *Manchester Guardian*, 2 August 1938.

72 F. D. Bradbrooke, 'Air Transport – The Air Road to the Isles', *Aeroplane*, 6 July 1938, edited slightly to increase clarity.

73 'Manchester's Air Link with Amsterdam – A Journey from Ringway and Back', *Manchester Guardian*, 29 June 1938.

74 Today this relationship is seen in the operation of the internet and social media.

75 Stroud, *Railway Air Services*, 64.

76 Derek Aldcroft, 'Britain's Internal Airways – The Pioneer Stage of the 1930s', *Business History* 6, no. 2 (1964): 113–23.

77 *Manchester (Ringway) Airport – Official Opening and Air Display*, 49.

78 Air Ministry, *Report of the Committee to Consider the Development of Civil Aviation in the United Kingdom*.

79 Ibid., 37.

Chapter 9

1 Malcolm Muggeridge, *The Thirties* (London: Hamish Hamilton, 1940); Robert Graves and Alan Hodge, *The Long Week-End: A Social History of Great Britain 1918-1939* (London: Faber and Faber, 1941).

2 Hamilton, *Modern England*.

3 Martin Petter, '"Temporary Gentlemen" in the Aftermath of the Great War: Rank, Status and the Ex-officer Problem', *Historical Journal* 37, no. 1 (1994): 127–52.

4 *Harrow Times*, 16 December 2013.

5 Derek Wood, *Project Cancelled: A Searching Criticism of the Abandonment of Britain's Advanced Aircraft Projects* (London: Macdonald and Jane's, 1975).

6 Daniel K. Benjamin and Levis A. Kochin, 'Searching for an Explanation of Unemployment in Interwar Britain', *Journal of Political Economy* 87, no. 3 (1979): 441–78; Sue Bowden, 'The New Consumerism', in Paul Johnson (ed.), *Twentieth-Century Britain, Economic, Cultural and Social Change* (London: Longman, 1994), 242–60.

7 1931 Census, visionofbritain.org.uk, [accessed 25 January 2010] and Abercrombie, *Greater London Plan 1944*, 188. A precise definition of where London's suburbia stops is problematic, but I have used Abercrombie's calculations that consider Surrey, Middlesex and the inner parts of Essex and Kent as suburbanized.

8 Plowden, *The Motor Car and Politics 1896-1970*, 456.

BIBLIOGRAPHY

Primary sources

Archives

British Library.
Glasgow City Archives.
Historic England.
House of Commons Parliamentary Papers.
Hulton Archive.
Kent County Council Archives.
National Aerospace Library.
National Library of Scotland, Moving Image Archive.
RIBA Archives.
RIBA Drawings and Archives Collections at the V&A.
Suffolk Record Office.
The National Archives.
Trafford Local Studies Archives.

Ephemera

Valentine's Snapshots. '12 Real Photographs, Empire Exhibition Scotland', 1938.
W. A. & A. C. Churchman. 'Modern Wonders' Cigarette Card Set, 1938.
W. D. & H. O. Wills. 'Speed' Cigarette Card Set, 1938.

Books before 1950

Abercrombie, L. P. *Greater London Plan 1944*. London: HMSO, 1945.
Air Ministry. *Report of the Committee to Consider the Development of Civil Aviation in the United Kingdom*. London: HMSO, 1937.
Anon. *Airports and Airways 1937*. London: Royal Institute of British Architects, 1937.
Anon. *Empire Exhibition, Scotland-1938, Official Guide*. Glasgow: Corporation of Glasgow, 1938.
Anon. *Shell-Mex House*. London: Shell-Mex Ltd, 1935.
Anon. *Straightaway Review 1938*. London: Straight Corporation Limited, 1938.
Anon. *The People's Year Book 1939*. Stockport: Co-operative Wholesale Society, 1939.

Architecture Club. *Recent English Architecture 1920–1940*. London: Country Life, 1947.

British Broadcasting Corporation. *BBC Handbook 1939*. London: British Broadcasting Corporation, 1939.

British Broadcasting Corporation. *Television Again*. London: British Broadcasting Corporation, 1946.

British Broadcasting Corporation. *The London Television Station, Alexandra Palace*. London: British Broadcasting Corporation, 1937.

Brunner, Christopher. *The Problem of Motor Transport. An Economic Analy*sis. London: Ernest Benn Ltd, 1928.

Burns, Delisle C. *Leisure in the Modern World*. London: The Century Co., 1932.

Burton, Miles. *The Charabanc Mystery*. London: Collins, 1934.

Casson, Hugh. *New Sights of London*. Westminster: London Transport, 1938.

Cloud, Yvonne *Beside the Seaside, Six Variations*. London: John Lane, The Bodley Head, 1934.

Clunn, Harold P. *The Face of the Home Counties*. London: Spring Books, [1936] 1959.

Cobham, Alan J. *Report on the Present Situation with Regard to the Establishment of Aerodromes in Great Britain* and *Northern Ireland*, presented to the Secretary of State for Air, 9 January 1931.

Corporation of the City of Glasgow. *Industrial Enterprise*. Glasgow: United Publishing Company, 1938.

Cronin, A. J. *The Citadel*. London: Gollancz, 1937.

Cronin, A. J. *The Stars Look Down*. London: Gollancz, 1936.

Cross, Beryl M. *The Modern Girl's Beauty Book*. London: Sir Isaac Pitman & Sons, 1938.

Crossland, John R. *The Modern Marvels Encyclopedia*. London: Collins, 1938.

Golding, Harry. *The Wonder Book of Empire for Boys and Girls*. London: Ward, Lock & Co., 1915.

Golding, Harry. *The Wonder Book of Why & What? Answers to Children's Questions*. London: Ward, Lock & Co., 1921.

Golding, Harry (ed.). *The Wonder Book of Do You Know?* London: Ward, Lock & Co., 1934.

Golding, Harry (ed.). *The Wonder Book of Inventions*. London: Ward, Lock & Co., 1930.

Graves, Charles. *And the Greeks*. London: Geoffrey Bles, 1930.

Graves, Robert and Hodge, Alan. *The Long Week-End: A Social History of Great Britain 1918–1939*. London: Faber and Faber, 1941.

Greenwood, Walter. *Love on the Dole*. London: Jonathan Cape, 1933.

Hamilton, Cicely. *Modern England*. London: Dent, 1938.

International Office Machines Research Limited. *Office Machine Manual. A Loose Leaf Reference on Office Machines and Appliances*. London: IOMRL, 1938.

Joad, C. E. M. *The Book of Joad*. London: Faber and Faber, 1935.

Low, Archibald M. *Conquering Space and Time*. London: T. Nelson & Sons, 1937.

Low, Archibald M. *Our Wonderful World of To-Morrow. A Scientific Forecast of the Men, Women, and the World of the Future*. London: Ward, Lock & Co., 1934.

Low, Archibald M. *What New Wonders! The Story of the Pasadena Telescope*. London: Herbert Joseph, 1938.

Madge, Charles and Harrisson, Tom *Britain by Mass-Observation* Harmondsworth: Penguin, 1939.

Mais, S. P. B. *The Home Counties*. London: Batsford, 1942.

Martindale, Hilda. *Women Servants of the State, 1870–1938. A History of Women in the Civil Service*. London: Allen and Unwin, 1938.

Mass-Observation. *The Pub and the People: A Worktown Study*. London: Victor Gollancz Ltd., 1943.

McMinnies, W. G. *Signpost to the Road Houses, Country Clubs and Better and Brighter Inns and Hotels of England*. London: Simpkin Marshall, 1935.

Ministry of Transport. *Road Traffic Census 1938 Report*. London: HMSO, 1939.

Morton, H. V. *In Search of England*. London: Methuen, 1927.

Muggeridge, Malcolm. *The Thirties*. London: Hamish Hamilton, 1940.

Oliver, Basil. *The Renaissance of the English Public House*. London: Faber and Faber 1947.

Orwell, George. *The Lion and the Unicorn: Socialism and the English Genius*. London: Secker and Warburg, 1941.

Orwell, George. *The Road to Wigan Pier*. London: Gollancz, 1937.

Pendrill, Charles. *The Adelphi; or, old Durham House in the Strand*. London: Sheldon Press, 1934.

Priestley, J. B. *English Journey*. London: Heinemann, 1934.

Priestley, J. B. *Let the People Sing*. London: Heinemann, 1939.

Rasmussen, Steen Eiler. *London: The Unique City*. London: Jonathan Cape, 1948.

Shaw, George Bernard. *The Intelligent Woman's Guide to Socialism and Capitalism*. New Brunswick, NJ: Transaction Publishers, [1928] 1984.

Simpson, H. W. *Modern Office Management*. London: Pitman, 1937.

Society of Motor Manufacturers and Traders, Ltd. Statistical Dept. *The Motor Industry of Great Britain* 1937. London: SMMT, 1937.

Summerson, John Newenham. *Georgian London*. London: Pleiades Books, 1945.

Wheeler, Harold (ed.). *Marvels of the Modern World*. London: Odhams Press Limited, 1938.

Williams-Ellis, Clough. *England and the Octopus*. London: Geoffrey Bles, 1928.

Williams-Ellis, Clough and Summerson, John Newenham. *Architecture Here and Now*. London: T. Nelson and Sons, Ltd, 1934.

Articles before 1950

Bamber, George 'Empire Exhibition Glasgow', *Kodak*, September 1938, 194–5.

Borthwick, Alastair. 'Building Scotland's Exhibition', *Listener*, 2 March 1938.

Bradbrooke, F. D. 'Air Transport – The Air Road to the Isles', *Aeroplane*, 6 July 1938.

Byron, Robert. 'The Destruction of Georgian London', *New Statesman and Nation*, 11 December 1937.

Cock, Gerald. 'Television Today', *Listener*, 2 February 1938.

Dickson, Harold. 'The Spirit and Splendour of Empire', in *A Souvenir of the Empire Exhibition 1938*. Glasgow: The Daily Record and Evening News, 1938.

Kelmsley (Lord). 'Youth and the Exhibition', *A Souvenir of the Empire Exhibition 1938*. Glasgow: The Daily Record and Evening News, 1938.

Massey Philip. 'The Expenditure of 1,360 British Middle-Class Households in 1938-9', *Journal of the Royal Statistical Society* 105, no. 3 (1942): 159–96.

Richardson, Norah, 'Review of S. P. B. Mais, *The Home Counties*', *Journal of the Royal Society of the Arts*, 27 October 1944.

Ryan, Bryce and Gross, Neal C. 'The Diffusion of Hybrid Seed Corn in Two Iowa Communities', *Rural Sociology*, 8, no. 15 (1943): 15–24.

Summerson, John. 'Architecture at the Empire Exhibition', *Listener*, 18 May 1938.

Traub, E. H. 'English and Continental Television', *Journal of the Television Society*, December 1938.

Booklets, brochures and programmes

Air Ministry. *Guide to Croydon Aerodrome: (the Air Port of London)*. London 1929.

Ferranti. *Ferranti Television – 'Masters of Power'*, 1938.

G. E. C. *G. E. C. Television*. 1938.

H. M. V. *His Master's Voice' Television: The Birth of Television for Home Entertainment*. 1937.

Ipswich Airport. *Suffolk Air Day*. 9 July 1938.

Manchester (Ringway) Airport. *Official Opening and Air Display*. 25 June 1938.

Manchester Municipal Information Bureau. *Manchester Airport, Ringway*. undated 1940s.

Marconi EMI. *The Marconi EMI Emitron Camera*.

Modern Woman booklets:
    'Good Looks', 1938.
    'Good Manners', 1938.
    'Home Laundry Work', 1938.
    'Interior Decoration', 1938.
    'Party Games', 1938.
    'The Domestic Worker', 1938.

Murphy. *Murphy Television*. 1938.

PYE. *PYE Television*. 1938.

Radiolympia. *On Television – You See It Better Than If You Were There!*, August 1938.

Radiolympia. *Television in Your Home – The Receivers You Can Buy – A Complete Guide*, 1938.

Railway Air Services. *General Timetable*. 1938.

Scotland Calling. Marketing Brochure. 1937.

Skinners. *Motor Coach Tours from Hastings and St. Leonards*. Gloucester: British Publishing Co., 1937.

Southend Flying Club. *At Home*. 27 August 1938.

Ultra. *Ultra Television – The Gift of Sight*. 1938.

Speeches

Baldwin, Stanley. 'What England Means to Me', speech to the Royal Society of St George, 6 May 1924.

Edward, Prince of Wales. 'Think in Terms of 250 m.p.h.', speech reported in *Flight*, 14 December 1933.

Conference papers

Ashley Hall, R. 'Organisation of Air Transport in Great Britain', Aerodrome Owners Association Conference. 1937.
Volk, M. H. 'Some Practical Suggestions on Aerodrome Organization and Management', Aerodrome Owners Association Conference. 1938.

Amateur films from National Library of Scotland, Moving Image Archive

1938 Glasgow Empire Exhibition [film] Dir. Mr Laidlaw, 1938 (ref. 5653).
Empire Exhibition [film] Dir. Don McLachlan, 1938 (ref. 8686).
Empire Exhibition [film] Dir. Jimmy McKenzie and Joe McRobert, 1938 (ref. 0065).
Empire Exhibition [film] Dir. unknown, 1938 (ref. 8782).
Glasgow Empire Exhibition [film] Dir, unknown, 1938 (ref. 6710).
Visit to the Empire Exhibition [film] Dir. D. Campbell, 1938 (ref. 3035).

Commercial films

Housing Problems [film], Dir. Arthur Elton, UK, British Commercial Gas Association, 1935.
I See Ice [film], Dir. Anthony Kimmins, UK, Associated Talking Pictures, 1938.
It's in the Air [film], Dir. Anthony Kimmins, UK, Associated Talking Pictures, 1938.
Lightening Coach Tours [film], UK, It's Marty, BBC television broadcast 1968.
Passport to Pimlico [film], Dir. Henry Cornelius, UK, Ealing Studios, 1949.
Roadways [film], Dir. A. Cavalcanti, UK, S. Legg and W. Coldstream, GPO Film Unit, 1937.
Sing As We Go [film], Dir. Basil Dean, UK, Associated Talking Pictures, 1934.
The *Gang Show* [film], Dir. Alfred J. Goulding, UK, Herbert Wilcox Productions, 1937.
The *Lady Vanishes* [film], Dir. Alfred Hitchcock, UK, Gainsborough Pictures, 1938.

Newsreels

King George VI Opens Scottish Exhibition [film], UK, British Movietone, 1938.
Movietone Reviews 1938 [film], UK, British Movietone, 1938.
Review of the Year [film], UK, British Pathé, 1938.
Scottish Exhibition [film], UK, British Pathé, 1938.
Towards 100% [film], UK, British Pathé, 1937.

Magazines

A. B. C. Railway Guide.
Aeroplane.
Amateur Photographer and Cinematographer.
Architect and Building News.
Architect's Journal.
Architectural Review.
Armchair Science.
Autocar.
Boy's Own Paper.
Builder.
Country Life.
Discovery.
Flight.
Girls' Cinema.
Gramophone.
Illustrated London News.
John Bull.
Kinematograph Weekly.
Kodak.
Lilliput.
Listener.
Modern Boy.
Modern Woman.
Modern Wonder.
Motor Coach A. B. C.
New Statesman and Nation.
Picturegoer.
Picture Post.
Popular Flying.
Radio Pictorial.
Radio Times.
Reader's Digest.
Spectator.
Television and Short-Wave World.
Weekly Illustrated.
Wireless World.
Wireless World & Radio Review.
Woman.

Newspapers

Daily Dispatch.
Daily Mail.
Daily Mirror.
Daily Record.

Daily Telegraph.
Dundee Courier.
Harrow Times.
Lancashire Evening Post.
Manchester Guardian.
Midland Daily Telegraph.
New York Times.
Observer.
Sunday Post.
Surrey Comet.
Times.
Weekly News.

Memoirs

Borthwick, Alastair and BBC Scotland. *The Empire Exhibition Fifty Years On: A Personal Reminiscence.* Edinburgh: Mainstream, 1988.

Bragg, Stanley E. *Down Memory Lane: Thoughts of the Adelphi: Being Reminiscences of his Time in Collcutt & Hamp's Office During the Rebuilding of the Adelphi, Westminster, in 1934'.* London: Unpublished, 1984, RIBA archive, BrS/1.

Cobham, Alan J. Sir. *A Time to Fly.* London: Shepheard-Walwyn, 1978.

Hopkinson, Tom. *Picture Post 1938–50.* London: Allen Lane, The Penguin Press, 1970.

Jenkins, Clare (ed.). *The Bumper Book of Beanos: South Yorkshire People Reminisce About Works Outings, Trips to the Seaside and Other Merry Sprees.* Castleford: Yorkshire Art Circus in Association with Sheffield City Libraries and Ventura Holidays, 1988.

Newby, Eric. *A Traveller's Life.* London: Pan, 1982.

Secondary sources

Books

Abraham, Barry and Jones, Les. *Manchester Airport – Ringway Remembered.* Stroud: Tempus, 2001.

Aldcroft, Derek H. *British Railways in Transition.* London: Macmillan, 1968.

Aldgate, Anthony and Richards, Jeffrey. *Best of British: Cinema and Society from 1930 to Present.* London: I. B. Tauris, 1999.

Allan, David G. C. *The Adelphi Past and Present: A History and a Guide.* London: Calder Walker, 2001.

Anderson, Gregory (ed.). *The White-blouse Revolution: Female Office Workers Since 1870.* Manchester: Manchester University Press, 1988.

Anon. *Basil Spence: Buildings & Projects.* London: RIBA, 2012.

Anon. *Glasgow's Greatest Exhibition: Recreating the 1938 Empire Exhibition.* Edinburgh: RIAS, 2008.

Armes, Roy. *On Video*. London: Routledge, [1988] 1995.

Arnold, Guy. *Held Fast for England: G. A. Henty, Imperialist Boy's Writer*. London: Hamish Hamilton, 1980.

Atkinson, Harriet. *The Festival of Britain: A Land and its People*. London: I. B. Tauris, 2012.

Ballaster, Ros. Women's *Worlds: Ideology, Femininity and the Woman's Magazine*. London: Macmillan, 1991.

Barker, Paul. *The Freedoms of Suburbia*. London: Frances Lincoln, 2009.

Beaven, Brad. *Leisure, Citizenship and Working-Class Men in Britain, 1850–1945*. Manchester: Manchester University Press, 2005.

Bennett, Tessa. *Antiques and Their Values — Cigarette Cards*. Galashiels: Lyle Publications, 1982.

Benton, Charlotte, Benton, Tim and Wood, Ghislaine. *Art Deco 1910–1939*. London: V&A, 2003.

Berman, Marshall. *All That is Solid Melts into Air: The Experience of Modernity*. London: Penguin, [1982] 1988.

Blom, Philipp. *The Vertigo Years: Change and Culture in the West, 1900–1914*. London: Weidenfeld & Nicolson, 2008.

Bloom, Clive. *Bestsellers: Popular Fiction Since 1900*. Basingstoke: Palgrave, 2002.

Bloom, Ursula. *He Lit the Lamp*. London: Burke, 1958.

Boyd, Kelly. *Manliness and the Boys' Story Paper in Britain: A Cultural History, 1855–1940*. Basingstoke: Palgrave Macmillan, 2003.

Branson, Noreen. *Britain in the Nineteen Thirties*. London: Weidenfeld and Nicolson, 1971.

Bret, David. *George Formby: A Troubled Genius*. London: Robson, 1999.

Briggs, Asa. *The History of Broadcasting in the United Kingdom, Volume 2*. London: Oxford University Press, 1965.

Burnett, John. *A Social History of Housing, 1815–1985*. London: Methuen, 1986.

Burns, R. W. *British Television, the Formative Years*. London: Peter Peregrinus Ltd., 1986.

Caffrey, Kate. *'37- '39: Last Look Round*. London: Gordon & Cremonesi, 1978.

Campbell, Neil, Davies, Jude and McKay, George. *Issues in Americanisation and Culture*. Edinburgh: Edinburgh University Press, 2004.

Carey, John. *The Intellectuals and the Masses: Pride and Prejudice Among the Literary Intelligentsia, 1880–1939*. London: Faber, 1992.

Clapson, Mark. *Suburban Century: Social Change and Urban Growth in England and the United States*. Oxford: Berg, 2003.

Cleeve, Brian. *1938, A World Vanishing*. London: Buchan & Enright, 1982.

Cluett, Douglas, Nash, Joanna and Learmonth, Bob. *Croydon Airport: The Great Days, 1928–1939*. Sutton: London Borough of Sutton Libraries and Art Services, 1980.

Cortada, James W. *Before the Computer*. Princeton, NJ: Princeton University Press, 1993.

Costigliola, Frank. *Awkward Dominion: American Political, Economic, and Cultural Relations with Europe, 1919–1933*. Ithaca, NY: Cornell University Press, 1984.

Crampsey, Robert A. *The Empire Exhibition of 1938: The Last Durbar*. Edinburgh: Mainstream, 1988.

Crisell, Andrew. *An Introductory History of British Broadcasting*. London: Routledge, 1997.

Croft, Andy. *Red Letter Days: British Fiction in the 1930s*. London: Lawrence & Wishart, 1990.

Cross, Gary S. and Walton, John K. *The Playful Crowd: Pleasure Places in the Twentieth Century*. New York: Columbia University Press, 2005.

Cruddas, A. C. *Those Fabulous Flying Years: Joy-Riding and Flying Circuses Between the Wars*. Tunbridge Wells: Air-Britain Historians, 2003.

Daunton, M. J. and Rieger, Bernhard. *Meanings of Modernity: Britain from the Late-Victorian Era to World War II*. Oxford: Berg, 2001.

De Grazia, Victoria. *Irresistible Empire: America's Advance through Twentieth-Century Europe*. Cambridge, MA: Belknap, 2005.

Delgado, Alan. *The Annual Outing and Other Excursions*. London: Allen and Unwin, 1977.

Dennis, Richard. *Cities in Modernity: Representations and Productions of Metropolitan Space, 1840–1930*. Cambridge: Cambridge University Press, 2008.

Dümpelmann, Sonja. *Flights of Imagination: Aviation, Landscape, Design*. Charlottesville, VA: University of Virginia Press, 2014.

Edwards, Brian. *Basil Spence, 1907–1976*. Edinburgh: Rutland Press, 1995.

Fisher, Kate. *Birth Control, Sex, and Marriage in Britain 1918–1960*. Oxford: Oxford University Press, 2006.

Floud, Roderick and Johnson, Paul (eds). *The Cambridge Economic History of Modern Britain (Volume 1)*. Cambridge: Cambridge University Press, 2004.

Forty, Adrian. *Objects of Desire: Design and Society, 1750–1980*. London: Thames and Hudson, 1986.

Gardiner, Juliet. *The Thirties: An Intimate History*. London: Harper Press, 2010.

Gardner, Charles Joseph Thomas. *Fifty Years of Brooklands*. London: Heinemann, 1956.

Gilbert, David, Matless, David and Short, Brian (eds). *Geographies of British Modernity: Space and Society in the Twentieth Century*. Oxford: Blackwell, 2003.

Gillies, Midge. *Amy Johnson*. London: Weidenfeld & Nicolson, 2003.

Gold, John Robert. *The Experience of Modernism: Modern Architects and the Future City, 1928–53*. London: E & FN Spon, 1997.

Gordon, Alastair. *Naked Airport: A Cultural History of the World's Most Revolutionary Structure*. New York: H. Holt, 2004.

Gourvish, Terry. *Dolphin Square: The History of a Unique Building*. London: Bloomsbury, 2014.

Gutzke, David W. *Pubs and Progressives: Reinventing the Public House in England, 1896–1960*. DeKalb, IL: Northern Illinois University, 2006.

Gutzke, David W. and Law, Michael John. *The Roadhouse Comes to Britain: Drinking, Driving and Dancing, 1925–1955*. London: Bloomsbury Academic, 2017.

Hallett, Michael. *Stefan Lorant: Godfather of Photojournalism*. Lanham, MD: Scarecrow, 2006.

Hallett, Michael. *The Real Story of Picture Post*. Birmingham: ARTicle Press, 1994.

Hamilton Patrick. *Mr. Stimpson and Mr. Gorse*. London: Constable, 1953.

Herbert, Stephen. *A History of Early Television*. London: Routledge, 2004.

Hern, Anthony. *The Seaside Holiday. The History of the English Seaside Resort*. London: Cresset Press, 1967.

Highmore, Ben. *Everyday Life and Cultural Theory: An Introduction*. New York: Routledge, 2001.

Hilton, Matthew. *Smoking in British Popular Culture 1800–2000: Perfect Pleasures*. Manchester: Manchester University Press, 2000.

Hoggart, Richard. *The Uses of Literacy: Aspects of Working-Class Life, with Special Reference to Publications and Entertainments*. London: Chatto and Windus, 1957.

Hopkins, P. D. *Minster-in-Thanet: An Outline History for the Visitor*. Minster: Minster Parish Council, 1985.

Houlbrook, Matt. *Queer London: Perils and Pleasures in the Sexual Metropolis, 1918–1957*. Chicago, IL: University of Chicago Press, 2005.

Hubble, Nick. *Mass-Observation and Everyday Life*. London: Palgrave Macmillan, 2010.

Huggins, Mike and Williams, Jack. *Sport and the English 1918–1939*. London: Routledge, 2006.

Jackson, Alan A. *Semi-Detached London: Suburban Development, Life and Transport, 1900–39*. London: Allen & Unwin, 1973.

Jackson, Alan A. *The Middle Classes 1900–1950*. Nairn: David St. John Thomas, 1991.

James, Robert. *Popular Culture and Working-Class Taste in Britain, 1930–1939*. Manchester: Manchester University Press, 2010.

Jennings, Charles. *The Fast Set: Three Extraordinary Men and Their Race for the Land Speed Record*. London: Little, Brown, 2004.

Jones, Edward and Woodward, Christopher. *A Guide to the Architecture of London*. London: Seven Dials, 2000.

Jones, Stephen G. *Workers at Play: A Social and Economic History of Leisure, 1918–1939*. London: Routledge & Kegan Paul, 1986.

Kaika, Maria. *City of Flows: Modernity, Nature, and the City*. Abingdon: Routledge, 2005.

Kane, Josephine. *The Architecture of Pleasure: British Amusement Parks 1900–1939*. Farnham: Ashgate, 2013.

Kee, Robert. *The Picture Post Album*. London: Barrie & Jenkins, 1989.

Kinchin, Per. *Glasgow's Great Exhibitions: 1888, 1901, 1911, 1938, 1988*. Wendlebury: White Cockade, 1988.

Kynaston, David. *Modernity Britain: 1957–1962*. London: Bloomsbury, 2013.

Law, Michael John. *1930s London – The Modern City*. Canterbury: Yellowback, 2015.

Law, Michael John. *The Experience of Suburban Modernity*. Manchester: Manchester University Press, 2014.

Learmonth, Bob, Nash, Joanna and Cluett, Douglas. *First Croydon Airport, 1915–1928*. Sutton: Sutton Libraries and Art Services, 1977.

LeMahieu, D. L. *A Culture for Democracy: Mass Communication and the Cultivated Mind in Britain Between the Wars*. Oxford: Clarendon, 1988.

Light, Alison. *Forever England: Femininity, Literature and Conservatism Between the Wars*. London: Routledge, 1991.

Lockwood, Stan. *Kaleidoscope of Char-a-bancs and Coaches*. London: Marshall Harris & Baldwin, 1980.

London Cigarette Card Company (The). *The Complete Catalogue of British Cigarette Cards*. Exeter: Webb & Bower, 1981.

Marcou, David J. *All the Best: Britain's Picture Post Magazine, Best Mirror and Old Friend to Many, 1938–57*. La Crosse: DigiCOPY, 2013.

Matless, David. *Landscape and Englishness*. London: Reaktion, 1998.

McKean, Charles. *The Scottish Thirties: An Architectural Introduction*. Edinburgh: Scottish Academic, 1987.

McKibbin, Ross. *Classes and Cultures: England, 1918–1951*. Oxford: Oxford University Press, 1998.

Mort, Frank. *Capital Affairs: London and the Making of the Permissive Society*. New Haven, CT: Yale University Press, 2010.

Moss, Graham. *The Post Office and the Empire Exhibition, 1938*. Ross-shire: Scottish Postal History Society, 1988.

Munby, D. L. *Inland Transport Statistics, Great Britain, 1900-1970*. Oxford: Oxford University Press, 1978.

Murray, Martin. *The Story of Cigarette Cards*. London: Murray Cards (International) Ltd, 1987.

Napper, Lawrence. *British Cinema and Middlebrow Culture in the Interwar Years*. Exeter: University of Exeter Press, 2009.

Nava, Mica and O'Shea, Alan (eds). Modern *Times: Reflections on a Century of English Modernity*. London: Routledge, 1996.

Nott, James. *Music for the People: Popular Music in Britain between the Wars*. Oxford: Oxford University Press, 2002.

Nye, David E. *American Technological Sublime*. Cambridge, MA: MIT Press, 1994.

O'Connell, Sean. *The Car and British society: Class, Gender and Motoring 1896-1939*. Manchester: Manchester University Press, 1998.

Ogborn, Miles. *Indian Ink: Script and Print in the Making of the English East India Company*. Chicago, IL: University of Chicago Press, 2007.

Ogborn, Miles. *Spaces of Modernity: London's Geographies, 1680–1780*. London: The Guilford Press, 1998.

Oliver, David. *Hendon Aerodrome – A History*. Shrewsbury: Airlife Publishing, 1994.

Oliver, Paul, Davis, Ian and Bentley, Ian. *Dunroamin: The Suburban Semi and its Enemies*. London: Barrie & Jenkins, 1981.

Overy, Richard. *The Morbid Age: Britain Between the Wars*. London: Allen Lane, 2009.

Peter, Bruce. *Form Follows Fun: Modernism and Modernity in British Pleasure Architecture 1925–1940*. London: Routledge, 2007.

Plowden William. *The Motor Car and Politics 1896–1970*. London: The Bodley Head, 1971.

Powers, Alan. *Modern – The Modern Movement in Britain*. London: Merrell, 2007.

Powers, Alan. *Oliver Hill: Architect and Lover of Life 1887–1968*. London: Methuen, 1989.

Pugh, Martin. '*We Danced all Night*': A Social History of Britain Between the Wars. London: Bodley Head, 2008.

Reed, David. *The Popular Magazine in Britain and the United States 1880–1960*. London: The British Library, 1997.

Richards, Jeffrey. *The Age of the Dream Palace: Cinema and Society in Britain, 1930–1939*. London: Routledge, 1989.

Rieger, Bernhard. *Technology and the Culture of Modernity in Britain and Germany, 1890–1945*. Cambridge: Cambridge University Press, 2005.

Rogers, Everett M. *Diffusion of Innovations*. New York: The Free Press, 1995.

Rose, Jonathan. *The Intellectual Life of the British Working Classes*. New Haven, CT: Yale University Press, 2001.

Rydell, Robert W. *Buffalo Bill in Bologna: The Americanization of the World, 1869–1922*. Chicago: University of Chicago Press, 2005.

Savage, Christopher and Barker, T. C. *Economic History of Transport in Britain*. Abingdon: Routledge, 1959.

Savage, Jon. *Teenage: The Creation of Youth Culture*. London: Chatto & Windus, 2007.

Scannell, Paddy. *A Social History of British Broadcasting, Volume 1, 1922-1939 – Serving the Nation*. Oxford: Basil Blackwell, 1991.

Scholefield, R. A. *Manchester Airport*. Stroud: Sutton Publishing Limited, 1998.

Scott, Peter. *The Making of the Modern British Home: The Suburban Semi and Family Life between the Wars*. Oxford: Oxford University Press, 2013.

Simmons, Jack. *The Victorian Railway*. London: Thames and Hudson, 1991.

Singleton, Thomas. *The Story of Scophony*. London: Royal Television Society, 1988.

Sterling, Christopher H. (ed.). *Encyclopedia of Journalism*. London: Sage, 2009.

Stevenson, John. *British Society, 1914–45*. Harmondsworth: Penguin, 1984.

Stevenson, John. *The Slump*. London: Quartet, 1979.

Street, Seán. *Historical Dictionary of British Radio*. Oxford: The Scarecrow Press, 2006.

Stroud, John. *Railway Air Services*. Shepperton: Ian Allan Ltd, 1987.

Taylor, David. *Bright Young People: The Rise and Fall of a Generation, 1918–1940*. London: Chatto & Windus, 2007.

Tebbutt, Melanie. *Being Boys: Youth, Leisure and Identity in the Inter-War Years*. Manchester: Manchester University Press, 2012.

Thacker, Andrew. *Moving through Modernity: Space and Geography in Modernism*. Manchester: Manchester University Press, 2003.

Thompson, E. P. *The Making of the English Working Class*. London: Gollancz, 1963.

Thorold, Peter. *The Motoring Age: The Automobile and Britain 1896–1939*. London: Profile, 2003.

Turner, Barry. *Beacon for Change: How the 1951 Festival of Britain Helped to Shape a New Age*. London: Aurum, 2011.

Virilio, Paul. *The Original Accident*. Cambridge: Polity, 2007.

Walford, Rex. *The Growth of 'New London' in Suburban Middlesex (1918-1945) and the Response of the Church of Eng*land. Lampeter: Edwin Mellen Press, 2007.

Walton, John K. *The British Seaside: Holidays and Resorts in the Twentieth Century*. Manchester: Manchester University Press, 2000.

Walvin, James. *Beside the Seaside: A Social History of the Popular Seaside Holiday*. London: Viking, 1978.

Weightman, Gavin. *'Picture Post' Britain*. London: Collins & Brown, 1991.

Williams, Raymond. *Keywords: A Vocabulary of Culture and Society*. London: Fontana, 1976.

Wolmar, Christian. *Fire & Steam: A New History of the Railways in Britain*. London: Atlantic Books, 2007.

Wood, Derek. *Project Cancelled: A Searching Criticism of the Abandonment of Britain's Advanced Aircraft Proje*cts. London: Macdonald and Jane's, 1975.

Woodham, Jonathan M. *A Dictionary of Modern Design*. Oxford: Oxford University Press, 2004.

Worpole, Ken. *Dockers and Detectives: Popular Reading, Popular Writing*. London: Verso, 1983.

Chapters in edited collections

Aitken, Ian. 'The British Documentary Movement in the 1930s', in *Land of Promise – The British Documentary Movement 1930–1950*. London: BFI, undated, 8–11.

Baxendale, John. 'Priestley and the Highbrows', in Brown, Erica and Grover, Mary (eds), *Middlebrow Literary Cultures*. Basingstoke: Palgrave Macmillan, 2012, 69–81.

Bowden, Sue. 'The New Consumerism', in Johnson, Paul (ed.), *Twentieth-Century Britain, Economic, Cultural and Social Change*. London: Longman, 1994, 242–60.

Bracewell, Michael. 'Morecambe: The Sunset Coast', in Feigel, Lara and Harris, Alexandra (eds), *Modernism on Sea: Art and Culture at the British Seaside*. Witney: Peter Lang, 2009, 35–44.

Edwards, Brian. 'Exhibition Design', in Long, Philip and Thomas, Jane (eds), *Basil Spence: Architect*. Edinburgh: National Galleries of Scotland in Association with the Royal Commission on the Ancient and Historical Monuments of Scotland, 2007, 49–61.

Gerhard, Dietrich. 'Periodization in History', in Wiener, Philip P. (ed.), *Dictionary of the History of Ideas*. New York: Scribner's, 1973, 476–8.

Gibson, Bob. 'From the Charabanc to the Gay Hostess', in Leisure Studies Association (Great Britain). *Recording Leisure Lives: Holidays and Tourism in 20th Century Britain*. Eastbourne: Leisure Studies Association, 2011, 99–118.

Hall, Stuart. 'The Social Eye of Picture Post', in Centre for Contemporary Cultural Studies, *Working Papers in Cultural Studies*. Birmingham: University of Birmingham, 1971, 71–120.

Kohl, Stephan. 'Rural England: An Invention of the Motor Industries?', in Burden, Robert and Kohl, Stephan (eds), *Landscape and Englishness*. New York: Editions Rodopi, 2006, 185–206.

Lewis, Jane. E. 'Women Clerical Workers', in Anderson, Gregory (ed.), *The White-Blouse Revolution: Female Office Workers Since 1870*. Manchester: Manchester University Press, 1988, 27–47.

MacKenzie, John M. 'The Second City of Empire', in Driver, Felix and Gilbert, David. (eds), *Imperial Cities: Landscape, Display and Identity*. Manchester: Manchester University Press, 1999, 215–37.

McArthur, Colin. 'The Glasgow Empire Exhibition', in Bennett, Tony, Mercer, Colin and Woollacott, Janet (eds), *Popular Culture and Social Relations*. Milton Keynes: Open University Press, 1986, 117–34.

Voigt, Wolfgang. 'From the Hippodrome to the Aerodrome, from the Air Station to the Terminal: European Airports 1909–45', in Zukowsky, John (ed.), *Building for Air Travel*. Chicago, IL: Art Institute of Chicago, 1996, 27–51.

Conference papers

Langhamer Claire. '"Who the Hell are Ordinary People?", Ordinariness as a Category of Historical Analysis', Lecture to the Royal Historical Society, 10 February 2017.

Street, Seán. 'Pre-War UK Commercial Radio and the BBC', Radio Studies Conference, York University, Toronto, July 2009.

Journal articles

Adey, Peter. 'Airports and Air-mindedness: Spacing, Timing and Using the
    Liverpool Airport, 1929–1939', *Social & Cultural Geography* 7, no. 3 (2006):
    343–63.
Aldcroft, Derek. 'Britain's Internal Airways – The Pioneer Stage of the 1930s',
    Business History 6, no. 2 (1964): 113–23.
Armstrong, John and Williams, David M. 'The Steamboat and Popular Tourism',
    Journal of Transport History 26, no. 1 (2005): 61–77.
Baxter, J. Neil. 'Thomas S. Tait and the Glasgow Empire Exhibition 1938', *Thirties
    Society Journal* 4 (1984): 26–30.
Bednarek, Janet R. Daly. 'The Flying Machine in the Garden: Parks and Airports,
    1919–1938', *Technology and Culture* 46, no. 2 (2005): 350–73.
Benjamin, Daniel K. and Kochin, Levis A. 'Searching for an Explanation of
    Unemployment in Interwar Britain', *Journal of Political Economy* 87, no. 3
    (1979): 441–78.
Bingham, Adrian. '"An Era of Domesticity"? Histories of Women and Gender in
    Interwar Britain', *Cultural and Social History* 1 (2004): 225–33.
Bowler, Peter J. 'Discovering Science from an Armchair: Popular Science in
    British Magazines of the Interwar Years', *Annals of Science* 73, no. 1 (2016):
    89–107.
Britton, Sarah. '"Come and See the Empire by the All Red Route!": Anti-
    imperialism and Exhibitions in Interwar Britain', *History Workshop Journal* 69,
    no. 1 (2010): 68–89.
Britton, Sarah. 'Urban Futures/Rural Pasts', *Cultural and Social History* 8, no. 2
    (2011): 213–32.
Broadberry, Stephen and Ghosal, Sayantan. 'From the Counting House to the
    Modern Office: Explaining Anglo-American Productivity Differences in Services,
    1870–1990', *Journal of Economic History* 62, no. 4 (2002): 967–98.
Campbell-Kelly, Martin. 'Large-scale Data Processing in the Prudential, 1850–
    1930', *Accounting, Business & Financial History* 2, no. 2 (1992): 117–40.
Cantor, Geoffrey. 'Emotional Reactions to the Great Exhibition of 1851', *Journal of
    Victorian Culture* 20, no. 2 (2015): 230–45.
Conway, Rebecca. 'Making the Mill Girl Modern?: Beauty, Industry, and the
    Popular Newspaper in 1930's England', *Twentieth Century British History* 24,
    no. 4 (2013): 518–41.
Giles, Judy. '"Playing Hard to Get": Working-class Women, Sexuality and
    Respectability in Britain, 1918–40', *Women's History Review* 1 (1992): 239–55.
Glancy, Mark. '"Temporary American citizens"? British Audiences, Hollywood
    films and the Threat of Americanisation in the 1920s', *Historical Journal of
    Film, Radio and Television* 26, no.4 (2006): 461–84.
Holmes, Su. 'The "Give-away" Shows – Who is Really Paying?': "Ordinary" People
    and the Development of the British Quiz Show', *Journal of British Cinema and
    Television* 3, no. 2 (2006): 266–83.
Holmes, Su. '"You Don't Need Influence … All You Need is Your First
    Opportunity!": The Early Broadcast Talent Show and the BBC', *Critical Studies
    in Television: The International Journal of Television Studies* 9, no. 1 (2014):
    23–42.

Jeans, D. N. 'Planning and the Myth of the English Countryside in the Interwar Period', *Rural History* 1, no. 2 (1990): 249–64.

King, John. 'Gatwick's Beehive: A Forgotten Development', *Thirties Society* 2 (1982): 25–8.

Law, Michael John. 'Charabancs and Social Class in 1930s Britain', *Journal of Transport History* 36, no. 1 (2015): 41–57.

Law, Michael John. '"The Car Indispensable" The Hidden Influence of the Car in Inter-War Suburban London', *Journal of Historical Geography* 38, no. 4 (2012): 424–33.

Law, Michael John. 'Turning Night Into Day: Transgression and Americanization at the English Inter-War Roadhouse', *Journal of Historical Geography* 35, no. 3 (2009): 473–94.

Lopez Galviz, C. 'Mobilities at a Standstill: Regulating Circulation in London c. 1863-1870', *Journal of Historical Geography* 42 (2013): 62–76.

Maier, Charles S. 'Consigning the Twentieth Century to History: Alternative Narratives for the Modern Era', *American Historical Review* 105, no. 3 (2000): 807–31.

Moores, Shaun. '"The Box on the Dresser": Memories of Early Radio and Everyday life', *Media, Culture and Society* 10 (1988): 23–40.

Myerscough, John. 'Airport Provision in the Inter-War Years', *Journal of Contemporary History* 20 (1985): 41–70.

Nicholson, H. Norris. 'In Amateur Hands: Framing Time and Space in Home-Movies', *History Workshop Journal* 43, Spring (1997): 198–212.

Petter, Martin. '"Temporary Gentlemen" in the Aftermath of the Great War: Rank, Status and the Ex-officer Problem', *Historical Journal* 37, no. 1 (1994): 127–52.

Pike, David. '"Down by the Dark Arches": A Cultural History of the Adelphi', *London Journal* 27, no. 1 (2002): 19–41.

Pope, Rex. 'Railway Companies and Resort Hotels Between the Wars', *Journal of Transport History* 22, no. 1 (2001): 62–73.

Sheller, Mimi. 'Automotive Emotions – Feeling the Car', *Theory, Culture & Society* 21, nos. 4/5 (2005): 221–42.

Smith, Jason Scott. 'The Strange History of the Decade: Modernity, Nostalgia and the Perils of Periodization', *Journal of Social History* 32, no. 2, Winter (1998): 263–85.

Szczelkun, Stefan. 'Public History: The Value of Home Movies', *Oral History*, Autumn (2000): 94–8.

Taylor, John. 'Kodak and the "English" Market Between the Wars', *Journal of Design History* 7, no. 1 (1994): 29–42.

Taylor, Matthew. 'Beyond the Maximum Wage: The Earnings of Football Professionals in England, 1900–39', *Soccer & Society* 2, no. 3 (2001): 101–18.

Tinkler, Penny and Warsh, Cheryl Krasnick. 'Feminine Modernity in Interwar Britain and North America: Corsets, Cars, and Cigarettes', *Journal of Women's History* 20, no. 3 (2008): 133–43.

Trenouth, John. 'Behind the Cameras: No. 2 – The Emitron Camera', *405 Alive* 25, First Quarter (1995): 34–54.

Urry, John. 'The "System" of Automobility', *Theory, Culture & Society* 21, nos. 4/5 (2004): 25–39.

Walton, John. 'The Origins of the Modern Package Tour?: British Motor-coach Tours in Europe, 1930–70', *Journal of Transport History* 32, no. 2 (2011): 145–63.

Waters, Chris. 'Beyond "Americanization" Rethinking Anglo-American Cultural Exchange between the War', *Cultural and Social History* 4 (2007): 451–9.

Theses

Andrewes, Frazer. 'A Culture of Speed: The Dilemma of Being Modern in 1930s Australia', Ph.D. Thesis, University of Melbourne, 2003.

Holland, Jessica. 'An English Sensibility: The Architecture of Oliver Hill', Ph.D. Thesis, University of Portsmouth, 2011.

Websites

http://bufvc.ac.uk [accessed 15 August 2015].
http://thecroydoncitizen.com [accessed 4 March 2012].
http://tampax.com [accessed 21 September 2016].
http://timetableworld.com [accessed 20 November 2015].
http://whirligig-tv.co.uk/radio/downyourway.htm [accessed 28 May 2015].
maps.google.com [accessed 6 January 2014].
www.basilspence.org.uk/work/buildings/empire-exhibition [accessed 9 August 2014].
www.brownie.camera [accessed 26 August 2016
www.earlytelevision.org/ [accessed 29 May 2016].
www.empireexhibition.com/html/atlanticRestaurant.html [accessed 11 December 2015].
www.freemaptools.com [accessed 6 January 2016].
www.historicengland.org.uk/ [accessed 19 April 2014].
www.hse.gov.uk/contact/faqs/toilets.htm [accessed 24 March 2016].
www.ici.com/History via wayback machine at archive.org [accessed 17 August 2014].
www.lightstraw.co.uk/ate/tass/telex1.html [accessed 26 April 2014].
www.measuringworth.com [accessed 11 December 2015].
www.oed.com [accessed 25 May 2016].
www.rgd.org.uk [accessed 9 April 2015].
www.sounds.bl.uk [accessed 2 August 2014].
www.tvhistory.tv/magazines1.htm [accessed 1 May 2015].
www.visionofbritain.org.uk [accessed 25 January 2010 and 4 November 2013].

INDEX